A Parent's Guide to Innovative Education

A Parent's Guide to Innovative Education

Working With Teachers, Schools, and Your Children for Real Learning

ANNE WESCOTT DODD

The Noble Press, Inc.

CHICAGO

Printed in the United States of America

Library of Congress Cataloging-in-Publication Data

Dodd, Anne W.
A parent's guide to innovative education : working with teachers, schools, and your children for real learning / Anne Wescott Dodd.
p. cm.
Includes bibliographical references (p. 263).
ISBN 1-879360-16-0 : $12.95
1. Teaching. 2. Learning. 3. Education—United States—Parent participation. 4. Home and school—United States. I. Title.
LB1025.3.D63 1992
371.3—dc20 91-51219
CIP

Noble Press books are available in bulk at discount prices. Single copies are available prepaid direct from the publisher.

The Noble Press, Inc.
213 W. Institute Place, Suite 508
Chicago, Illinois 60610
(800) 486-7737

DEDICATION

For

Archie H. Wescott and in memory of
Felicia Ferrara Wescott,
my first teachers;

Vickie Dodd Gehm and Suzan Dodd de los Heros,
first teachers;

and their "students," my grandchildren:

Kristen, Cori, and Casey; Eric,
Marcus, and Sara;

and James H. Dodd, first teacher, former teacher,
loyal critic, and friend.

Contents

Acknowledgments

I COULD NOT HAVE written this book without the help of many people—far too many to list here—for I would have to include all of the students I have taught in public schools in Maine and in California, at the University of Maine at Augusta, Colby College, and Bates College; professional colleagues and friends; my own teachers; and others from whom I've learned formally and informally. Some individuals who made specific contributions to this project, however, do deserve special mention: Barbara Bartels, Lois Berge, Norm Berge, Evariste Bernier, Lorrie Blake, Susan Bradford, Suzanne Burnham, Rev. Linda Campbell-Marshall, Heather Carson, Beth Cherry-Anderson, Norine Clarke, Cheryl Cluff, Kelly Cluff, Adrienne Ehlert, Vickie Gehm, Renay Goodkin, Bethany Gott, Judith Guerette, Robin Hansen, Nancy Heiser, Suzan de los Heros, Richard Hollis, Diana Holdsworth, Todd Jepson, Rochelle Johnson, Eileen Laine, Shannon Laitala, Jane Lamb, Eileen Landay, Martin McDonough, Mia McFarlane, Rev. Paul E. Marshall, Lucretia McDine, Margaret Mrstik, Jim Nichols, Betsy Parsons, Leslee Smith, Dany Tracy, Shelley Vadeboncoeur, Carol Wishcamper, and, of course, Jim Dodd. I offer my thanks and appreciation to them and to David Driver, Doug Seibold, and all at Noble Press for their help and encouragement.

Preface

YOU MAY NOT think of yourself as a teacher, but as a parent you are the first and most influential teacher your child will ever have. Any parent can benefit from knowing more about learning and teaching. What you learn about education from this book should help you in working with your children at home, but it should also help you evaluate both present practices and proposed changes in our nation's schools. In this book I explain some new ways of thinking about education. Many people believe we can fix schools by going back to the way things were in the "good old days." They're wrong.

When I began teaching, first in Maine and then in Southern California, I was the authority in the classroom, a benevolent dictator, because that's what teachers were supposed to be. My students sat in rows. I talked. They listened. Everyone did the same assignments at the same times in the same ways. My supervisors gave me excellent evaluations, but I knew something was wrong. Bright students grubbed for grades or froze on tests. Poorer students struggled to keep up or complained about being bored and came late to class.

As I tried to understand what wasn't working, I continued my own education, earning an M.A. in English and a C.A.S. in Educational Administration. Reflecting on my own feelings as a student was probably more helpful, in terms of gaining new insights about learning and teaching, than the information I got from my post-graduate classes.

As a high school assistant principal and middle school principal, I had to deal with the problems of those students who weren't successful. It was clear that their negative feelings about school were often exacerbated by teachers who focused entirely on subject matter, seemingly unaware of the role the human element plays in the process of learning.

I now teach education courses to students in a liberal arts college, and also teach writing courses for non-traditional students (usually adults returning to school after many years) in an off-campus center of a public university. I've seen how traditional teaching has limited the achievement of many students while leaving scars on others. In Chapter Two, and in other places throughout the book, you'll find excerpts from the writings of both former students and friends of mine, some of which were originally written for class assignments and some of which were done expressly for this book. [These people have given me permission to quote them, though some requested that I not use their real names, to which I agreed.] Their memories of school and teachers may help shed light on your own experiences, and convince you that the same mistakes should not be perpetuated in the educations of your children.

Classroom changes must come first. Special programs created to address specific problems almost always cost a lot of money, and they usually have little effect on what happens in the individual classrooms where children spend most of their time. While drastic changes in school structure and culture will ultimately be needed, the place to begin is in the classroom. If teachers adopt different classroom practices, then programs for potential dropouts and many remedial classes won't be needed. The money saved can be used to reduce class sizes, thereby making it easier for teachers to know their students as people.

Of course, such changes will force the system itself to change. For example, making classes smaller means finding space for more classes, and none may be available. That doesn't mean, however, that we'll need to build more schools. Some communities already have discovered that space limitations can be overcome by keeping schools open year-round and staggering student attendance. Over time, the educational system can be transformed in ways that will benefit everyone in the community. One possible vision of how public education might look in the future is sketched out in Chapter Twelve. School improvement doesn't have to cost more. With some creative thinking, education will not only become better, but also more cost-effective.

Change can seem threatening. We all share a fear of the unknown. But when the new becomes more familiar, we often wonder what we were so afraid of in the first place. My goal in writing this book is to make new ways of thinking about education more familiar to you, so that you can work toward getting your children the best education possible. Armed with specific information about teaching and learning, you will be in a better position to evaluate the quality of an educational system, lobby for changes that will help improve our schools, and—as your children's first teacher—help them learn to love and respect learning.

BRUNSWICK, MAINE
MARCH, 1992

Chapter One

Reforms That Work: An Introduction

"WHAT IS ALL THIS talk about school reform and restructuring? Why can't schools just get back to teaching the basics? School shouldn't be all fun and games. Kids today need more discipline! I'll bet a national test would make schools get down to business."

"The papers my son brings home from school are filled with misspelled words the teacher hasn't corrected. Doesn't that teacher know he'll never get a job if he misspells words on the job application?"

"My daughter is in eighth grade and she still hasn't learned the parts of speech. If she doesn't learn correct grammar, she's never going to learn to write well."

"The math teacher put the kids in my daughter's class in small groups. They're supposed to teach each other. That's ridiculous! What are we paying teachers for?"

"My son's history teacher doesn't even use a textbook. The kids do projects all the time. I want my son to learn dates, facts, all the important things we learned when we were in school. How can he do that without a textbook?"

"I couldn't believe it! The English teacher asked the students what books they wanted to read. Naturally no one wanted to read Shakespeare. Children don't always know what's good for them. Teachers should teach students what they need to know. After all, my boss doesn't ask me what I'd like to do."

"This year they've done away with grouping at the middle school my kids attend. The special ed kids are mixed in with everyone else. I don't see how anyone will be able to learn very much. The kids who have trouble learning should be in a class by themselves so they can learn at their own pace and not hold the other kids back."

If you have children in school, you may believe that they will learn more in a no-nonsense traditional school where teachers make sure everyone learns the basics. I used to think it was important to mark every error students made, to make all the decisions about what and how students would learn, and to do most of the talking in class so students wouldn't get any misinformation from classmates who might be as confused as they were. I taught the parts of speech and gave weekly spelling tests. I thought students learned best when they were assigned to separate classes based on their ability levels. If I had been told then that the teachers described in the quotations above were more effective than the teachers I knew who were doing things the old way, I would never have believed it. I know better now, and this book explains why.

I was forced to reexamine my ideas about teaching and learning because of students like Vickie and Fred, who were in my seventh-grade English and social studies classes. Vickie was bright, articulate, and eager to learn. School tests pegged her IQ at over 150. She had many friends and enthusiastically participated in class. She wrote wonderfully imaginative stories and voluntarily read books from the library on the topics we studied in class. Vickie was the type of student teachers want to clone. Thus, I was shocked and confused to find during the unit test on Egypt that Vickie was using information she had written on her hands to answer the questions. She knew the stuff. Why did she feel she had to cheat?

I didn't grab her paper, tear it up, and record a zero in the gradebook as many teachers might have done. Instead, I took her aside and in private asked her why. From the words she managed to choke out among the sobs, I figured out that she froze on tests. Her parents demanded she do well in school and that meant earning nothing less than A's. Vickie was so worried about getting the answers right that she couldn't gain access to what she knew. Crib notes were the only way she felt she could survive.

Unlike Vickie, Fred didn't appear too interested in learning much of anything. Chubby and plain, he smiled a lot, but he often forgot his book and rarely did his homework. His test scores were low, and so he was grouped in a smaller class with others who were labeled "slow." To be honest, this good-natured do-nothing drove me a little crazy since my constant reminders and periodic detentions produced no results.

As the year went on, I got to know Fred better and learned that he loved industrial arts. He didn't like social studies because reading for him was like deciphering hieroglyphics. All he got from struggling to make sense of the watered-down textbook was a long list of names and dates he couldn't remember. Fred saw the Egyptians not as people who had actually lived but as meaningless facts to memorize for a test. That he didn't or couldn't learn all these bits and pieces of information was evident in his low grade on the unit test.

Fred surprised me, however, when we later turned to ancient Greece. As an experiment, I asked students to choose for study some aspect of ancient Greece and do independent projects. Many students wrote stories or reports, some very colorfully illustrated. With the help of his IA teacher, Fred constructed a model of a Greek temple. When he brought the finished project in and explained what he had done, I noticed that his eyes, which had seemed dull and lazy, were bright and alive. Even more amazing to me was the knowledge of ancient Greece Fred had gained in the process of working on the temple. The Egyptians never lived for Fred, but the Greeks certainly did.

I was just a beginner when Vickie and Fred were my students. They were like hundreds of others students I've come in contact with over the years. They attended a junior high school that had an excellent reputation and represented the old ways of teaching and testing. Their stories show what's wrong with these types of schools, and why reform efforts that package old ideas in new programs are part of the problem, and not part of the solution. Old wine gone bad is still vinegar, even when poured in fancy new bottles.

Schools based on a new way of thinking about teaching and learning would have been better for both Vickie and Fred. You may be the parent of a child who, like Vickie or Fred, is having difficulty in school, or one who's simply not doing as well as you would like. Or maybe your child is getting all A's in honors classes but is motivated only by grades because the required assignments, although sometimes intellectually challenging, are not personally meaningful. Or you may be a property owner whose children are all grown up. You support education but can't afford to pay higher taxes. In any case, if you got a fairly good education in a traditional school, you may think the schools would be better off if they went back to the basics as you remember them. What you may not realize, however, is that a Model-T education, even when it's done well, won't prepare today's students for tomorrow's world.

Like the old Soviet economy, American education desperately needs *perestroika*. Restructuring, however, requires a change in traditional beliefs about education. Just as people in what used to be the USSR must have faith in an economic system they don't understand, Americans must believe in teaching methods most of us never experienced. Classrooms—not schools—should be the first focus of reform. Contrary to what many "experts" say, we can make many of these changes without spending a lot of money.

When the Department of Education published *A Nation at Risk* in 1983, proclaiming "a rising tide of mediocrity" in our public schools, we responded by turning our attention to educational reform. To that end we've witnessed reports and recommendations for change from many other national, state, and private groups, along with legislative mandates and policy changes that have resulted in more testing of both students and teachers, increased graduation requirements for students, higher certification standards for teachers, more time in school, and stronger and more specific curriculum guidelines in many states and local school districts. More recently, we've been told that schools also need to be restructured; parents should be free to choose which schools their children attend; schools themselves need more autonomy; and teachers must be empowered.

Given all the energy, effort, and money that have been expended, we might expect to see improved student test scores, but that has not been the case. Tests given in 1988 to fourth-, eighth-, and eleventh-graders across the nation by the National

Assessment of Educational Progress (NAEP) revealed that reading skills were up only slightly and writing skills had not improved at all since the early Seventies. Average scores on the Scholastic Aptitude Test (SAT), which had been increasing in recent years, were slightly lower in 1991.

While policy makers express their disappointment and concern, they are unlikely to come up with any solutions. Recent history shows that when something doesn't work, politicians and administrators believe they can make it work if, with greater determination and more money, they do more of the same. The situation is rather like trying to make someone understand what we have said by repeating the same message over and over with the same words in a progressively louder and louder voice. That method doesn't work in education any more than it does in communication. If someone doesn't understand, or a strategy doesn't work, common sense should tell us that we should not continue to repeat ourselves. Instead we need to try something else–phrase the message differently or figure out another approach.

Lorraine McDonnell, senior political scientist at the Rand Corporation, believes that efforts to make the schools more accountable have motivated them–but in the wrong direction. "I've certainly seen schools . . . that have changed their behavior. . . . But many have changed in ways we feel are inappropriate." There's plenty of evidence to support McDonnell's view, and we'll continue to be frustrated by the state of public education unless we sharpen the focus of school improvement efforts. If we want better schools for America's kids, we must work together to chart a new course for school reform.

Ironically, many recent efforts to improve education have actually made things worse. Take testing, for example. Most standardized tests focus on measuring students' ability to recall isolated bits of information and perform relatively simple operations out of context, rather than their ability to think creatively, solve complex problems, or apply knowledge in meaningful ways. The increased attention given to test scores, including the publication of district and school scores in newspapers, has resulted in more pressure on teachers to "teach to the tests." Thus, rather than engaging students in personally challenging learning experiences that will motivate them to work hard and do well, teachers are making school even more boring and irrelevant for students. At the same time students fail to get the knowledge they will need to be successful in the future, they also learn even less of the material they must know in order to do well on the standardized tests.

Perhaps our desire for the quick fix is one reason schools haven't improved. We seem to believe that every problem can be solved with a new program. We have created special courses to teach self-esteem, "aspirations compacts" to get kids to set higher goals for themselves, alternative programs for potential dropouts and teen mothers, and school-business partnerships. Although these programs may actually help some kids, a large part of their appeal is that they provide the illusion that something is being done to solve the problem. After one of these programs is featured on the evening news, we snap off our TV sets and never once think about applying what really does work in these special programs to all the students who sit, forgotten, in regular classrooms everywhere.

Though there's nothing inherently wrong with any of these efforts, they add to the bureaucratic burden schools already carry, and they don't change what most needs to be changed. Moreover, some of these reforms have been cut as states have been forced to deal with budget shortfalls. In my state, Maine, politicians eliminated the legislation-mandated statewide student testing program as a cost-saving measure. That no one fought very hard to keep this once highly touted program shows how fickle public opinion can be.

So what will work? The answer is simple and a lot less costly than much of what has already been tried. We must change the way we think about the education process and direct our resources toward helping individual teachers learn new and more effective ways of teaching and relating to the students in their classrooms. The heart of education is the classroom. Unless good things happen there, we'll continue to be disappointed with student achievement, no matter how many peripheral reforms we adopt. The reforms we most need are those that directly support the academic and personal growth of teachers and students in individual classrooms. It's also worth noting that unlike special programs, classroom change—once institutionalized—will be relatively safe from budget axes in the future because there is no cost beyond the money teachers are paid in salaries.

Classroom change, of course, is where reform should begin, but that is not where it should end. There are many other complex issues that must be addressed. As Jonathan Kozol shows in his recent book, *Savage Inequalities*, some children in America are not being given equal educational opportunities. Children who live in middle-class suburbs have more comfortable and better-equipped buildings, more books and materials, and more highly qualified teachers than children who attend inner-city schools. Because school districts with more money can provide better working conditions and higher salaries than financially strapped urban districts or poor rural districts in isolated areas, they can attract better teachers. But resolving these inequities will be neither quick nor easy. Some states that have attempted to change school funding formulas have discovered how difficult implementing such a plan can be even after one has been agreed on. But while the battles over how to reallocate scarce dollars continue, students can get a better education if teachers improve their classroom practice—even in the poorest of schools.

There are many other changes that should be considered. Schools would benefit from being smaller; every school should be small enough to feel more like a community of classroom families than a factory or prison. In smaller schools there would be much less need for bureaucratic processes and procedures; many administrative positions could be cut. Class sizes should also be smaller; the elimination of many special programs (and the administrators who supervise them) would allow schools to reduce class sizes at no increase in cost. With fewer students, teachers could more easily change their classroom practices to accommodate the abilities, learning styles, and interests of students from a wide variety of backgrounds. The school schedule should be more flexible; bells and buzzers are not conducive to learning.

Schools should also find ways to establish links with community and social service agencies so that services are not duplicated, and to involve everyone in the community—businesses, senior citizens, colleges, and universities—with the school in some way. Students need to see the connections among their different subject areas, their school and community, and their school work and "real life." Changes like these would result in schools where students want to learn. They would see that education is valued by everyone in the community.

Other people who participate in the process must also assume responsibility for education. Parents must support what their children are doing in school and do more to foster their learning at home. In addition, we need adults who are willing to be mentors for children lacking the family support that's often a given in most middle- and upper-class homes—this is especially true for teenage males who live with their mothers in single-parent households. To make the right changes, however, we first need a public that understands teaching and learning in a new way. Without this consensus we will still be spinning our educational wheels into the next century.

Giving up our old ideas about teaching and learning will not be easy. The media could certainly help in changing people's attitudes about education. We would all benefit from a media campaign devised to promote learning as a personal and complex process rather than a simple transmission of information. The results of current tests show that forcing students to play Trivial Pursuit with cultural literacy hasn't worked. A well-planned, long-term public relations campaign could change the nation's consciousness. We've seen advertising and public service announcements work when it meant saving lives from drunk driving and smoking. Should we do any less for the lives of America's children?

Changing the way we think about teaching and learning may also help lead to a resolution of some of our most difficult societal problems, such as substance abuse and child abuse. Our best hope lies in education, but not in education as we have come to know it. It's not a matter of stuffing more and more information into kids' heads about the dangers of crack or the threat of AIDS. What the schools must do—and what we as a society must work to achieve—is to make sure students grow as much personally as they do academically. Teaching methods that engage students in active learning will help them develop self-esteem and a sense of belonging. These qualities are necessary if students are to achieve, and thereby avoid destructive habits and behaviors. Teachers can encourage students to grow as individuals *at the same time* they help them to gain academic knowledge and skills. To do this, however, they must view teaching as more than just trafficking in facts.

We all learn in different ways. I attended a conference once where the speaker, in describing different learning styles, said that some of us are like powerboats while others are like sailboats. Powerboat people like efficiency and want to get right to the point. They will take the shortest route in order to reach their destination in the shortest time. Sailboat people, on the other hand, like to stop and look around, to explore. Even when they're headed to the same place as the powerboats, they'll take longer getting there because they'll choose to follow a circuitous route and may even stop along the way. I think there are some rowboats among us, too. Rowboat people will take a direct route, but they'll have to work very hard pushing and pulling on the oars to move. It will take them a long time to go any distance. But if they continue at a slow and steady pace, they can go wherever the powerboats and sailboats do.

Schools are organized and classes are taught, usually, to favor powerboats. But powerboats with big engines sometimes get bored because the rest of the fleet isn't moving fast enough. Creative-thinking sailboats often get in trouble for wanting to do things their own way. Rowboats end up with failing grades and may be placed in special education classes. But all the boats could work together in the same class if teachers stopped expecting everyone to do the same assignments in the same way at the same time. When students use their strengths to work with classmates who are different, they develop confidence in themselves and help their classmates do the same. Since all the boats sail in the same waters out in the real world, we shouldn't separate them in school. Teachers who have learned to think about teaching in new ways have found the means to personalize learning for different kinds of students.

The idea that schools can accomplish so much more, and do so without large increases in school funding, may appear ridiculous to some. But by thinking about science in new ways—

considering the big picture and overall process instead of looking more closely at the smaller individual elements—theorists in the new study of chaos have already made exciting discoveries in many different fields. There is order in chaos; complex results can come from simple beginnings, and small differences in input can result in enormous differences in output. What's true in science is just as true in education.

Although it may appear chaotic to work toward changing what happens in thousands of individual classrooms without having a detailed master plan prescribing everything each teacher must do, there will be common patterns among many teachers doing seemingly random things. Although the education system as a whole is very complex, the information we collect on what students across the country do essentially depends upon the interactions of individual students with their respective teachers. And a seemingly simple change in the way teachers teach and relate to students can result in enormous increases in student achievement.

I am convinced that teachers can make incredible gains, even with students on whom others have completely given up. I've seen it happen with my own students and with those of other teachers, time and time again. And when teachers change the way they teach in order to reach the most unmotivated and the least able students, they find that the average and gifted students learn more as well. What's more, as students become more actively involved in learning, they assume more responsibility for themselves, set and reach higher goals, and become more concerned about learning for the joy of learning than they are about the grades they get.

Many of these suggestions sound like echoes from the late Sixties and Seventies, when free schools and student choice were in vogue, but in fact they are very different. Too much of what was tried in those years lacked structure. In trying to make school more relevant to students, many teachers let anything go. When we realized that this do-your-own-thing approach resulted in an erosion of standards and little attention to what we considered basic to a good education, we overreacted by forcing schools back to the old teach-and-test tradition. We moved from a focus on personal process to an emphasis on specified outcomes. Now, however, some teachers have learned that students learn more when we give as much attention to the process of learning as we do to its product.

Teaching strategies that engage students in doing and thinking also increase their motivation. Writing can be used in any subject as a tool for learning and communicating, not just for evaluating what students have or have not learned. Informal writing—"talking on paper"—and cooperative learning activities make it possible for students to process information in a way that allows them to remember it longer and better apply it in the future. As students learn in more active and personal ways, they also gain confidence in their abilities to learn on their own and with other students. Because teachers who use these teaching strategies also get to know students as individuals—even when they teach over a hundred students a day—the students respond to their caring and concern by working longer and harder.

When teachers capitalize on students' normal human desire for social interaction by creating small-group learning activities, they increase the number of "teachers" in the room: students can and do learn as much, sometimes more, from each other as from the teacher. These activities also help students develop interpersonal skills that are invaluable on the job or in the home, where getting along with others is just as important as being able to read and write. Studies also have shown that cooperative learning can reduce stereotyping and prejudice.

If some teachers have already discovered how well these methods work, why haven't all teachers adopted them? No one welcomes change, and change comes more slowly to institutions than it does to individuals. But perhaps an even greater obstacle than the natural resistance to change in any form is the fact that too few educators—administrators and teachers—and members of the general public understand what should be changed and why. Sometimes teachers have tried small groups, for example, when they lacked the background to make them work effectively. Instead of figuring out why they failed and trying again, they go back to what they've always done: lectures, teacher-led discussions, and worksheets.

Students often prefer these familiar methods, too, because they aren't comfortable with change, especially when they don't understand what they're doing and why. Under pressure and deadlines to do too much in too little time, teachers often make the mistake of not providing explanations when they want kids to do something–even though knowing "why" can make a big difference in how things turn out.

When parents don't understand a new approach, they make it difficult for schools to adopt changes that would enhance student learning. For instance, when one school adopted a problem-solving approach for teaching math, a parent complained that his child wasn't doing "real math." He eventually pulled the child out of the public school and placed him in a private one.

Despite the fads that have come and gone–"new" math, open classrooms, and the like–public schools have changed little in a hundred years. And while the schools might have worked well for the country's needs at the turn of the century, nearly everyone agrees that they're not working well enough today to prepare students to live in the twenty-first century. But if we hope to implement change in schools that desperately need it, we first need to understand what we must do differently, and why a new approach will work when so many other innovations have failed or been forgotten. Then we need to marshall all of our resources and work together to make it happen. We have no time to waste, and thoughtlessly scattering our efforts here and there will not work any better now than it has in the past.

The strength of the nation depends on the quality of our schools. Students who believe in themselves and have the support and encouragement of others will succeed in school and in life. If you understand what teachers must do, then you can encourage their efforts in your own way–as a parent, a school board member, or an interested citizen.

If you think the support of informed citizens doesn't make a difference, consider what happened to Bill Nave, Maine's 1990 Teacher of the Year and one of four finalists for the national award. Recognized for his work with high school dropouts in an alternative program, Nave says his philosophy is very simple: "Every student is of infinite worth and value and is capable of learning. We need to structure schools so that learning can take place." Although Nave was hailed by the governor as a model for other teachers, only a few years ago he was forced to resign from a teaching position in another community in the state for using the *same* methods that now earn him praise! Nave refused to follow a schoolwide discipline approach that required teachers to write the offending students' names on the board, to which checks would be added for each subsequent offense. Three checks would usually warrant a consequence, such as staying in at recess or after school. (This discipline model has been adopted by many schools across the nation, but it also has been the target of much criticism from those teachers who realize that humiliating students in front of their classmates creates more problems than it solves.)

Nave points out that the schools have become too caught up in their own structure and tradition—one reason students become turned off by school and drop out. "Economically, it's a lot more cost effective to teach them now than it is to support them later through the Department of Human Services or through the penal system," he said, and of course he's right.

If there are dedicated teachers using effective but innovative methods in your local school, they need your support. Each year administrators resistant to change drive good teachers like Bill Nave out. And many of these talented and dedicated people don't find positions in other schools—they leave teaching altogether. You can help good teachers stay in teaching by finding out who they are and being ready to rally local support, should the need arise, to prevent unwise administrators from getting rid of them.

Even if their jobs are not in jeopardy, these teachers may feel lonely and unappreciated in schools where everyone else goes about teaching in the same old ways with little enthusiasm and no desire for change. Parents who take the time to say "I like what you're doing for my child" can help these teachers feel good enough about their work to continue, despite the fact that the principal and other teachers may not agree with their methods.

Whatever you can learn about teaching and learning will help you educate your own children in many diverse, informal ways. Parents are, after all, children's first and most influential teachers. You also will be able to evaluate the quality of the teaching in your children's schools and see what changes are likely to enhance classroom learning. Sometimes parents know instinctively that a particular teaching method is not working, but they don't know what teachers could do instead. If your children are fortunate enough to have teachers who already use the methods described here, you'll be able to support their efforts by working with your children at home to reinforce what they are doing, and perhaps also by explaining the strategies to other parents who still believe that old-fashioned methods are better.

Chapter Two

Looking Back

WE ALL HAVE a tendency to remember things as better than they were, and our school days are no exception. Your clearest memories of school are probably friends and social activities, not teachers and courses. How much time did your teachers spend teaching things you haven't used since you got out of school? How much of what you need to know and do today did you learn outside of school or on your own? Which teachers do you remember? Which ones made a difference in your life?

Because most people have not really thought about their education and how it has affected their lives, they fail to support teachers using techniques they themselves never experienced in school. We tend to judge schools on the basis of our own experience. If your teachers emphasized correct spelling on every assignment, for example, you may be unhappy when your child brings home a paper with misspelled words the teacher didn't mark. Too much concern with spelling, however, can be a barrier to more important learning. You may be able to understand why many teachers are doing things differently today by reflecting on your own education and considering what worked and what didn't.

Just so that you can get in touch with your own school days, take some time to read over the questions below. One of the major reasons the changes we've made to improve schools haven't made them more effective is that we've continued to do more of what *hasn't* worked, rather than thoughtfully considering how to devise better ways of teaching. After doing this little "test," and then reading the responses of other adults who tried it, you'll see why the kind of school we remember is not the kind of school we need today.

How many hours would you guess you spent learning grammar in English or in a foreign language? How much do you remember now? Try labeling all the parts of speech (noun, pronoun, verb, adjective, adverb, conjunction, preposition, and interjection) and the functions of words (subject, predicate, object of preposition, direct object, indirect object, predicate adjective, predicate nominative) in the following sentence: AFTER SWINGING FROM TREE TO TREE, THE MONKEY WAS EXHAUSTED WHEN HE JUMPED TO THE GROUND.

Now try a math question. We all sat through endless hours of math instruction and completed pages and pages of homework. Solve this: If $35\ rt + 8 = 42\ rt$, then $rt =$ ________.

Here's a social studies question. Remember, American history and government are graduation requirements in most schools. What is the Missouri Compromise and when was it signed? If you were stumped by that question, try this one instead: List in order the steps a bill must go through before becoming a federal law.

And last, but not least, a question from biology, another course that's usually required of all students: What is the difference between *mitosis* and *meiosis*?

If you're curious, you can easily find the right answers using a standard reference work—if not your children's own textbooks. But that's not important here. Instead, think about how you felt as you tried to answer the questions. Consider your feelings and thoughts as you answered them, and consider how useful that knowledge is for you today. Did you struggle to remember what you're sure you once knew but can't fully recall now? How important is knowing the answers to these questions in your present life? How many times since you left school, for example, have you had occasion to use the parts of speech? Which questions were relatively easy for you, even now?

Can you remember a classroom activity or project you worked on that you'll never forget because you really enjoyed doing it? What made it special or meaningful? Why does it stand out from the hundreds of other assignments and projects you did in school?

Think about your teachers, those you remember as being

good teachers and those who weren't so effective. Choose the teachers you remember most vividly, good and bad. Try to recall specific memories of being in their classes.

The exercise you just did is a good example of how teachers can help students connect what they study with their own lives. If teachers start with what students already know about a subject, they can make the new information personally meaningful and thus increase the possibility that students will understand and remember it.

If you were a student in my class right now and we were doing a unit on schools, I would ask you to share your responses to these questions with other students in the class. Since you're reading a book, however, and can't participate in a class discussion, I asked a few other people I know to take a crack at these questions and then write down their responses. The ideas presented in the rest of this book will make more sense to you if you relate them to your own experiences in school.

Diana, who's been out of school for several years, said, "After looking over the questions, I felt as though I'd lost some grey cells—couldn't recall the answers to all the subject matter, though I remembered more than I thought I would after thinking about it for a few minutes. I believe the reason I don't recall all the answers now is because . . . in those days . . . the point was pleasing the teacher and getting by, not learning something that would empower me at a later date, or even at the time."

Suzanne, a college senior who is student teaching, said, "I think I knew all of the answers to the questions at one point in my life. . . . It was a little frustrating to know I *knew* the answers at one point but now had no real idea of what the answers are. I certainly have not had occasion to use the parts of speech since I learned them, except now to teach them to others who will have no occasion to use them. It seems that we should focus on writing ability and not on memorization of useless knowledge, such as parts of speech."

Todd has been teaching at a private school for two years. "I feel somewhat dumb trying to answer these questions. I'm not sure how right I am. In math and science especially I am quite ignorant. . . . The history questions were tough even after I taught U.S. history last year!"

Ellen, much older than Todd and not a teacher, said she didn't use the specifics of anything she learned, but her English teachers must have been effective. When she reads articles or books, typos jump from the page. She said, "When I listen to speakers from commercials or political candidates, some grammatical errors– 'between you and I,' 'me and Jimmy were married in 1984'–almost make my teeth hurt."

Rochelle said, "My first reaction to many of the questions was 'This is stupid.' I reacted this way because I didn't know the answers. I felt threatened . . . I never have been good at trivia, which is what many of these questions are. The math question was the easiest . . . it just required logic, not factual knowledge."

Kelly isn't good at trivia either. She said, "I felt like I was playing Trivial Pursuit when I tried to answer. . . . As for using the information in my present life, I would have to say that would be very seldom except when I play Trivial Pursuit. Then I usually get the answer wrong, so I suppose it doesn't matter what I learned in the first place."

Evariste, who graduated from high school about fifteen years ago, said, "Looking back over these questions I find I cannot any longer answer most of them off the top of my head. I find this embarrassing, as I always do whenever I consider matters that rely on my memory. . . . I have looked back over my school history and those subjects that I had the most trouble with have the same link: memorization required. I recall suffering through memorization of the alphabet. My father and my sister tutored me for several weeks until I could say the alphabet." Evariste described in some detail the problems he had with spelling, times tables, and fractions, and then comments, "I am wondering if I have a learning disability or if I am just lazy."

Perhaps the saddest comment came from Eileen, who said simply, "I could remember suffering."

The people who volunteered to do this exercise all went to college. They were students who were successful in school–and yet they mentioned feeling frustrated, dumb, and embarrassed. Imagine how much worse students who don't do well must feel.

It's clear that schools need to be more concerned with students' feelings. But these responses also show that if we use or see value in knowing the information we learn, we remember it. Schools shouldn't teach only the content that we'll have practical use for immediately or later on. But they should make sure that students spend enough time developing skills in areas that will directly benefit them when they're out in the workplace, and that they teach those skills within a meaningful context.

The study of grammar and writing illustrates this point well. Research studies have shown that there is little or no connection between knowledge of formal grammar and the ability to write well. Yet if your schools were like mine, you devoted countless hours to completing grammar exercises and worksheets and going over them in class. Actual writing assignments, however, at best, amounted to one short essay per week and one longer research paper per year. The teacher dutifully marked up your finished theme with red ink, returned it to you with a grade, and told you to avoid making the same mistakes again. She probably spent hours explaining the parts of speech and punctuation rules but only minutes talking about your essays. Although she showed you models of good essays, you rarely (if ever) discussed *how* to go about writing one, and didn't spend any class time at all learning how to revise an essay you were in the process of writing.

You later learned that being able to write clearly and coherently was a necessary and useful skill on the job, but while school may have helped you get the commas in most of the right places, you probably had to learn on your own how to make what you had to say clear and understandable to others. The school's focus on literary essays and surface correctness didn't give you much preparation for writing office memos and reports to higher-ups. There's quite a difference between explaining the imagery in *The Adventures of Huckleberry Finn* to a teacher and clarifying the new policy on insurance benefits for factory workers. This isn't to say that schools should teach students how to write only for business purposes, but that they should reconsider how much time they spend teaching content in isolation. They must help students see the practical applications of what they study. Wouldn't you have been better off if your English teachers spent one hour on grammar study for every four hours on writing, rather than the other way around?

In many ways, I've become more and more resentful of my own teachers—although it wasn't their fault they didn't know how to do things any differently. I now know that writing is a complex process that can't be reduced to the simple formula essay form I was taught: begin with an introductory paragraph that includes a "thesis statement," follow with paragraphs that each begin with a topic sentence and develop one sub-point of the thesis, and conclude with a paragraph that summarizes what you have just written. (The formula essay may be quite useful in some situations, such as writing the answer to an essay question in a history class.) Because I could often construct these formula essays in my head, I was able to write final copy on the first draft. Since my teachers never looked at anything but the final draft, that's all I usually did—unless I had to copy a page over because of a crossed-out word or ink smudge.

Old habits die hard, and although I teach my own writing classes differently, I find it hard to practice what I preach. Because the process of writing often means doing many drafts, I should have learned to get my ideas down on paper first and gone back to revise them later on. I now find writing more difficult, because when taking on ambitious projects—such as this book—I still try to write final copy on the first draft. My own students are learning to write in a much more realistic and productive way. They won't develop the bad habits I was taught and now must struggle to break.

What's true for English courses is also true for other subjects. Students need to learn what they'll use after they leave school. They need to know why what they are studying is important to know. And they need to be taught in ways that will support rather than hinder what they'll be doing in real life. It isn't enough for the teacher to say, as parents so often do, "Do it because I said so."

Are your children's teachers giving them enough practical knowledge and developing the skills they'll need later in life? Do your children see value and purpose in what they study? Are your children's teachers preparing them for real-life activities or just giving them lots of practice doing things they'll use only in school? Are they teaching them skills in context–punctuation of their own writing, for example–or having them practice on "dummy exercises?"

In talking with adults, I've discovered that poor teaching seems to handicap students only when they have trouble learning a subject. If you're naturally good at math and science, for example, you'll catch on even when the teacher is dull and uninspiring. It takes an effective teacher, however, to help you learn a subject that is difficult for you. Math phobia or an aversion to writing may be the result of teachers who don't deal well with students' anxiety and lack of natural ability. They teach their subject as if it could be learned and understood by everyone in the same way at the same pace.

Diana said, "Geometry was my real downfall. My head doesn't work three-dimensionally. I just never got it. It made me feel hopelessly stupid, and it is only in my later years, when I realized that some people are simply not designed to deal with certain modes of thinking, that I can forgive myself for not having been good in this area."

Geometry never made any sense to me either. I can still hear the teacher's monotone voice and see him standing by the blackboard, his hand holding the string from which the piece of chalk he used to draw circles dangled as he spoke. He never once explained the connection of geometry to anything in the real world. Thirty years later I watched a public television program and was surprised to learn that no one would ever have been able to sail away from the sight of land had it not been for geometry. What a remarkable development! Without geometry, we wouldn't have been able to navigate across oceans. Geometry might not have been any easier for me if my teacher had taken some time to explain its connection to history–which I loved–or the real world. I am sure that if he had, though, I would have tried harder to learn it.

Suzanne didn't do well in math either: "I don't have an analytical mind, I've decided. I began taking [math] courses thinking I didn't have to study, which was wrong. Doing the homework was not enough. . . . Knowledge is built upon mastery of the previous level. Since I hadn't mastered the other earlier material, I was soon lost. I obviously did not realize the value and necessity of studying to understand the subject–it didn't *always* just come to me in an instant."

Anna, in writing about a journal article she read for her education class, also mentioned math: "Math is not a whole-concept thing to me. I always think of it as–you learn one thing and then you move on to the next thing, and none of it will ever be used after you take it in school. As Lauren Resnick points out, this kind of learning is 'contradictory to the goal of having children come to believe that mathematics is an organized system of thought that they are capable of figuring out.' This helps me understand why in high school I got straight A's in math, but as soon as I got to calculus I failed. I had come to believe that 'mathematics [was] a collection of questions to which one can find the answer in about a minute or not at all.' This is why calculus and complex problems were so frustrating to me."

It's surprising what details people remember. Shelley hated algebra, and she remembers little of the class twenty-four years ago except that the teacher was boring and a girl named Audrey sat near her. Diana's memories are more personal and painful. "Being shy and terribly insecure, I always hated being called on in large classes, though I enjoyed small ones with intelligent, sensitive teachers. I had a terror of getting the answers wrong when called on. I always had a sense that there was more than one right answer, that things were not all black and white, but the world of school said otherwise. I felt either stupid or superior, depending on my mood at the time. . . . In seventh grade [math] we had time tests every morning. . . . While a timer ticked away the five minutes or whatever it was, I used to sit and stare at the numbers until they became a haze of little black strokes, listening to the tick-tick of that damned clock, waiting for my nerves to get jangled for good by the final BUZZZ."

My own math phobia can be blamed on the way I was taught math. My teachers never helped me understand the purpose of what we were learning, and, like Anna, I never realized that mathematics was a way of thinking. Before long I convinced myself that since I was incapable of learning math, there was no point in trying to understand it. I would just concentrate on passing the required courses, which I was able to do in my high school by going back two afternoons a week for extra help. Even though I'm sure I failed nearly every test, my teachers gave me "courtesy passing grades," as they did to most students who showed they were trying. My presence at the extra help sessions enabled me to fulfill the school's graduation requirements even though I knew next to nothing about math.

Kelly also had a tough time in math. "My [algebra] teacher tortured me by making me sit at the front of the class and would constantly ask me questions I certainly couldn't figure out. I did my homework every night. . . . I studied, paid attention to the teacher, and worked my butt off. After all my efforts, I still only managed to receive C's. . . . To this day I do not understand why there are letters in a math problem!" Many algebra teachers would probably be astonished to find out that after a whole year in their course, a student with a passing grade didn't understand such a basic principle!

Todd cites physics and math as the subjects in which he had the most difficulty. "Physics I didn't like because of the math, formulas and equations coupled with the step-by-step processes it took to properly figure out problems. I always got frustrated in math because the examples we did in class and the ones that were in the book seemed to be designed perfectly for solving. Then the ones in the homework didn't seem to fit the supposed 'flawless' method we learned in class. Ugh!"

History was Rochelle's least favorite subject. "I *hated* memorization. I do not have a photographic memory and learning battles and names and dates of treaties really bothered me. I hated the reading most of the time because often it was a cold listing of facts. I took one history course that I enjoyed. The teacher treated the course . . . as if she were . . . telling a story. Although I don't remember everything, I have fond memories. What's odd is that although I cannot recall facts about history, I feel like I have a decent hold on it. Most of what I do remember about history is from reading novels. I feel like I have learned most of the history I know through novels, movies, and discussions with friends."

Sometimes we assume that good students excel at everything, but the truth is that each of us has different strengths and weaknesses. Rita, who felt comfortable and successful in academic classes, said, "I never ended up liking art or woodshop or classes like that, not for the reason that I did not think they were important, but because I didn't do well in them. Our projects were always graded and since my projects were always lopsided or very messy, I did not receive good grades. I suppose I had a hard time following directions. Thus, since middle school, I have always hated art just because I'm not good at it. Being graded on final products but not on effort can result in really turning a student away from a certain subject area."

Fear may inhibit learning, but we'll often learn certain things for utilitarian reasons, both in and out of school. Diana said, "Math subjects were anathema. Once again, math just seemed to be a lot of laws and rules that I would happily apply and forget once I'd gotten a decent enough grade not to ruin my average." And her feelings about grammar labels weren't much different. Since she was praised for writing well, she said, "I had a kind of chauvinistic view that I didn't need to learn these silly labels. It was only in later life that I have bothered learning any of the parts of speech, etc., if only to hold my own at meetings and cocktail parties."

Marlene wrote about doing the same grammar exercises over and over, year after year. "Things like this happened in other classes besides English. It's disgusting the amount of time we wasted. People in my upper-level classes were pretty conforming and we did all the work, no matter how trivial. But I can see how many kids can get bored and frustrated in school and maybe eventually leave for good. Even if they do stick around, they probably won't learn much that will help them later in life."

Ask your children to talk about the subjects they're having difficulty with. Are their feelings similar to what yours were? Teachers *can* engage and involve students in meaningful learning activities, using a variety of approaches so that students with different learning styles can be taught effectively—even in the same class. When teachers develop better strategies for teaching and relating to students, fewer students will end up with negative attitudes about any subject.

The people who shared their school memories with me talked about boring classes and hours spent doing homework exercises, dittoed worksheets, quizzes and exams, routine essays and research papers—most of which have faded from memory, along with much of the knowledge required to complete them. Still, most of them clearly remembered some of the school work they did, even many years later. Compare these highlights with your own memories of special projects and assignments.

My memory list includes writing two haiku that won a first prize in a high school poetry contest, a story—about the evils of alcohol—I wrote in class and later read to a meeting of the Women's Christian Temperance Union, and a model of the solar system I constructed when I was in elementary school. I'm sure I remember these because I worked on all of them by myself. They were mine, not the teacher's, and they gave me a chance to be creative. But in each case I could feel proud of my accomplishment, and others also recognized my achievements. I often wish I had had more opportunities in school to get such good feelings.

Diana's memories are similar. "I made a stained glass window when I was about ten years old. . . . It took months and was tedious in a sense, because all the other kids had chosen shorter, easier projects and got theirs done first, but it was beautiful when it was finished, and my parents still have it in their living room." In fifth grade Diana made the cover for the class yearbook, "a painting of yet another stained glass window, and the entire school applauded me at the assembly where the painting was displayed."

Barbara mentioned a paper she did for her junior history class on Joe Hill—was he set up because of his beliefs or was he guilty of murder? "It was the biggest [project] I'd ever done. I remember going to the Boston Public Library and to Brandeis University to research it. I felt very old—and I did very well." Rochelle, too, remembered research papers because she "looked upon them as detective work." And Linda fondly recalled term papers, because she liked the discovery process and the tangible product at the end.

Todd remembered two projects he did in school. "One was a biology project where we examined many living organisms. We dissected everything from worms to fetal pigs. I distinctly remember taking the intestines out of pigs, unraveling them, and measuring them—they were over five feet long! Also, the smell of formaldehyde still lurks in my nose! I also remember writing a report on the first atomic bomb for my U.S. history class. I read several books about the bombs and how they worked. I drew diagrams and I even carved two little wooden models to represent the 'Fat Man' and 'Little Boy' bombs. I remember slicing my thumb nearly off while whittling these models. I got A's on both projects. I think these stand out in my mind because, first, they interested me, and second, because they were both hands-on."

Evariste favored assignments that allowed him to work independently and be creative. One project involved asking people to respond to a political cartoon on abortion which he admits he didn't understand. "The responses I got when I asked people to explain it, and also say whether it was for or against abortion, were divergent. Everyone who looked at it was just as confused as I was. I learned a most valuable lesson that I will carry with me for the rest of my life, and that was something like: the exact same words can mean one thing to one person and something very different to the next. . . . "

Norine clearly remembers her third-grade class almost a half-century ago, because everyone worked together to build a village that covered the entire classroom floor. Houses lined the black paper streets. "I even remember being chided for painting my house red and blue–no one *ever* puts those two colors together." In seventh grade she wrote a journal of an imaginary trip across the United States, using information obtained from writing to publicity bureaus and looking everywhere for pictures to use like photographs. Geography became real and personal.

The assignments or projects people remember with pleasure have some common characteristics. The students were interested in the subject; they had a personal investment in the assignment; they were actively involved; and, because the product was a result of their own hard work, they could feel proud of what they had accomplished. Recognition from others–whether in the form of a high grade or praise–only seemed to make these projects even more memorable.

Good assignments and good teachers often go hand in hand, but students will tolerate and even work hard to do well on boring assignments for teachers they respect and care about. In fact, in response to the question, "What projects did I enjoy?" Evariste wrote, "It is easier for me to consider the teachers first. I mean, if I consider teachers that I remember fondly, I naturally think of some of the assignments I did for them. As I think of teachers who did not inspire me in any way, I can't even recall what we studied."

Put good teachers and good assignments together, and you have the formula for lifelong learning. What were your teachers like? How much did the person who taught a subject have to do with how you felt about the subject, then and now? Was your life changed–for better or worse–by a teacher?

There's no question that teachers make a difference. Unfortunately that difference isn't always positive, and some of us may never get over the negative effects caused by a teacher in whose class we sat many years ago.

Leslee remembered a computer teacher who inspired students–to fear. "The 'Iron Man' he was often called. . . . I was really nervous so I tried not to talk and sat right down at my desk. He'd give us homework assignments and we had to create programs that would *run* successfully. We had a computer at home, but it was entirely different from the school computers. To this day I'll never forget how upset I got in that class. He would have us work on programs in class, and it never failed that I messed up so that the screen was full of jumbled work. He would sigh and let the whole class know I'd messed up again. I have always wanted to do the best I could at everything. Therefore, I became very anxiety-ridden and cried whenever I got a homework assignment."

She continued, "I got an upperclassman to help me and I started getting A's on my homework. He asked me who had been helping me. This man made an entire year nerve-wracking for me. He was very sarcastic and let every student know they would never be able to solve the problems he assigned. He was so proud when he was the *only* one to know the answer. Some students were very good on computers and could always solve the programs. He would get very angry and mark their papers 'short cuts' and give them low grades. Ever since that class, I have had a mortal fear of computers. Every time I try to work on one, 'SYNTAX ERROR' flashes before my eyes." Leslee's teacher not only didn't teach her, he also turned her off to learning about computers on her own.

Bethany will never forget her art teacher. "[She] should have used her influence to help people instead of deter them. Instead . . . she discouraged anything people did. . . . I remember one instance when I was stretching a canvas across a frame for a silk screening project and she grabbed it out of my hands, heaved a deep sigh, and told me that I couldn't even do that right. Maybe she was having a particularly rotten day, though I don't think she acted much different than usual, but for someone like myself with little confidence as it was, she didn't help." Teachers often forget how fragile self-confidence can be, and how much students need it to take the risks necessary to learn. One experience like Bethany's is all it takes to make some students give up on a subject for a year, and sometimes altogether.

Jim said, "In the middle grades I had a teacher who was just mean. I cannot now think of her without tagging 'witch' onto her name. . . . A workbook with both printed and written words was enough to single a student out for criticism. . . . She refused to let one student use the restroom during class, then failed to intervene when the predictable occurred. The rest of us sat heads down over our lessons in pained silence. In that kind of environment, no . . . progress was made in writing." In tenth grade Jim's English teacher was "caught in a time lock." She taped a sheet of red paper over the clock because "she didn't want us anticipating the end of class. She bored me nearly out of my mind."

Ellen put her Algebra I teacher at the top of her "worst" list because "he tended to take out all his frustrations in life on his students. He had no patience for students who didn't share his love of baseball. He was extremely sexist and made no secret of his preference for athletes."

Todd said, "The worst teacher I had was Mr. P., who taught me French during sophomore year. I had really enjoyed French I with Mr. R. and was looking forward to learning how to speak French better. However, this man completely turned me off. . . . He only taught the phonetics to us, and wrote strange symbols on the board and tried to explain them but couldn't. The class was huge and rather rowdy. He had no control over anyone. . . . People cheated like crazy. . . . I think I knew less French after two years than I did after only one year because we never got to speak it. He would often teach for ten or fifteen minutes and then give us the remaining thirty minutes to work on homework or do nothing."

Suzanne said her Algebra II teacher "just could not teach. . . . I remember this man asking us if we had any problems with the homework. . . . He dutifully filled up both the front and side board with a difficult problem—and then came up with the wrong answer. He 'explained' things too quickly for me to follow and then couldn't solve the problems himself. . . . After this happened, he would scratch his head, look over his work for a few minutes, and then say, 'Hmm, well. Tell you what. I'll take it home and work on it, and ask my wife what she thinks, and I'll let you know tomorrow.' This was of little help to me. Homework was still assigned . . . built on that day's work, and when tomorrow came, the answer usually didn't."

Some poor teachers were also unforgettable characters. Cheryl's driver ed teacher "kind of snuffled when he talked. He had a big red nose that often dripped and he didn't smell very good. . . . Mr. H. would put his hands in his baggy trousers, turn around from the class, and scratch his groin—you could tell by the way his shoulders would hunch up and down. . . . He didn't teach us anything. He just had us read the book. He didn't show a lot of enthusiasm or interest in his students. I was just a job to him, and that showed." Cheryl must have practiced driving with this teacher, but it's worth noting that her strongest memories are from the classroom part of the course.

Rather than describing a particular teacher, Rochelle listed the qualities her worst teachers shared: "sarcastic, cold in speaking, bored and therefore boring, teased kids . . . teachers who didn't listen to students' ideas."

Similarly, Evariste said, "I remember dullness, boredom, disdain for the subject . . . even disdain for the students. The worst teachers I remember did not want to be teaching. . . . Some I do recall, vividly, were downright hateful—even sadistic; they seemed to take pleasure only in the belittlement of their students. It amazes me . . . that I did not protest. . . . I am sure well-adjusted, self-confident adults would never have put up with such brutality."

But there are teachers we remember fondly—and a relationship with one special teacher can make a lifelong difference in how we feel about ourselves or about an area of knowledge.

Cheryl recalled a teacher she had decades ago in the fourth grade: "Mrs. P. was a roly-poly Santa Claus type and treated all her students like ducklings with herself as Mother Duck. She would find something special about every student and then she would find some way to make that student shine. Glen, a very thin, tall boy with thick glasses and blond hair that stuck up all over, and I were known as the class artists. Mrs. P. arranged for us to go to the second grade [classroom] . . . and draw birds on the chalkboard with colored chalk. This was a very big deal because children rarely got to even write on the chalkboard. . . . One of us did a robin, the other a bluebird. It took all day. . . . The pictures stayed on the upper part of the chalkboard all year. I remember how proud I was. When I walked by the second-grade classroom, I would always peek in just to see if the pictures were still there."

Juanita found math difficult because she was told as a little girl that "girls don't do well in arithmetic." Her fear dissolved in high school when her female math teacher exclaimed, "Math is my life—I wouldn't want to live without it!" This teacher inspired Juanita to earn an A in geometry.

Beth never cared for science "because it was a lot of complicated and useless nonsense," but that all changed with Mr. G. in seventh grade. "He was a show, not just tell, teacher. When we learned about electricity, we got a *feel* for it. Our class gathered around an electrically charged battery and held hands. Mr. G. asked for a volunteer/victim to hold one end of a wire that was connected to the battery while he held the other wire. He then flipped a switch and we felt electricity flowing through our hands. What a weird sensation!"

"The subject that stays with me to this day," Beth continued, "is astronomy. We each had to choose a planet or constellation (I chose Jupiter) and do a report. Before we started, he took each of us out at night . . . and showed us where our subject was in the sky. . . . Mr. G. spent many hours at this, as you can imagine, with twenty-eight students. . . . Now I look at the night sky with fascination . . . and always think of Mr. G. He was also interested in his students' lives. . . . I loved that man and will never forget him as long as there are stars in the sky!"

Dany's biology teacher stood out from all the other teachers. Although she taught a required subject, she got students interested by focusing on what they most wanted to learn. "I was Mrs. H.'s student assistant in my senior year. In a sense I was a microcosm of her class. She was interested in what school was doing for me . . . [and wanted] to help me learn or reach my goals. She made me responsible for everything behind the scenes of her class. She trusted me as much as I trusted her. . . . She cared enough to make learning interesting for each student, going so far as to make special assignments for students."

Norm remembered someone who helped him when he needed it: "My most admired teacher was Mr. D. in high school chemistry and physics. I entered both classes late due to working on a farm in Vermont until mid-October. He was able to extract my best efforts to catch up and excel."

After having several teachers who discouraged students, including one who was so concerned about order and appearance that she made students feel like "soldiers in desk row formation," Jim awakened from "the dulling effect of past teachers" in eleventh-grade English. After he got the lowest score on a grammar test, he discovered to his relief that the teacher's goal was "to get us to write. I found myself in . . . a renaissance class. We wanted to be involved. We read books out loud. Students acted out parts in the books. A year before I had discovered the state library. . . . What an amazing place. . . . In Mrs. M.'s class I was given an A on a term paper, of all things. Her class was a peak. . . . "

Rob said his best teacher "distinguished himself by his hard work. Unlike most teachers, he came to school a half-hour early and left typically three hours after [classes ended]. Even after teaching similar courses year in, year out, he seemed to try new things." In Honors English "we usually got into a circle and talked about some great literature. He was great at facilitating discussion. We felt comfortable with him . . . so that we would feel free to go out on a limb seeking knowledge. We did group work. . . . In fact, we once used a group-effort exam. Teams of four would work on a test in a closed-book session. *We* chose this option. . . . On top of the reading we had a five-page paper every two weeks. I felt motivated not just by the grade but by wanting to excel."

Barbara remembered two very different English teachers. "I hated my sophomore English teacher at first. She was very organized. I remember an assignment—three poems, Joyce Kilmer's 'Trees,' William Carlos Williams' 'So much depends upon/a red wheelbarrow,' and a third poem that it turned out had been written by a computer. We discussed which was the best poem—and I, having picked the poem I had fallen for years before, 'Trees,' was crestfallen to discover that she found it flawed—an impossible contortion of images. To this day I can explain what's wrong with that poem. . . . By the end of sophomore year I remember cautiously approaching her and telling her I had not liked her at first—but that year I had learned a lot—and changed my mind."

The next year Barbara had an English teacher who replaced her sophomore instructor's carefully structured way of teaching with "seeming chaos" and "casual excitement." Mr. C.'s American literature class was "wild." "Gone were the meticulously written-out assignments—and with it any sense that we were proceeding with any order or going in any direction. As we finished our book or project, it seemed like he would say 'what next' and dream up something new. Only when I finally taught American lit myself did I realize . . . we had somehow covered the territory. . . . We even read all of *Moby Dick*. But in contrast to weekly vocabulary lists . . . there was a reverence for words, for sentences. . . . We wrote aphorisms and poems. . . . He convinced his friend, the poet Anne Sexton, to come to class for two or three weeks. . . . [she] talked about her poems and her craziness. I remember wanting to be just like her. . . . That was possibly the most important event in high school for me, though at the time I probably didn't know it—or didn't know that every town didn't have a poet like Anne Sexton in it."

The best teacher Todd ever had in high school was his biology teacher. Mrs. T. "somehow had the ability to make it very interesting. She could relate topics of discussion to our everyday lives. . . . She used up-to-date vocabulary that we . . . could understand and appreciate. . . . One class I distinctly remember talking about digestion. . . . She used French fries as an example of a food that filled us up fast, but also digested quickly and made us feel hungry soon after eating them. She then discussed the food breakdown process and how the grease on the fries broke down. . . . Every time I went to McDonald's after that I guiltily ate my fries knowing that I'd be hungry soon after munching them down . . . and I was! Now I knew why!"

Although the best teachers use different methods, they have common characteristics. Rochelle in fact listed the qualities of her best teachers rather than describe a specific person: "fun, excited about their field and about teaching, interested in each student's personal growth, spent time talking with each student individually—even if just for a minute, taught things that the students were interested in, caring and *honest* about themselves."

Evariste echoed Rochelle: " . . . the best teachers . . . genuinely liked what they were doing. They gave their students time; they really cared. They were animated, enjoyed talking about the subject—even if their delivery was boring. . . . They were knowledgeable and confident about their subject. I could quite easily give you a list I always keep in my head of the best who taught me. It is far harder to come up with a list of those who weren't good. . . . it is unfortunate that the list of bad teachers I've had over the years is much longer than the list of good ones . . . [but] I have trouble remembering those individuals and the assignments they gave me. . . ."

Studies have shown that teachers who inspire students both respect and care for them; are demanding; express humor, joy, exuberance; are fair, motivating, encouraging, sincere, understanding, and friendly—characteristics that are apparent in the memories of good teachers that people shared with me for this book.

If we want schools to do a better job of teaching students, it's clear that better teachers are essential. No reform effort will succeed unless it addresses ways to help less-effective teachers develop better ways of teaching and relating to students. The iron-fisted schoolmarm or schoolmaster of the past who tolerated no nonsense, made every kid toe the line, and drilled students in "the three R's" is unlikely to be successful teaching students today. Likewise the teachers who make no demands on students and encourage creativity without setting any standards for quality are unlikely to enable students to learn what they need to know. What we need is balance.

I hope you have begun to see that *what* is taught is often less important than *how* it is taught. Critics read Chester Finn and Diane Ravitch's book, *What 17-Year-Olds Know,* and conclude that the schools aren't teaching history because kids don't know when the Civil War took place. Perhaps the real problem, however, is that because the information is taught in a way that is confusing or boring to students, they remember the dates long enough to pass the unit test and then forget them. No one remembers much of anything unless it is personally meaningful, and too few teachers use methods that encourage students to make content part of their personal knowledge base.

Often students leave school with erroneous or incomplete understandings. Remember Kelly, who after a year in an algebra class still doesn't know why there are letters in math problems? In my high school English classes Shakespeare was taught as a foreign language. Because my teachers spent so much time going over the plays line by line, I learned how to "translate," but I never realized that the plays were great stories with human characters. I dutifully memorized what I needed to pass the tests but never saw that reading Shakespeare could be enjoyable or enriching. I might still believe that's all there was to Shakespeare if I hadn't later taken a graduate course in which we got beyond line-by-line analysis. Curriculum change alone will not improve schools, because what students learn also depends on how they are taught.

Students aren't always taught to think in school. Anna, a student in an undergraduate education course, wrote: "In a way I have self-taught myself to think. In high school everything was handed to me—concepts were repeated over and over again, my paper topics and information were extremely specific, and the teacher as a concrete source of information was always available. I did not need to think in high school and frankly I rarely did! I was capable of learning to think, and I probably did know how but I had no reason to do it."

Anna also pointed out that the thinking students do in school sometimes results from their learning to play the school game. "I have to ask myself, have I learned to think in college? And I must answer no. There have been a few extremely unorthodox classes that caused me to think, and I must admit I have been uncomfortable with them. . . . Even though liberal arts majors may be successful in college, this does not mean they have been taught to think, but they have learned how to get good grades. Perhaps even this skill reveals some thinking and problem-solving ability."

In fact, finding new ways to play the school game and outwit teachers may generate more thinking than classroom assignments. Susan, for example, who got caught doing something she wasn't supposed to be doing in class, wrote "The assignment was writing 500 times I wouldn't do that in class. Well, after all, necessity is the mother of invention, so the teacher got it handwritten 250 times and 250 carbon copies of the original. I must have satisfied the teacher because I never did get called on it." Susan had to write a science term paper in tenth grade. "Science wasn't my best subject and I put it off until the last minute despite warnings of the teacher that it had to be our own work and no way could we copy it out of textbooks . . . and not get caught. Well, I did, and he didn't. . . . I love a challenge!"

When teachers don't make learning purposeful and meaningful for students, they encourage students like Susan to spend time thinking of new ways to beat the system. When the focus is on rote memorization, regurgitation, and rules, students must learn to think on their own. But some students think so little about thinking itself that they sometimes don't realize when they *aren't* thinking. A college student disagreed with a textbook author who pointed out that what students *don't* study in school affects them as much as what they do study. She wrote, "If we do not read any women writers in a literature course, I do not think 'Woman writers aren't important.' I just don't think of them at all." I responded to her comments by writing, "And what does *that* say? That they don't exist at all?"

Bright students become very frustrated in classes where

teachers use only a fact-recall method of teaching. Rochelle wrote about one of her college classes for which the students were expected to do assigned readings before they came to class. "We do the reading and go to class to have the teacher recite exactly what we read. The other day the teacher was going over a section that included a drawing. She turned with chalk to the board and said, 'I am going to draw the diagram on the board. There is a better one in the book, but doing this will make me feel useful.' If that teacher needs to draw a duplicate diagram of one that was in our assigned reading to feel useful, something is not right. . . . Redundancy is useless, except perhaps in a review." Rochelle cared about her grades, so she learned the material no matter how it was taught, but other students gave up on the class and perhaps the subject altogether.

When teachers begin to think of teaching and learning as more than stuffing information into students' heads and measuring how much sticks, they become more concerned with establishing positive relationships with students. Their classrooms become places where students want to be. We all have to work together to help the others learn and grow. Remember, too, that the people quoted in this chapter for the most part were students who did well in school, not the ones who failed or dropped out, and consider how much more important better teachers are for the at-risk kids filling our schools today.

Suggestions for Parents

Spend some time every day talking with your children about school. Ask them what they did, what they learned, and, most important, how they felt. Encourage them to talk about whether they feel frustrated or stupid, and help them figure out ways to deal with these situations so that negative feelings don't overwhelm them.

Help children connect their school learning with real life. If teachers don't make the connections, you can help by talking about how you use school knowledge in your job or by showing how math concepts apply to the family budget.

Teach children new strategies for learning subjects that are difficult for them. Make memorizing facts a family game. Let children develop creative thinking skills by making up their own learning games. If your children's teachers emphasize memorization, such as lists of dates and events or definitions of words, you can at least help children make the task fun. While memorizing facts and words out of context isn't the best way to learn, memorization practice won't hurt, and doing something together helps strengthen the family unit.

Help children make sense of isolated bits of knowledge. Creating a time line for the period they're studying in history will give them a better sense of specific dates and events as well as reinforce their memory of them. They can increase their vocabulary by reading widely and taking time to figure out the meanings of unfamiliar words by considering the context in which they are used, or by looking for roots new words may share with words they already know.

Share your school experiences with your children. Sometimes parents give children the impression that they always did well in school. Children need to know that they aren't the only ones who have had a tough time learning a particular concept or topic. Not understanding something right away doesn't mean they'll never get it. Be careful, though, not to pass on a negative bias to your children. Studies have shown that girls often do poorly in math because many adults think of math as a "boys' subject." Mothers who didn't do well in math may inadvertently let daughters think they probably won't do well either, and the children end up not trying very hard to learn.

Help your children develop healthy and positive views of themselves. When children have trouble in one area, they can convince themselves that they're dumb about everything. Remind them of the things they do well and explain that if they believe they can do something, they usually can. (The children's story of the little engine that could is a good message for children of all ages.) Learning a difficult concept or skill may take time. In the meantime they need to know it's O.K. to make mistakes because that's how we learn. Everyone has different strengths and weaknesses, but persistence can make up for a lack of natural ability. Children who get discouraged quickly need to learn that sticking with a challenging task will pay off in the end. If one strategy doesn't work, they should try another approach.

Finally, don't forget that your children learn from what you do. Let them see you learning something new and sticking with it until you get it. If you serve as a model of lifelong learning, your children are more likely to become lifelong learners, too.

Chapter Three

Real Learning

WHICH ONE OF the following would best indicate to you that your child has learned what *photosynthesis* is?

A. The child spells and pronounces the word correctly.
B. The child gives a complete definition using words he or she read in the textbook or heard from the teacher.
C. The child gives a complete definition in his or her own words.
D. The child explains an example of photosynthesis that was discussed in class.
E. The child tells you his or her friend's mother must not have done very well in science. She bought a plant to put in a back room where there is only one small, high window and is upset with the store for selling her an unhealthy plant.

All of these responses indicate some degree of learning, but E is probably the best indication of what might be called "real" learning, because it indicates that the child both understands and can apply the concept. A and B are good examples of "rote" learning —the kind of learning children are often asked to do in school. The problem with rote learning is that even though children can memorize and repeat what has been taught, they may have no understanding of its meaning. C and D are closer to real learning, but if children do not see how what has been learned can be applied outside the classroom, they may be unable to use that knowledge. If schools are to prepare students to meet the unknown demands of the twenty-first century, they must help children learn in ways that will enable them to use their knowledge in new and creative ways. The fullest and best use of knowledge is the ability to recognize how it can be used to explain circumstances, predict consequences, or solve problems in unfamiliar situations. Why then do schools often emphasize rote rather than real learning?

Americans are very practical people. We like order, efficiency, and results. We measure progress in terms of profit and loss, the growth of the GNP, and the Dow Jones average–figures that can be neatly plotted on graphs and charts. But while it makes sense to determine how well a car salesman has performed by considering the number of vehicles he sells, we can't apply these same techniques to learning and teaching. We won't improve our schools until we stop thinking of learning solely as the acquisition of information. Besides the fact that learning is much more complex than manufacturing widgets, the schools have time to teach only a tiny part of what there is to know.

Moreover, knowledge continues to increase. As Dr. Robert Hilliard of the U.S. Federal Communications Commission points out: "By the time a child today graduates from college, the amount of knowledge in the world will be four times as great [as it is now]. By the time that child is fifty years old, it will be thirty-two times as great and 97 percent of everything known in the world will have been learned since the time he was born."

It is true that we need to make sure students get some basic information, but if they are to retain facts and figures, they need to use what they learn. Consider how you remember information in everyday situations. You have memorized, with no apparent effort, the phone numbers of friends and family members you call frequently. But if you only occasionally have a question for your banker, you probably have to look up the number every time you call. If you get tired of leafing through the phone book, you might make a conscious effort to learn the bank's phone number. If we're motivated enough and there's a good reason for remembering something, all of us are capable of rote memorization.

Although they are often compared, our brains aren't exactly like computers, capable of storing vast amounts of isolated bits of information that we can easily retrieve. High motivation makes it possible for us to remember some isolated facts, but most of what we know is remembered in the context of experience. Before the invention of the printing press, information was passed from one generation to another in the form of stories and songs.

If early peoples had tried to pass on what they knew in bits and pieces instead of weaving knowledge fragments into meaningful wholes – songs and stories that others could experience – little of what they knew would have remained. Because storytelling is a very effective way to learn, it has generated renewed interest among educators today.

Songs and stories, however, are simulated experience. The best teacher is firsthand experience, and much of what we've learned we didn't learn in school but on our own. Computers, for example, weren't widely available until recently, so many of us learned to use them in a variety of informal ways. Perhaps your own experience was similar to mine.

As a math phobic who erroneously thought that computers had a lot to do with math, I resisted going near one. I feared I was incapable of ever learning to use something so complicated. It helped, then, that the first time I saw one up close, a gentle and knowledgeable woman briefly explained how to turn it on and off, what the disk and disk drive were for, and gave me short, simple exercises that even I could do successfully right away. Soon I purchased an Apple IIe and set about learning to use a word-processing program. I went through the tutorial that came with the software, but I found my interest lagging because the tutorial didn't yield a product I could use. I decided I would only learn how the computer functioned by working on a real project. Since I was in the process of revising the teacher handbook at the school where I was the principal, I figured typing the handbook myself and saving it to a disk would not only make it easier to update the handbook the next year, but would also give me the opportunity to learn to use the word processing program.

The handbook probably contained only twenty-five typewritten pages. It took me much longer to do them on the computer than it would have on the electric typewriter, but I learned what I wanted to know through trial and error. I frequently had to stop and search for answers in the manual. And when something didn't work as the manual said it should, I had to retrace my steps to figure out what I'd done wrong. It was a very long, frustrating, and laborious process, but when I'd finished the handbook, I understood the basics of the program and had internalized much of the process.

If you'd like an immediate simulation of how awkward and frustrating learning can be in the beginning, try writing with your non-dominant hand. Even when writing or printing your name, something you've done thousands of times without even thinking, you now have to consider the shape of each individual letter. And the pen won't easily go where you want it to because your muscles are not trained for this task. When you first learned to write with your favored hand you went through this same process, but with time and lots of practice your handwriting became almost automatic. Today you may have to pause to think about the spelling of a word but not the formation of a letter. Suppose that when you first learned to write, your teachers only assigned hundreds of pages of handwriting exercises. Would you have learned to write? Probably not. Although we may remember filling line after line with push-pulls and evenly spaced repetitions of the alphabet, our handwriting eventually became automatic because we also wrote real sentences and stories that made sense to us.

Real learning is personalized and process-oriented. What we learn through active involvement stays with us, but unless we continue to use what we learn, we can't always retrieve it when we want to. It's been said that no one ever forgets how to ride a bicycle, but if you don't go near a bike for twenty years, you'll be a little shaky. You won't feel comfortable until you relearn and practice what you knew before. Having once learned something in a meaningful way, we usually find we can fairly quickly bring it back without going through the same long process it took to learn it in the first place.

Rote-learned information, however, is not easily recaptured, especially when there's little or nothing to connect the bits and pieces. Some of us as kids memorized the state capitols or U.S. presidents. If you did, see how many you can remember now. Try learning them again and see what happens. That kind of knowledge won't usually come back with a quick refresher but must be relearned with almost as much effort as it was the first time.

Real learning is a complex process that is personally meaningful, not a simple matter of memorization or drills. Take reading, for example. While knowing the sounds of the letters can help in reading, students are not learning to read when they do phonics drills. Because of the way reading is often taught in schools, students not only don't learn to read, they are also turned off to it. We should be concerned not only with the number of illiterates but also the growing number of aliterates—those who can but do not choose to read.

The way schools approach the teaching of reading can make a big difference, both in regard to whether students learn to read as well as whether they learn to *enjoy* reading. One of my friends, the mother of a six-year-old, is very concerned about her son's progress in first grade. He loved kindergarten and found school exciting because the teacher engaged the kids in a variety of interesting learning activities. He had looked forward to first grade because he was anxious to do "big kids' work." But instead of moving from talking about pictures and stories that were meaningful to him to being able to read and talk about the words that tell the stories on the printed page, his first-grade teacher has suffocated the class with worksheets. The little boy who loved school last year begs to stay home now, in part because he's learning *about* reading instead of learning to read. Students need to practice reading skills by reading stories and discovering the meanings inherent in the words, just as they need to practice handwriting skills by combining the letters and words into sentences that say something. Real reading (understanding the meaning of the words) is very different from rote reading (saying the words without knowing what they mean).

Teachers often misunderstand the reason children don't do well in school. One parent was called in for a conference with her daughter's second grade teacher because the girl was so far behind in her work. The teacher was concerned, and rightly so, that the child had failed to do over twenty assignments. Why the teacher hadn't talked to the child about the problem long before is hard to imagine. The parent quickly found out that the missing worksheets were in the child's desk. "The worksheets were boring," her daughter told her. "I already knew everything that was on them." If this child's teacher had given her students real books to read rather than worksheets to fill in, everyone would have been better off.

If we tried to teach people to use computers with the graded books and worksheets used to teach reading, many would learn to hate computers without ever learning much about them. Imagine spending days and weeks completing worksheets that asked you to label the parts of the computers and having to work through teacher-designed dummy projects like the tutorials that come with most software programs. Neither of those activities would be too bad if they served merely as an introduction. But if you rarely got to do anything with the computer that *you* considered important or interesting, how long would you continue to exert any effort? How much frustration would you be willing to tolerate when you hit a snag? Learning to operate a computer requires using it; learning to read requires a great deal of time spent actually reading. And because no one will devote much time to something that is neither interesting nor purposeful, many of the methods teachers have used for years actually turn kids off to learning.

"Purpose" is a key word here. Good students often learn because they create purpose where there otherwise would be none. Successful students quickly figure out how to play the school game and are willing to suffer through meaningless drills and assignments because they want good grades. Their parents expect them to do well in school, and they have role models in their lives of people for whom education was the grounds for later success. Disadvantaged students, on the other hand, may lack both role models and family support. Less able students never can figure out the strategies needed for classroom success. When getting an A on a test becomes the sole purpose for learning, students rarely learn to love learning for its own sake. What they do learn often doesn't stick; once the test is over, what's the point in remembering?

Perhaps you are thinking: since traditional methods worked for me when I was in school, why do we need something different now? One answer is that times have changed. Schools must now compete with TV, video games, and other new activities. The worksheets, drills, and watered-down stories we endured can't match the excitement of a Nintendo game or TV thriller.

Teachers must look for new ways to interest students in learning. But schools shouldn't try to entertain children. Instead they should offer children an antidote to the quickly vanishing images on the TV screen. Schools should get children to slow down, to stop and think, to reflect, and to connect what they learn in school with what they already know.

Another reason why teaching methods should change is that schools have never worked for all students. In the Fifties it was common for many students to quit school after eighth grade, if not before. I can remember a boy named Donald who was in my class in the sixth, seventh, and eighth grades. Today he would be in special education classes, but back then he just sat in the back of the room. Teachers kept the big, lumbering boy busy, doing what I didn't know. They never called on him to respond in class and he rarely did the same assignments we did, unless we went outside for phys ed or worked on an art project. Because Donald was good-natured, we never made fun of him, but we all knew Donald wasn't very bright.

Looking back now, I wonder if he ever learned anything in school. The teachers didn't have time to work with him one-on-one, and there were no tutors or aides in the school. Donald marked time until the end of eighth grade, got a diploma at graduation, and then disappeared. He didn't move on to high school with the rest of us. I have no idea what ever happened to him. Years later I realized that what Donald got wasn't a diploma at all but a certificate of attendance, a piece of paper schools routinely gave to students who "served their time" but were unable, usually because of limited ability, to complete the requirements for graduation. Donald and his parents must have known that he'd been shortchanged, but the rest of the graduation audience, including all of his classmates, never gave him a thought.

If the students who didn't do well in school in the Fifties and Sixties did go on to high school, they were unseen by students in college preparatory classes. Even today most high school classes are tracked, and students of differing ability levels have few opportunities to mix. In fact, in some high schools college-bound students are assigned to classes on special wings or floors, so they don't even pass vocational or general students in the halls. And even when all students take phys ed or eat lunch at the same time, they often don't talk to one another because they congregate with their own friends. Since the less-able, the less-motivated, or less-advantaged students are invisible to those who do fairly well, no one notices when school doesn't work for them. If you were one of the fortunate who made it in school despite the fact that teachers used methods that made learning a chore, you probably have no idea how many students weren't so lucky.

If you haven't spent time in a public school as an adult and know only the children who come from families similar to your own, you should spend at least one day in a school where you can see a cross-section of the school population. You will see many children who aren't learning. If we do not find ways to help these children succeed in school, we will pay for their failure through unemployment, welfare, and crime.

Unfortunately, the kids we didn't notice when we went to school aren't as invisible today. When schools fail to help them, they affect the quality of life for all of us, because many of them become drug abusers, vandals, teenage mothers, and dropouts. While schools have little or no control over the environment these kids must face outside of school, they could do a much better job of preventing these problems by changing the way they teach. Real learning can work where rote learning has failed.

Many teachers have learned to create classrooms where all kids enjoy learning. Many first-grade teachers, for example, have discovered a way to make learning to read and write exciting and enjoyable by throwing away the worksheets and the basal readers. They let students choose individual books to read, encourage them to write their own stories and read them to classmates, and give them lots of opportunities to talk with each other and the teacher about the reading, writing, and learning they are doing together. Classrooms come alive and kids are turned on to reading and learning. "Whole language" is the term educators currently use to describe these classrooms, where teachers engage students in using their own spoken and written language to learn in every subject. These teachers perform a very different role from that of traditional teachers. They are guides or facilitators of learning rather than sources of information that must be stuffed into students' heads.

Parents are often uncomfortable with whole language classrooms even when their children show progress and are excited about learning. This is because parents think of learning as a neat and orderly process, where students learn *x* and pass a test, move on to *y* and pass another test, and so on in every subject. But when we consider curriculum as the content and skills students must master, and set up schools as a series of grades children must pass through, we are viewing learning as a logical, linear process. Unfortunately, most people don't learn this way.

In fact, breaking down academic subjects into fragments to be measured on achievement tests actually works against good education. Our rigid belief that knowledge can be artificially organized and delivered to students step by step results in some students who can't or won't learn, and thus an increasing number of dropouts.

Learning is a messy process. Knowledge can't always be neatly packaged, especially if students are to learn how to use what they know in situations outside of school. The solutions to real-life problems require the integration and application of knowledge gained both from academic study in many disciplines and personal experience. Real-life problems are interdisciplinary and don't fit the tidy subject area compartments we've devised for schools.

Learning outside of school is a complex and ongoing process by which we try to make sense of the world. We constantly assimilate new knowledge and experiences by extracting what seems essential or important from them. Then we connect this new knowledge to what we already know, making it personally meaningful enough for us to remember it.

The personal connection is easy to understand if you think of valuable lessons you've learned from firsthand experience. If you ever took advantage of a mail-order bargain that seemed too good to pass up and received shoddy merchandise, you'll think twice before ordering anything again without first checking out the company. You may have been told many times to read the fine print before signing anything and paid little attention, but you'll never forget that advice in the future if your failure to do so ends up costing you a few hundred of your hard-earned dollars. While school lessons can't duplicate the power of real-life experience, teachers have found ways to help students make personal connections as they learn history, math, and other subjects.

But because learning is a very personal activity, no two individuals will find the same meaning or learn the same things from any life experience or classroom assignment. If we think of learning as a spiral rather than a line, it becomes clear why we gain new perspectives or new knowledge when we read the same book again or visit a place a second time. Our knowledge about any topic becomes richer and deeper each time we consider or come in contact with it.

Because students have many different learning styles, teachers should use a variety of methods and activities. Yet, as John Goodlad and many others report, in most classrooms students sit passively and listen to the teacher talk, or work quietly at their desks doing the same assignment in the same way—a classroom situation that guarantees some students won't learn, and others won't learn as much as they could.

You may have read about the difference between the two halves of the brain, but have you considered how this relates to school assignments and individual learning? The left hemisphere relies primarily on language in thinking and remembering, while the right draws on images. Though all of us use both halves of our brains just as we use both hands, we may favor one more than the other. If we're good at music, poetry, and art, for example, we depend on the more intuitive right brain. On the other hand, if we're quick to see logical connections and solve problems in an organized, sequential manner, then we lean to the left brain.

The functions and interaction of the two halves of the brain are much more complex than I have described them here, and there is much about them we do not know. People have learned to compensate for damage to parts of one hemisphere of the brain by "retooling" parts of the other with intensive therapy. Since teachers cannot provide the sort of one-on-one instruction that health professionals do in the case of a brain-damaged accident victim, it would seem that schools would provide a number of ways for students to figure out what learning strategies work best for them. That, however, is not the case.

Schools are oriented toward left-brain activities. The whole curriculum depends heavily on written language and on students learning it in an organized and structured way, using left-mode activities to do so. While it seems to make sense to set up a curriculum in a logical, sequential manner, such a plan ignores students who learn best using right-brain techniques. If a student remembers images much better than she does words, she will likely have trouble remembering the information in a chapter from her history book, especially if she depends on answers she has written to the questions on a study guide, or notes on the lectures—all left-brain techniques. However, if her teacher shows her how she can outline the chapter by constructing her own visual map [see example of concept map on next page], she might be able to recall the details as part of a larger image. Every time teachers make the whole class do a left-brain-dependent assignment, such as a traditional outline of a textbook chapter or answering the questions at the end of a chapter, they're at best wasting the time of "right-brain" students; at worst, they're setting them up to fail.

The parents of a sixteen-year-old girl became concerned when her grades began to drop and she started skipping school. They took her to a counselor. Because the therapist determined that drugs and alcohol were not involved, they arranged to have a battery of tests given to help determine what the problem was. The tests revealed that although the girl could read and write very well, she had a problem with short-term memory—exactly what someone needs in traditional schools, where so much depends on remembering information. It's not surprising that a student who got consistently low grades on such tests would soon lose interest in school.

As a result of the academic evaluation, the girl was given special help in the resource room, but this effort caused further problems. Because her friends looked down on special education students, she tried to hide the fact that she went to the resource room instead of study hall. It was another blow to her self-confidence, and would have been totally unnecessary if her teachers had used both right- and left-brained teaching strate-

How did mass production and the growth of corporations aid industry?

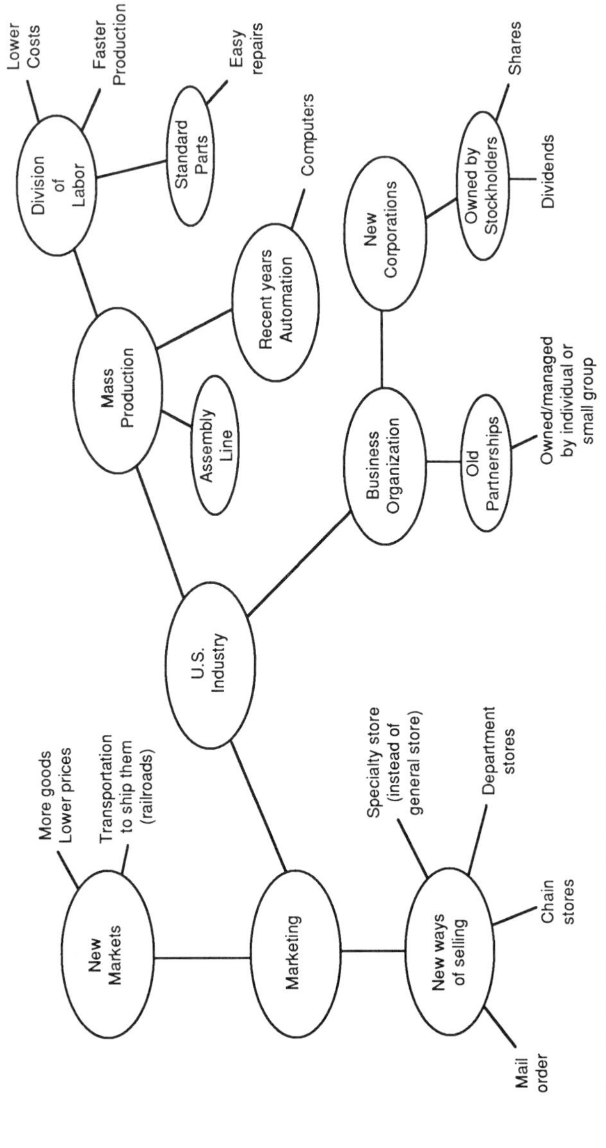

From chapter 22, pp. 460—464. This Is America's Story, 4th edition. Boston: Houghton Mifflin Co., 1981.

gies, and graded students on activities and projects as well as traditional tests. Why? This teenager was very artistic and creative—very right-brained—but she hadn't been taught to organize information in a visual way in order to remember it. Instead she wasted hours studying notes and outlines, working very hard but still flunking the tests. And if her parents hadn't intervened when she began skipping school, she might have become another dropout statistic. After a summer of reading and working with her mother on learning styles, and with the help of a structured home support system to encourage regular study habits, she eventually made the honor roll. But too many students lack that kind of parental support, and the costs to society are enormous.

In addition to accommodating both right-brain- and left-brain-dominant students, teachers should also consider that students favor different "channels" for receiving and sharing what they have learned with others: visual (seeing), auditory (hearing), kinesthetic (moving and touching), or a combination of these. You can see how listening to the teacher explain a new math concept and watching her do examples on the board will not do much for a student who learns kinesthetically. That's why some math programs now involve young children in manipulating rods and other objects as they learn about numbers.

After studying what several other people had discovered about learning styles and doing her own research at a suburban Chicago high school, Bernice McCarthy classified learners into four categories. She has written a book for educators and conducts workshops across the country to show teachers how they can plan lessons that include activities for learners in all four categories. (McCarthy's model is given as an example. Other people categorize and describe learning styles in varying ways.)

Imaginative learners look for personal meaning and judge things in relation to values. They are cooperative and social and learn through social interaction as well as by watching, sensing, and feeling. The teacher must make sure these students have a reason to learn.

Analytic learners seek intellectual competence. They want to learn the facts and how to verify them. They learn by watching, but teachers must give them time to think through the facts so they can gain a conceptual understanding of what they study.

Common sense learners like finding solutions to problems and prefer trying things out. They judge things by their usefulness and want to make things happen. They are kinesthetically aware, so teachers can keep them motivated by showing them how things work and letting them try some things on their own.

Dynamic learners are fascinated by hidden possibilities. They sometimes tend to disregard authority because they prefer discovering things on their own, but they are usually enthusiastic and adventuresome. Teachers can capitalize on these qualities by letting them teach themselves or others.

Because few students will fit precisely into these learning-style packages, however, teachers should plan units with techniques and activities for all four types. That way every student will be able to shine at some point. All students will be able to stretch their intellectual muscles in a variety of ways, and come to appreciate the different strengths of their classmates. Whether students are powerboats, sailboats, or rowboats, they all can get to the same destination, but they will take different routes and arrive at different times. If we continue to expect that all kids can get to the same place by the same route in the same amount of time, we're going to continue to be frustrated by the problem of the students who fail. We have organized our schools like production lines. The product isn't faulty; the production system is.

Gender can also affect student achievement. For several years now Myra and David Sadker and others have called attention to classroom inequities as they relate to gender. Because males generally get more attention and more time to talk than females, girls lose out. Their self-esteem, educational attainment, and eventual career choice and income are affected. Schools have made some changes to ensure that girls have the same opportunities as boys. They've added athletic programs, provided workshops for teachers to make them aware of gender bias in classroom practices, expanded the curriculum to include the study of more female writers, and made special efforts to encourage girls to take more math and science courses and consider traditionally male careers, such as engineering and architecture.

But despite all these efforts, and even though women's roles in society have become more broadly defined, there is more the schools—and society—need to do.

Linda Silverman describes how social pressures and school practices reduce the number of girls who are identified as gifted as they move up through the grades. She explains why schools should be concerned with what she calls "the strange case of the disappearing girl." The Sadkers and Sharon Steindam, who term gender "our national blind spot," note that "males outperform females substantially on all subsections of the Scholastic Aptitude Test (SAT) and ACT (American College Testing Program)" and girls get only 36 percent of the more than 6,000 National Merit Scholarships awarded each year. Girls, say the Sadkers and Steindam, "are the only group who enter school scoring ahead and twelve years later leave school scoring behind."

Carol Gilligan and other researchers believe that males and females perceive the world differently; they have different ways of knowing and hold different values. Because females must compete in a society and educational system developed and dominated by males, they are at a disadvantage. While fully explaining these complex gender issues is beyond the scope of this book, perhaps an example can show why some of the changes I propose here are likely to foster educational achievement among girls. Studies show that females value relationships more highly than males; they are interested in making and maintaining connections. Thus, many girls learn better when they are given opportunities to learn cooperatively rather than being forced to compete against their classmates for grades. The practice of writing journal entries allows girls to process what they learn and make connections between themselves and the subject.

Because the teaching methods described here enable teachers to personalize the curriculum for all students, they not only will help females learn better, they also will help students from different cultural and ethnic backgrounds who, like females, have previously been excluded from the curriculum.

Researchers have also proposed new theories that expand or redefine how we have traditionally viewed intelligence. Robert Sternberg, a professor of psychology and education at Yale, has developed what he calls "a triarchic theory of intelligence." For years we have relied on IQ tests that measure only what Sternberg refers to as "componential" intelligence, but he began to notice that analytical and critical thinking weren't all a student needed in order to be successful in a graduate program. Students who ranked high on these measures often weren't able to come up with good ideas on their own, whereas some students who didn't have such high test scores were superb creative thinkers and could combine disparate experiences in insightful ways. Sternberg termed this second kind of intelligence "experiential." The third part of his theory looks at intelligence in relation to an individual's external world—that is, people who are street smart in the everyday world. Even when these students don't do well on traditional tests, they succeed in situations that require adapting to and manipulating their environment in very practical ways. Sternberg calls this third type of intelligence "contextual."

Because Sternberg doesn't favor one kind of intelligence over another, and believes that everyone should learn to capitalize on strengths and improve weaknesses, he has written a book, *Intelligence Applied*, to explain a training program based on his theory.

Sternberg has also considered differences in thinking and learning styles by comparing mental activity to the forms and functions of governments. His theory of mental self-government maintains that some people prefer using the "legislative" function of the mind, which is concerned with creating, formulating, imagining, and planning. Others prefer the "executive"—implementing and doing—or the "judicial"—judging, evaluating, and comparing. He notes that although everyone uses all three functions, they are usually more comfortable with one function than the others. Any subject can be taught in a way that is congruent with any style, but as Sternberg points out, teaching styles usually reflect teachers' own preferred thinking functions. Thus, teachers must vary the ways they present information and make assignments so that every student gets the chance to use the function he or she favors.

Like the functions, the forms of mental self-government also differ. A student who prefers a "monarchic" form tends to focus on one goal or task at a time. A student who is comfortable dealing with multiple goals, each of which may have a different priority, favors a "hierarchic" form. The "oligarchic" form describes the student who likes dealing with multiple goals that are all equally important. Sternberg includes a fourth form, "anarchic," to cover those students who perform best when situations are unstructured and they can solve problems in unusual and insightful ways. Students with anarchic styles, as one might expect, are usually happiest in alternative schools, because they often resist authority and don't like rules and regulations.

It is possible for teachers to expand classroom options to accommodate students whose favored styles are different from their own, and from those of other students in the class. Even anarchic students can do well in a class where the teacher engages students in a variety of activities and gives them some freedom to make choices and work on their own. If, however, a monarchic, judicial teacher plans lessons and adopts a teaching approach which is very goal-oriented, many students in the class will do less well than they would if the teacher included some assignments that better suited their own particular styles. Sternberg advises teachers to be flexible. Students can use more than one style, but they differ in their ability to switch among them. And since all styles are necessary at different times in different situations, everyone benefits from becoming more able to move from one style to another.

Like Sternberg, Harvard psychologist Howard Gardner believes in multiple kinds of intelligence, but he lists seven categories instead of three:

linguistic—sensitivity to the meaning and order of words, and the varied use of language;

logical-mathematical—the ability to handle long chains of reasoning and to recognize patterns and order in the world;

spatial—the ability to perceive the visual world accurately, and to recreate, transform, or modify aspects of that world based on one's perceptions;

bodily-kinesthetic—a finely tuned ability to use the body and to handle objects;

musical—sensitivity to pitch, melody, rhythm, and tone;

interpersonal—the ability to notice and make distinctions among others;

intrapersonal—access to one's own "feeling life."

Gardner would replace traditional IQ tests, which yield a single score, with an evaluation that gave a profile of the learner in all seven "intelligences." Both Sternberg and Gardner, in transforming our narrow view of intelligence, give us good reason to rethink what students do in schools. As these men are practical theorists, they have joined together on a project to examine the kinds of "practical smarts" schoolchildren need to succeed, including their understanding of themselves and others, the academic tasks required of them, and the differing demands made by separate academic disciplines. The Key School, a public school in Indianapolis, has built a curriculum around the seven intelligences: children do an activity in each every day.

To understand that we need more people doing such research, we need only realize that success in school does not guarantee success in life. Haven't we all met someone who is very bright and knowledgeable, but with almost no common sense when it comes to dealing with people and practical matters? Shouldn't schools be doing more to help students develop in ways that will benefit them in their lives outside of school? Can they do that at the same time they focus on the acquisition of knowledge?

The answer to the last question is yes—if we view the subject matter as a vehicle for teaching students to think and solve problems on their own. Knowledge of a subject should not be an end in itself (as is too often the case in schools) but a natural outcome of the learning process.

We have made school learning too simple and thereby prevented many students from learning. Instead of allowing them to make their own discoveries and forge their own connections, we've taken the meaning out of learning by chopping knowledge into separate units. We teach students a punctuation rule or a math concept and ask them to apply their new knowledge by doing twenty sentences or problems that require only the use of that rule or concept they have just been taught. Students can easily complete such a dummy exercise with 100 percent accuracy. But a few days or weeks later, many will not recognize a situation that calls for using that same rule or concept. Students often spell a word correctly on a spelling test and misspell the same word when they later write a letter or essay. Bits and pieces of knowledge are useful only when students develop a conceptual framework that unites the fragments into a meaningful whole.

One way to help students learn strategies for organizing information is giving them practice in figuring out which rule or concept to apply when the choice isn't clear. Take the case of punctuation rules, for example. Instead of learning and practicing punctuation rules one by one, the teacher can provide them with an introductory overview of all the rules at once – knowing that most students won't understand all of them at that point – and then follow up with meaningful activities that require students to reconsider the rules on their own. Students will really learn and internalize the rules as they find and correct punctuation errors in their own writing – and help classmates in finding theirs.

Of course, this process is not as "efficient" as explaining a rule to the whole class and assigning a page in the handbook for everyone to complete. But students who are forced to go back to the handbook to find the rule they need for a specific sentence that they themselves have written will eventually learn all the rules they need to know. What's more, they'll find the process of learning these rules much more purposeful than inserting random commas in artificial sentences written by an anonymous textbook author. The teacher can make the process even more meaningful to students by having them write for real audiences. If students know that what they write will be seen by other students, parents, a newspaper editor, or the principal, they will be much more motivated to find and correct their errors than they would be if it were only going to be graded by the teacher. Finding and correcting errors in an original piece of writing, of course, is more complex than a textbook exercise, but it fosters students' ability to learn on their own – exactly what they'll have to do when they're out in the real world, where textbooks and teachers aren't around to make things simple. And they learn to think –

which, as Anna pointed out earlier, she was never required to do in high school.

It amazes me that we Americans think "programs" are the solutions for problems ranging from homelessness to substance abuse. This mindset has led to packaged curriculum programs designed to teach kids "how to think," and courses–believe it or not–on self-esteem. Thinking, like self-esteem, must be dealt with in context. You can't think about "nothing." Schools need to develop methods that will get students to think about whatever subject they are studying, and to use thinking to solve problems outside of school.

One elementary school's drug education efforts show why programs that don't take the "big picture" into account usually don't work. The underlying principle of the program was that students who developed self-confidence and self-esteem would be strong enough to say no to drugs when they were faced with the choice. A couple of times a week a counselor came into their regular class, and the children talked about their feelings as they participated in small group activities that were valuable and fun. The counselor did an excellent job of making these kids feel good about themselves and developing their ability to interact with others in a positive way. Sounds good, you're thinking. Well, the counselor spent only an hour or so a week with the kids. The rest of the time they were in class with their regular teacher–a strict, no-nonsense woman who rarely asked students what they thought, controlled their behavior and their assignments inflexibly, and meted out stiff penalties for the most minor infractions of classroom rules. She chiseled away at students' self-esteem and gave them almost no opportunity to demonstrate responsibility for themselves or make meaningful decisions. Whatever progress the counselor might have made with these kids was effectively cancelled out by the regular teacher. If we need a "program," it must be one that improves what happens in regular classrooms with ordinary teachers and students.

Schools often forget that people need a view of the big picture to make any sense out of the little pieces. One day my husband asked me to help him fold a huge piece of net he had used to cover a peach tree, to keep birds from eating the peaches before we could pick them. He grabbed one end and gave me the other. "Fold that over," he said, and I folded—but not the way he wanted me to. "Put that end over there!" he shouted, but I still couldn't figure out exactly what I was supposed to do. He was angry; I was frustrated. Clearly we weren't communicating. When we finally got the net folded, we were hardly speaking to each other. Only later did I realize what the problem was. No, it wasn't just that his directions weren't clear—although he could have done a better job of explaining what he wanted done. The real problem was that I didn't have a picture in my head of the process of folding he intended to use. Thus, the little bits and pieces he gave as directions made no sense at all to me. Had he first given me an overview of the way he expected to fold the net, then I could have seen what little steps I needed to take to get the job done.

Teachers and parents sometimes forget to give students an understanding of the big picture, and then they get frustrated when children fail to deal with the little pieces. It is this principle that led me to write an article about why so few students ever learn grammar. I called the article "The Big Mac Approach to Teaching Grammar," because the way we expect students to learn grammar in school is like eating a Big Mac one ingredient at a time. If you first taste a pickle, wait a minute, eat a bit of sesame seed bun, wait a minute, try some onion, wait a minute, nibble some hamburger, wait a minute . . . you'll never understand what a Big Mac tastes like. To know a Big Mac, you have to take a big bite and sample all the ingredients as part of the whole, all at once.

What does all of this have to do with grammar teaching? Consider that students spend several *years* learning grammar, bit by bit. Nouns and verbs first. Then pronouns. Adjectives and adverbs. Later conjunctions, prepositions, and interjections. They follow a parallel course with functions of words in a sentence: subject, verb, direct object, and so on. The problem is that none of this grammar makes any sense in isolation. Nor is it interesting when learned by studying simple sample sentences and doing exercises in grammar handbooks. And the repetition year after year is boring. Students either catch on or they don't, but by the time they've been exposed to all they need to know in order to analyze a real sentence and see how each word works as part of the whole, the teacher says, "Noun," and they turn off. They've heard it before, and even if they still don't understand, they don't care.

Grammar study can be fun. It's sort of like being a detective using your knowledge and clues from the sentence to figure out how each word in the sentence should be labeled. In order to do that, however, you have to have a sense of the whole. Understanding that research shows that a knowledge of grammar has little or nothing to do with learning to write well, I suggested in my article that we teach absolutely no formal grammar at all until students have developed to the point where they can handle abstract concepts. Ninth grade would be a good year to start, and that's when we should teach students everything. If they aren't turned off by having heard the same old stuff before, they'll find it interesting to see how each little word functions in terms of the whole sentence. Grammar study, when approached this way, also teaches students to think rather than merely memorize.

In getting a big picture of the way grammar works, students will be able to see that the little pieces make sense. It shouldn't take more than four weeks to get most students to learn a whole lot more about grammar than they learn now in eight or ten years. I know the method works because I've been able to teach students in my community college classes in a few hours. Without exception, my students have been amazed to discover that grammar isn't hard, that it makes sense, and that they can actually understand it. One veteran asked me, "Why didn't my high school teachers teach me this way?" Our present system not only doesn't make sense—it doesn't work.

Getting the big picture, or making sense of the parts by seeing how they fit together to make a whole, is essential to all learning. By trying to make what students should be learning in school easier to understand, we've made much of it meaningless. Learning about any subject in tiny bits and pieces is like studying the dots that form a television image instead of looking at the whole picture. And, speaking of television, maybe the reason so many people are unable to program their VCRs is that the instructions present the process one step at a time, never giving the consumer an overall sense of what's required so that individual steps make sense in terms of the whole.

Schools need to give students more opportunities to struggle and figure things out on their own, because that's the only way they'll learn to think. If we challenge them, more students may develop the intellectual habits that foster continued learning throughout their lives—without losing the wonder and curiosity they possess naturally, but which our schools usually manage to snuff out by grade four.

In his books and speeches, the late Richard P. Feynman, Nobel Prize-winning physicist, reveals the best qualities of a life-long learner. You may remember him from the commission that investigated the *Challenger* disaster. He was the man who put the rubber used on the faulty seal in a glass of ice water to show that freezing temperatures at the launch site could have caused the explosion. Feynman wondered about and questioned everything. He was always thinking. He once spent an incredible amount of time breaking the code on a Mayan artifact, even though he knew he could find a translation in the library because someone else had already done it. Learning and thinking for Feynman were often a form of play. Imagine how different schools would be if we nurtured students' curiosity so that they, too, would view intellectual challenges as recreation.

Frustration and confusion are a necessary part of the learning experience, not only because they simulate what happens in life (where solutions to problems—even the problems themselves—are neither clearly defined nor easily found), but also because the good feeling students get when they finally do succeed increases their self-confidence and prepares them to tackle new challenges. This doesn't mean that teachers should leave students on their own, without any help, to struggle and fail, but that they shouldn't be too quick to jump in and do what students themselves could do. Teachers should function as the safety net for students working on the high wire, ready to guide, encourage, and support them. They can also help students see that making mistakes is a necessary part of the learning process and that some problems merely have better answers than others, not necessarily right or wrong ones.

What teachers need to do is create carefully structured and creatively planned chaos. The skillful teacher realizes that planned classroom chaos is not random and unpredictable but has recognizable patterns. When students work together in small groups, an observer may not be able to see anything being accomplished if he only watches for one or two days. The patterns of the learning process only emerge over a longer period of time. Teachers who've used individual and group projects many times know from experience how small groups will function; it may seem unstructured, but in general the process will be predictable.

My introductory education course for college students considering education as a career illustrates how thinking of teaching in terms of chaos works. When I first began teaching the course, I realized that students could never learn in one semester more than a tiny part of what there was to know about education. Yet many of these liberal arts college students would end up teaching in private schools, and because this might be the only background they'd get for teaching before they began, it was important for me to help them develop a way of thinking about the process that could be a foundation for them to learn more on their own. Many wouldn't have the benefit of even a few weeks of student teaching.

The first semester I taught the course, I learned that my students were so used to teaching as transmission and so worried about their grade point averages that my "chaotic" teaching style made them very uncomfortable. They were so overwhelmed by all the ideas, names, terms, and so on that came up in their reading, they didn't know what was important enough to memorize. They enjoyed the free-flowing class discussions, but at the same time they were frustrated because I didn't tell them what they needed to know, and I raised issues and questions without giving them the "right" answers. They thought the class was interesting, but they figured they must not be learning anything because they hadn't memorized names, dates, and definitions to regurgitate on an exam. And, of course, fear played a big role, too. Some students worried that I would let them have fun during the semester and then zap them with picky factual questions on the exam.

What I had failed to do at the beginning of the semester was give them a big-picture understanding of how the course was organized and why. I didn't want to relieve their confusion—because that was necessary to their learning—but I did want to diminish their anxiety. And so I needed to explain my philosophy of learning and teaching.

In essence, I told them that learning is an endless journey, not a destination. Sometimes the route is smooth like an interstate highway, with many signs clearly marking the way. Although you can travel effortlessly to the next stopping point, you remember little of what you passed along the way.

Other routes are more confusing because there are many intersections and byways. Even though you may know where you want to go, getting there is often difficult and sometimes frustrating. On the long way around you may take a wrong turn or hit a deadend and get discouraged, but then there comes a moment when you surprise yourself with your ability to figure out what you need to do to move forward. Despite your personal struggle to find the way to your destination, you often decide that it was worth the hassle. You see what you'd never have seen on the interstate, but, more importantly, you remember what you experienced because you found the way yourself.

If learning is a journey and not a destination, then the teacher is a tour guide. If you travel on the interstate, the teacher need only mark the route on your map, get you started, and let you know when you've arrived at the next checkpoint. Some people may need a little extra help getting their cars started, others may have to stop for more fuel along the way, but the teacher's job is clearly defined and confined to making it possible for many travelers to get where they're going by using the same routes. Those who get there first with little or no difficulty even get prizes in the form of A's and B's.

The teacher's job encompasses far more, however, when you choose instead to make your trip on curved and hilly country roads or through crowded, signless city streets. The map the teacher gives you for such a trip is sometimes like a maze, not so carefully marked. Because the teacher has traveled in the area before and is familiar with many places along the way, the teacher can point out what you may not have noticed, sometimes a short cut, other times a landmark you might never have seen otherwise. Perhaps the teacher will take you to a place from which you can determine what you need to do or where you need to go next. Even more important on such a trip, the teacher as guide can support you when you get so discouraged you want to quit. The journey through such a circuitous route will take longer than zipping down the interstate, but you'll be rewarded with many rich and enduring memories from your trip, memories you'll appreciate even more after the journey's end.

Of course, there are many other ways to take this trip. You can make a learning journey entirely by yourself, with a guide there only when you need one, or with a guide who'll tell you everything you need or want to know. You can travel by yourself or you can go with friends who can make the trip more enjoyable or more frustrating, depending on how things go. When you travel with others, you have the same options for routes and guides. The choice you make will determine not only *how* you learn but also *what* you learn, how long you'll remember it, and whether this new knowledge will be integrated with what you already knew and what you have yet to learn.

In this class, I told my students, they wouldn't be traveling on the superhighway, so there would be a great deal to see and think about. I wouldn't tell them what they needed to know, but I was confident that such a seemingly random way to explore the territory–reading, thinking, writing, working on a group project, discussing whatever came up–would result in substantial learning. They themselves would put all the pieces together and see how they made sense. I promised not to trap them with a final exam which required a regurgitation of textbook trivia and asked them to trust me not to let them down.

Good teachers continually learn about teaching. I learned from the mistakes I made with that class, and now begin every course I teach (no matter what the subject area) by explaining not only my expectations as outlined on the course syllabus, but also why the course is organized the way it is.

Students are responsible for their own learning. The teacher can provide the opportunities, guidance, information, and encouragement, but in the end what and how any student learns is up to that individual. The teacher should be an example of a more experienced learner and should motivate and help students to learn. In that sense, perhaps the most effective teacher is one who poses questions for which students would like the answers—but does not necessarily give them those answers. People, process, and problem solving are more important than products and procedures.

Humans are very social beings, and because students can often learn as much from each other as they can from books or the teacher, they should also engage in collaborative learning activities. Learning is often more enjoyable, profitable, and meaningful when it is shared with others. And there's also a benefit for the real world as well: students develop skill in interpersonal relations that carry over to their personal and professional lives.

Moreover, because real learning cannot be forced on students by the teacher, the students should have some say about what they learn, how the class is run, and how they will be evaluated. However, since students usually take courses in an institutional setting, the teacher must follow some procedures, establish some standards, evaluate what students have learned in a given time period, and convert that judgment to a letter grade, which reflects not only what individual students have accomplished in relation to their goals, but also takes into account the accomplishments and achievements of the other students in their classes.

Teaching, then, must be broadly defined. It is much more than standing up in front of a class presenting information. Teaching is creating a dynamic, supportive classroom environment, and designing a variety of challenging assignments and activities that will actively engage students of varying abilities, interests, and learning styles. Teaching is encouraging students and helping them succeed. Most of all, teaching is providing an opportunity for students to learn how to learn on their own. The teacher's ultimate goal should be to help students reach the point where they no longer need the teacher at all.

I tell students that I've planned my course to reflect these beliefs. If they are used to a class where the teacher spells out exactly what they have to learn and do, they may have some difficulty accepting my teaching style. But just as they are often asked to suspend their disbelief in reading a work of fiction, I ask them to try to do the same when taking my course. I will ask them to evaluate what they have experienced and learned, and to give me specific feedback on my teaching, which I will use in planning future classes just as I have used suggestions from previous students in designing the present course.

One of the most exciting aspects of teaching is the continuing challenge to improve my teaching methods and course design, using student feedback and my own observations to make changes and try innovative approaches with each new group of students. As I work to become more effective, I get a chance to hone my own creative thinking and problem-solving skills. For example, when some students were unable to see what they had learned in my "chaotically taught" class, I didn't want to respond to the problem with a hundred-question exam at the end of the course. So I figured out another way to provide them with concrete evidence of what they had learned.

At the first class meeting I ask students to write a response to a hypothetical situation that requires the application of the knowledge and skills the course will cover. I collect these papers without discussing them. At the end of the semester I give students the same writing assignment. When they finish, I hand them their first versions and ask them to read them and then do free writings on what they notice. Even though they don't have numbers to quantify their learning–correctly answering 95 questions out of a hundred–they can see they have learned a substantial amount. They realize that in addition to learning terms and facts that would make good short-answer test questions, they have also developed a conceptual understanding of the material covered.

Here are some excerpts from the "freewrites" students in my introductory education class did after responding to a hypothetical classroom situation (with several problems they were asked to identify and solve), and then reading what they had written about handling the same situation at the beginning of the course.

"It has surprised me how much I learned in this course. In looking back on what I wrote at the beginning of the semester and on what I have written now, it is obvious that I have been able to develop my ideas much more fully now. I recognized more problems and found more solutions than I did at the beginning of the semester."

"I had ideas about what was wrong in the classroom scenario, but I didn't know how to fix them. I didn't have specific ways to motivate students. At the end of the class I had much more insight and many more concrete examples as to how I should go about teaching a class. I could see more difficulties, and each difficulty was more complex than a simple lack of communication and respect between teacher and students. There are many factors in a classroom that is falling apart, things I would not have seen or understood three months ago, but do so now."

"I had the problem identified right, but my solution was *horrible*! I would have gone in there like an army sergeant and demanded, 'This is my classroom, love it or leave it!' My guess is they would have left it. I couldn't blame them. Now I know how I could handle their misbehavior. I would be much more concerned with getting the students involved in learning, not just telling them what they need to know. . . ."

"After reading my freewrite from February, I have to smile. Although I knew little about teaching, I was intuitively able to pinpoint the problems and some solutions. I had no idea though how to attack a motivation problem but assumed I would by May. Well, it's May! I feel that by doing the exam and then reading my freewrite I have *realized* how much I've learned. That may sound elementary, but I think it doesn't happen enough. It was very rewarding for me to read exactly what I knew and didn't know in February and to realize that I learned what I wanted to learn and then so much more! I have so much enjoyed the amount of self-reflection that I have had to do in this class that I am finally motivated to start and keep a journal. Thanks."

As you can see from the students' comments, they not only talked about what they learned, they also reflected on the process of learning. The exercise forced them to look at *how* they learned, to demonstrate their ability to apply *what* they had learned, and to evaluate their own thinking—something students are rarely asked to do in school but must often do outside of school.

After many years of teaching a variety of students from grade seven through college, I truly believe in the value of not making it easy for students to learn. My students take more pride in what they do when it doesn't come too easily. And, surprisingly, most stop thinking about learning in terms of the grades they'll get and begin to learn just for the joy of learning. Of course, when that happens, they also put much more time and energy into the course. But there's even a more important reason why I make sure my students experience some confusion and discomfort as they learn: no one makes learning easy in the real world.

If education at any level is a preparation for life, then teachers must give students practice in learning on their own, help them to develop the skills they need to figure out what has to be done, and nurture their self-confidence so they won't quit when things aren't going well. One of the most important criteria by which we should measure teacher effectiveness is the degree to which they gradually make themselves unnecessary in the classroom. My greatest compliment came from the student who said, "You taught us without our knowing it."

Suggestions for Parents

One of the best ways parents can help children learn is simply to spend more time talking to them. Schedule some time for worthwhile conversation with children every day. As children explain what they have learned, they process the new information, clarifying it in their memories. Making connections with prior knowledge and framing questions for future knowledge will help them develop the habits of mind that distinguish lifelong learners.

Use the questions presented here as guides for discussing school work, TV programs, reading, personal experiences, or family trips. Remember that everything children do or experience is an occasion for learning. The last three questions can be used to frame a useful conversation about children's inappropriate behavior. While children do learn from suffering consequences for their misdeeds, in the long run they will benefit most from serious reflection on the experience. By considering factors such as other people's points of view or what they might have done instead, they are more likely to make better decisions in the future—to think before they act.

1. What did you learn . . . today in school? from that TV program? the book you just finished? that experience with your friend?
2. What does that remind you of?
3. In what ways is it similar to . . .?
4. How is it different?
5. What else would you like to know about that?
6. How could you go about finding out?
7. How do you think [another person] might feel about that?
8. What would happen if . . .?
9. What would you do if . . .?

To encourage children to expand their responses, say "Tell me more about . . ." Keep in mind that your overall aim is getting children comfortable with "thinking out loud." Try not to answer questions for your children without first letting them attempt to answer questions for themselves. Younger children are sometimes given fewer opportunities to learn because older siblings speak up before they get a chance to say anything. If that is a problem in your family, try to find time to have a private conversation with each child in addition to family discussions.

Chapter Four

Self-Esteem: The Key to Success

IN 1990, Nebraska authorities returned a convicted murderer named John Joubert to Maine so he could stand trial for the murder of an eleven-year-old boy that occurred eight years earlier. A newspaper story entitled "The Making of a Killer" detailed the twenty-six-year-old child murderer's history, and included comments from people who had known him when he was a boy attending Maine schools.

John Joubert came from a very troubled family. After his parents were divorced, he lived with his mother, who prevented him from making friends. As he spent more time alone, he became "less able to deal with real people in real situations." One of his elementary school teachers said, "He never fit in with the other kids. . . . He tried to do what the others did, but he was always sort of a failure. He had the ability. With just a little coaching and practice, he could have been just as good as the others."

A classmate recalled, "He was the kind of person a lot of people liked to pick on because he was small. People were mean to him. . . . " Other students made funny noises when he came into the room. He was the butt of schoolyard jokes and the object of ridicule.

It is clear from reading the entire article that John Joubert was severely disturbed from a very young age. Perhaps the schools couldn't have done anything to prevent him from murdering the two young boys in Nebraska. But one thing is clear: John Joubert lacked self-esteem. If his schools had been as concerned with students' self-concepts and sense of belonging as they no doubt were with their attendance records, grades, and test scores, would Joubert's later life have been different? Although it can't be answered, this question is well worth thinking about.

Some schools have begun programs designed to increase students' self-esteem. But self-esteem can't be directly taught; it must be developed. Special programs and activities, stickers, and gold stars are all nice, but they won't be enough to change the feelings of children who feel worthless because they come from dysfunctional families, or have been labeled as failures by their schools.

My dictionary defines self-esteem as "pride in oneself," but it doesn't go on to say anything about how children come to feel proud of themselves. One way to think about this process is in terms of the "Four C's": *care, confidence, competence,* and *control.* An increase in any one of the Four C's tends to raise the others. Children who have high levels of self-esteem believe in themselves because they know that others care about them. They feel confident enough to risk trying something new. Because they have developed competence in some areas, they believe they can eventually develop competence in others. They have seen that what they do does make a difference; thus, they have a sense that they have some control over what happens to them.

Developing students' self-esteem doesn't mean that teachers praise them for shoddy work; children are quick to spot and discount false praise. To foster real self-esteem, teachers must create classroom environments where all children feel they are valued, and provided with enough support and encouragement to be successful. Some children need more "scaffolding" than others. Because schools don't always help children to feel good about themselves and achieve results valued by others, many teenagers just drop out. School has actually taught them *not* to have pride in themselves.

The public spotlight has finally been turned more brightly on the problem of school dropouts. And it's about time. Our humane instincts should be enough motivation for us to help kids succeed in school, but even the most cold-hearted corporation head, whose main concern is the bottom line, must realize that our survival as a nation depends on our ability to make sure young people become contributing members of society. As a large portion of the population ages, the pool of young people shrinks. Thus, it's easy to see that we need to add every young person we can to the work force, or our country won't survive economically. We can't afford to have able-bodied men and women untrained or poorly educated for jobs that will be difficult to fill. Some already worry that the fewer workers of tomorrow will be unable to support a larger number of retirees.

If we don't reach these kids while they're in school, they may be lost to us forever. And their individual losses will become burdens on all of us. We'll be forced to deal with the consequences of welfare, crime, and other social ills.

Who are the kids who aren't making it? The kid who's high on drugs, the kid who can't read, the kid who's unmarried and pregnant at fourteen, the kid who skips classes and drops out of school—what they all have in common, regardless of whether they come from single-parent families on welfare or from two-parent households where both parents are busy professionals, is low self-esteem.

These kids have no purpose. They're letting life happen to them. They see themselves as failures because they've seldom, if ever, tasted success. No one cares about them so they don't care about themselves. Unloved and unconnected to others, they engage in destructive behavior. When their families fail to nurture them, they might find hope in the schools—but schools usually make matters worse.

The kids who spent too much time in my office when I was a high school assistant principal ten years ago are now the adults I read about in the paper. They're arrested time and time again for driving after their licenses have been suspended, for possessing or distributing drugs, for wife battering or child beating. And I am not surprised. I knew then they wouldn't make it. Instead of figuring out how we might reach these kids, we were making sure they learned punctuation rules and democratic principles—not so they could have better lives but so they could pass the necessary tests. When they didn't do their homework or came late to class, their teachers, having no time for a private conversation that might have led to some resolution of the immediate problem, recorded zeroes in the gradebook and handed out detention slips.

Imagine how school must feel to one of these kids. Maybe

there was no time for breakfast this morning because you had to help Mom get the younger ones ready for school. Even though you hurried, you arrived a minute after the late bell rang. Homeroom Teacher says, "Go to the office and get a slip. You know the rules." When you arrive at the office, Mrs. Secretary is joking with the captain of the football team, but she's frowning when she turns to you. "Second time this week. Wait for the vice-principal."

There are seven kids ahead of you so you wait your turn. You think maybe Mr. Vice-Principal will give you a chance to explain, but he's so harried all he does is growl, "Report for Saturday detention, eight to twelve. Suspension if you don't show." He's already dealing with the next kid, so you have no chance to say it'll have to be suspension because Mom's counting on you to babysit Saturday. At least now you have the necessary pass to get into your period one class. Trouble is you're twenty minutes late.

Period One Teacher gives you a nasty "Not you again" look as you drop the pass on his desk and take your seat, and continues talking to the class, "For tomorrow make sure you've memorized the qualifications and terms of office for the president, vice-president, senators, representatives, and the others we've talked about. We'll have a test on it." As the teacher tells everyone to open their books to page 101, you look at the meaningless lists the teacher has scrawled all over the board in the twenty minutes before you got there. You'll never be able to remember all those details. You tell yourself to focus on what the teacher's saying now. Period One Teacher says, "We'll go over the steps a bill must go through before it's a law." He reads aloud from the textbook, pausing every now and then to jot something on the board or to call on someone to repeat what he has just read. On the TV news you've caught glimpses of heated arguments between senators on proposed bills, but the teacher gives no indication that human emotions have anything to do with the process of making laws. His voice drones on. The room is hot and stuffy. You're supposed to listen and take notes, but it's hard to stay awake. You worry about Saturday and think about finding your friend at lunch. You need someone to talk to. Finally the bell rings and everyone rushes on to period two.

Period Two Teacher talks about how important it is for everyone to learn to write well, but for the third day this week you have a worksheet to do. Yesterday it was labeling parts of speech. Today you have to correct all the errors in a story someone else, probably the textbook author or the teacher herself, wrote. So far all you've had to write was one book report. The teacher wanted a complete summary of the plot so she could tell whether you'd read the whole book. "Stick to the facts," she said. "Don't waste time giving your opinion." You had thought you might do O.K. in this class, but when you got your book report back with red marks everywhere, you knew you were doomed. The teacher had given you a big red F for sentence fragments, misspelled words, and missing commas. She didn't say one word about the careful plot summary you had worked so hard on. Why bother playing the game, you decided, if there's no way you can win?

The rest of the day is no better. You get chewed out by the phys ed teacher for not having the right gym shorts, and you have no chance to explain that Mom can't get the money for them until next week. The math teacher tells you to report after school when he discovers your homework isn't done right. You wonder how you can do it later when you still don't understand the chapter, and you know he won't have any more patience after school than he does in class. He figures if kids pay attention in class they'll catch on, and if they don't it's their own fault. The study hall teacher makes you sit right beside her as a punishment for talking when all you were trying to do was borrow a pen from a friend when yours ran out of ink. The whole class gets blamed in science when the teacher can't find her gradebook, and she doesn't apologize when she later finds it buried under a pile of homework papers from the honors class.

Sometimes you wonder if you'd like science better if you were in the honors class. They get to do labs and stuff while all the general class does is watch filmstrips and fill in blanks on worksheets. Teachers always seem to like the kids better when they are in the honors class. But it's a waste of time to think about what will never happen. You're too stupid to be assigned to an honors class. Even though you had special reading classes all through elementary school, you still can't read very well. As soon as you realized the special classes were just for dumb kids, there didn't seem to be much point in working very hard. The special teachers were nice, though, so you pretended to do your work, but nothing made much sense. They told you that being in special classes would help you, but it was like wearing a sign that said you were dumb. The other kids made fun of you and didn't want you on their teams in phys ed, and the regular teachers didn't expect you to do very much. They seemed to think you'd be better off in a special class all day.

What can we do to prevent kids from feeling like the student profiled here? The answer really isn't all that complex. Students are people with very basic human needs. Your children's school experiences are probably much more positive than that of the teen described here, but one class or another may inspire similar feelings, perhaps because of a difficult subject or teacher. Many of the problems kids have in school stem from the fact that teachers or administrators—in their efforts to teach content or manage the institution—fail to pay enough attention to students' personal needs. Ironically, if schools focused more on reaching students personally, they would discover that academic achievement would increase and discipline problems would decrease as a matter of course. And everyone would benefit, not just the students who are at risk for dropping out.

When I read the opening sentence of an essay written by an eleventh-grade student for a statewide writing assessment, I chuckled. "Kids drop out of school because they have to go to the bathroom." What a ridiculous idea, I thought, but I continued reading to see where the student was going to go with it.

As the student explained in her essay, Joe was not doing very well in school and had been absent a lot, so when he asked the teacher for a bathroom pass, the teacher said no. Because Joe really had to go, he left without permission. Of course, the teacher reported him to the principal who in turn suspended him for three days for disobeying the teacher and cutting class. Joe decided he was fed up with being in trouble all the time so he never went back to school when the suspension was over.

While the need to use the bathroom wasn't the whole reason the student dropped out, it certainly was a contributing factor—the proverbial straw that broke the camel's back. But the student's essay made sense because it showed that, for many kids, school turns out to be a place where they are constantly put down and devalued as human beings. Even though rules and procedures are necessary to maintain an orderly and controlled learning environment, all too often students become victims of the system rather than being served by it.

What Abraham Maslow says about motivation and human needs in *Toward a Psychology of Being* applies to schools. Maslow categorizes needs in a hierarchy. He believes people must satisfy needs at one level before they will do anything toward setting or reaching goals at the next level. Using the bathroom, for example, is at the bottom because it is a physiological need. Academic achievement, the area with which schools concern themselves, is fairly high up on the list.

According to Maslow, people aren't motivated toward growth and development—what we expect from students in school—until their lower-level or deficiency needs have been taken care of. In simple terms, students can't learn math and history when they are hungry or cold (physiological needs), when they feel threatened (safety needs), when they feel that no one cares (love and belonging needs), or when they see themselves as failures (esteem needs). When schools don't first work to help students satisfy these lower-level needs, they waste their time trying to teach them anything. Once over this hurdle, however, Maslow believes that growth is a more or less forward development. The more one gets, the more one wants. If schools can make students feel that they belong and are capable, then students will learn because they want to learn.

We have only to talk with kids to see that the reasons they drop out or do poorly in school can often be traced to their school's lack of concern with satisfying their basic needs, usually those that have to do with love and belonging and self-esteem. Except for students like Joe, who wasn't allowed to use the bathroom when he needed to, the schools do a fairly good job of meeting physiological needs. The buildings are dry and warm (most of the time, anyway), and school breakfast and lunch programs are provided for students from poor families. In some urban schools where gangs and violence are major concerns, some students may worry about their safety, but for most students with problems in school, their unmet psychological–not physiological–needs keep them from doing well.

When we ate out at a family restaurant recently, our waitress was a young woman, now in her late twenties, who had dropped out of the local high school when she was a junior. I had known her when I was the assistant principal there, but even though I had chatted with her numerous times when she worked at the checkout in the grocery store, I had never known why she left high school. The restaurant wasn't very busy, so I asked her why she had changed jobs. "More money and better hours," she replied. Then she went on to tell me proudly that she had earned her GED [General Educational Development certificate, equivalent to a high school diploma]. "As soon as my kids are in school," she continued, "I plan to go back to school. I'd like to learn about computers and get a good job."

"What accounts for your positive attitude about school now?" I asked. "It was so different in high school."

"For one thing I want to set a good example for my kids, but I never would have quit in the first place if things had been different. When I started my junior year I was pregnant. I was having a lot of trouble with my legs swelling and stuff. My classes were all over the place, so I went in to see the guidance counselor about getting my schedule changed so I wouldn't have to climb the stairs so many times. He wouldn't even listen. He said, 'I have students who don't even have schedules yet. I don't have time to do anything about students who just want to make changes.' Well, I walked out in the hall feeling very tired and very discouraged. I figured if no one cares whether I'm here or not, I don't either. So I walked out the door and never went back."

A local paper here in Maine recently published an article about dropouts. A fifteen-year-old dropout told the reporter that even though she misses being with students her own age, she won't go back to school, because " . . . it wouldn't be worth it to go back. It makes me mad because I wasn't treated fair. I'm glad to leave it behind me." Her trouble began in the sixth grade when a classmate began calling her names. She ended up getting unfairly blamed for breaking rules, disrupting classes, and fighting. The next year she decided to start sticking up for herself. "I couldn't let teachers start chewing me out for no good reason. They decided I was talking back and I got a reputation for being mouthy." Even when she made conscious efforts to do better, it didn't work. "It always seemed so complicated. I never felt they were listening to me." Ironically when she's returned to the high school recently to meet friends, the teachers have been nice. "If they treated me like that when I was a student, I might not have left."

Another female dropout said, "Everybody has to go to school and fit in. If you don't, it's your fault and they don't help you. I wasn't interested in what we were being taught. I would ask, 'Why do we have to read this book?' or 'What are we learning this for?' But I never got an answer."

A male dropped out after his father died of a heart attack because he felt the school harassed him to do everything its way and overloaded him with anger and confusion. "Some of the teachers there, they didn't care at all. If you raised your hand and asked a question, they'd say, 'You should have been listening.' They would say it to make you feel stupid for asking."

A flurry of letters to the editor followed the publication of the story. School officials, feeling the article was biased, wrote several of them. The high school guidance director wrote, "It has been my observation that low self-esteem, substance abuse, dysfunction within the family, the desire for work and income, peer pressure, and lack of interest, which may be the result of unsuccessful experience in school, hold far more weight or validity than personal grievances with teaching staff." He's right, of course, but I can't help wondering why he can't see that the first item on his list—low self-esteem—leads to all the others. And if he reflected on what the students who were quoted in the article said, he should realize that if the teachers, along with teaching their subjects, had tried to meet students' needs for love, belonging, and esteem—Maslow's terms—then those students might still be in school, better equipped to deal with the other problems he mentioned.

The principal wrote, "I have the answer! Families need to value education as the vehicle that leads to opportunity." He then defended *all* the teachers and concluded, "It used to be true not so very many years ago that if a student caused a problem at school, he or she was in deep trouble on all fronts. Now it seems that if a student has a problem at school, the teacher is at fault." He's right. Times and people have changed, but we would do well to remember that the parents he complains about are themselves products of the schools. Shouldn't the schools share *some* of the responsibility for the way they deal with problems and respond to children's difficulties? Could it be that these parents were once students who felt put down and ignored by teachers?

A citizen responded, "Kids choose the easy way and drop out. Too bad, dropouts. Just blame yourselves for your noncompliance and your dismal future." Sure, students are responsible for their actions, but if schools from the very beginning make them feel like failures, is it all their fault when they make poor decisions as teenagers? I know one principal who, instead of finding ways to work toward solving problems with a difficult student, would haul the kid into his office, close the door, and say, "You're all done. Go clean out your locker." Fortunately for the principal none of these kids ever challenged him, because what he did was clearly against both state law and school board policy. These kids, however, were glad to get out of a place where nothing good ever happened. They got their stuff from their lockers, walked out the door, and were added to the school dropout statistics–and perhaps later to the lists of welfare recipients or prison inmates as well.

Among all the defensive and negative responses to the dropout article, one letter stood out. Four students in an alternative program for at-risk high school students wrote to defend their program (about which one of the dropouts quoted in the article commented negatively): "The atmosphere here is different. It seems to us that we learn more because the classes are smaller and there's more one-to-one attention. There's a family-like feeling here. We trust and care about each other. . . . Here we are treated like adults and therefore, we are expected to act like adults. There are no cliques here. If we do have problems, we deal with them and try to exist peacefully."

The kids in the alternative program, who appear to be doing well now, didn't make it in the regular school setting. Their description of the alternative program shows they're getting now what they didn't get before in the regular school program. Not surprisingly, one sees in their words that the psychological needs Maslow identified are being met. Why should we have to spend money to set up special programs for kids like these? Couldn't we work to establish a nurturing and supportive atmosphere that will foster achievement and success for all students in the regular classrooms?

A recent study asked dropouts to identify the factors that caused them to quit school before graduation, using a list of forty-five options. The most frequently cited problem, selected by 64 percent of the dropouts, was that counselors and teachers did not help them feel they belonged in school. Many said, "Most teachers didn't care whether or not I did well."

Under closer examination we can see that even when students give reasons such as pregnancy, outside jobs, or drug abuse, what they are really saying is, "I wanted someone to care about me. I wanted to feel like I belonged." Talk to a teenage mother and she'll say, "I have someone to love, and someone who loves me now." The kid who works for minimum wage at the gas station may not be getting rich, but it feels pretty good to know that someone trusts him to do a job, treats him like a person, and occasionally says, "Good work!" Real life for these kids, even when it's not great, feels a whole lot better than school.

By the time some students reach high school, it's too late to turn things around. Grading is one reason some students begin to lose confidence in themselves even before reaching high school. When younger students were asked what they thought about grades, their answers were predictable. The kids who were earning A's and B's thought grades were O.K. One eleven-year-old didn't agree. He thought the system at his ungraded elementary school was better than the letter grades he now gets in middle school. "It seemed like they knew you as an individual instead of just giving you letter grades. They also gave you more freedom toward grades because they let you make your own self-evaluation for how you think you have been progressing. I mean you do know yourself best. Also the people there couldn't say, 'Oh, I got an A, and you didn't,' because the grades were large reports on how you got better, not how you got worse, the grades wouldn't make you feel bad."

Another student said, "I think the grading system in my school is terrible. You study and work hard on a test and you still get a big fat F." Too many F's, and too much trouble with teachers who don't care and never listen over too many years, result in kids wanting to get out of school before they are really prepared to handle life. But grading isn't the only aspect of schools that can work against students developing self-esteem.

Grouping students by ability, either within the same class or in separate classes, also damages students' self-esteem. Studies show that while the higher-level students gain some academic benefit from special classes, the lower-level students lose out. Moreover, even the more able students don't always benefit. Peer and parental pressure drives some kids to suicide, and causes anorexia and other psychological or physiological problems in others. Ability grouping can also cause the more able students to develop arrogant, elitist attitudes.

When I first moved to a small town on the coast of Maine and was hired to teach at the local high school, I was surprised to learn that I would have the top-level senior English class. In my previous schools new teachers got only average or below-average classes, because teaching an honors class was a reward one had to earn by teaching for several years in the same school.

I soon found out why nobody else wanted to teach these students. They were capable and motivated to learn, but they weren't about to be told what to do by any teacher. Because the town was small, they had no competition and had been together from first grade on. In elementary school, where classes were heterogeneously grouped, they always had their own reading group. In high school, of course, they were scheduled into special advanced classes for every major subject. Because they were bright and had been together for many years, they knew how to manipulate teachers and the principal. By the time they were seniors, they believed they were better and smarter than other students and most teachers as well. Teaching them was an incredible challenge: there were twenty of them in a tightly knit group, and one of me.

The students declared war the first day, engaging me in a contest of wills. Had I tried to teach traditionally, I would have lost. But by involving them in group process activities and journal writing—both of which methods were new to them—I was able to break down their group defenses and reach them as individuals. By the time the second semester began, we had a positive and productive working relationship. When they locked me out of the room as an April Fool's Day joke, I pretended to be upset, but as I sat in the teachers' room and heard them through the thin wall enthusiastically and productively discussing the short story they'd read for homework, I was proud at how far we had come since September. I still treasure the gift those students gave me at the end of the year, a copy of *Winnie the Pooh* that they all signed.

Those senior English students didn't need me to show them that they needed to change their egotistical and elitist attitudes. They would have learned that lesson later in college anyway. Many capable students have trouble competing in colleges, where even a valedictorian may find that valedictorians are a dime a dozen. It's been said that good students learn in spite of the teaching they receive, and to an extent that's true. But even they would learn more if they were given the opportunities and the encouragement to do so.

Bright students can learn *more* when they aren't taught separately. One good way to learn is to teach. (I myself never really learned all the intricacies of the punctuation rules until the first year I had to teach them.) By giving bright students a chance to teach the ones who have difficulty learning, we not only help them thoroughly review and reinforce what they've been taught, we also help them develop a sense of social responsibility. Moreover, the process is synergistic: they increase their own self-esteem and self-confidence at the same time they help less able students increase theirs.

A survey of MacArthur fellows (winners of the so-called "genius awards"), who were asked about their own school experiences for a study on gifted education, supports this view. These individuals, who have demonstrated their uncommon abilities across a wide spectrum of creative pursuits indicated in their responses that the "opportunity to teach enhances student learning." Their responses also suggested four other important points: the "support of good teachers is crucial"; the "opportunity to be with supportive and challenging peers" is important; the "feature of the educational style favored is freedom but with appropriate structure"; and "the school system, public or private, most of the time rewards patterns of behavior inappropriate for an individual thinker, researcher, or artist."

Even when gifted programs do serve some students well, their very existence can be damaging to the students who aren't chosen for them. The gifted students in many schools get to do interesting and enjoyable activities that aren't part of the regular program–special projects, guest speakers, and field trips. Wouldn't all children benefit from visiting an art museum or going to a concert? Why don't average kids get to do any special projects? And how do those kids feel when they know others are involved in interesting and exciting activities from which they are excluded? Isn't it like giving candy or ice cream to some kids and forcing the others to watch enviously while they eat it? Consider what these programs can do to the self-esteem of kids who aren't included.

As the MacArthur fellow responses indicated, gifted students do benefit from interacting with other gifted students. In small schools, however, they may have few peers. States should consider establishing special summer programs like the ones already offered at some universities, such as the John Hopkins Talent Search, because these would give students from small schools the chance to learn with equally gifted students from other schools. Special residential schools like the North Carolina High School for Science and Mathematics are probably the best way to meet the needs of the small number of very highly gifted students. After-school and Saturday programs modeled after the Children's Palaces in China suggest another option. Children with special talents and interests pursue these activities with equally motivated students outside the school day, and perhaps off the school grounds. In my community a very active young people's theater–although not connected with the school–does a great deal to help children develop skill in the dramatic arts. With a little creative thinking, it's possible for schools to meet the needs of gifted students without creating problems for children who are less able.

Special programs for kids who have difficulty learning can also damage students' self-esteem. Because regular classroom instruction is too often not personalized for individual students, less able students often suffer high levels of frustration, anxiety, and tension. But special programs haven't always helped them much.

When it was first passed, P.L. 94–142 (the federal law that provided for special education classes and programs) was much needed by a segment of the student population that had been forgotten or ignored. But P.L. 94–142 has not lived up to its initial promise. Special education has become an enormous and costly maze of programs, personnel, and paperwork that no longer works as it was intended. Even though the law mandates that every student receive appropriate instruction in the least restrictive environment, with the intention that students will return to regular classroom placement as soon as possible, what actually happens is that students are labeled early. Too often that label sticks until the end of their school careers.

By being singled out for special instruction in a resource room, kids see themselves as dumber than other kids. Well-meaning teachers expect less from these students, and their expectations become a self-fulfilling prophecy: "these kids are slow so we'll give them special help, but we shouldn't expect too much because they are slow." The kids quickly get the message: "I'm not too smart so I can't do much." So they do enough to get by, and their test scores never improve enough for them to get back to regular classes in the mainstream.

Since many special ed programs require that students leave the regular class for part of the day, they cause further obstacles for both students and teachers. A speech therapist, for example, often works with students in several schools, so students have to leave their regular classes when the speech therapist can fit them in. There's no way to coordinate schedules among all the specialists and regular classroom teachers. Teachers have to stop whatever they're doing to remind students it's time to go, and when they return, teachers have to fill them in on what they missed and get them going on whatever the class is doing now. What students miss and misunderstand in regular instruction may cancel out the benefits of the one-on-one speech therapy.

A sixth-grade teacher told me that she is supposed to teach science and social studies to all the students in her self-contained class, but students regularly leave her room for lessons in the resource room, help from specialists, or conferences with the school psychologist or social worker. Because she has so many students coming and going all the time for these and other reasons, the whole class is together in the room for only twenty minutes out of an entire week. The interruptions in her teaching notwithstanding, there's no way these sixth graders can do anything meaningful in either social studies or science in the time available. Although it was never meant to do harm, special education has decimated curriculum and instruction for all students.

Perhaps the greatest benefit of special ed has been the psychological support students get from knowing that someone in the school truly cares about them as individuals. Special ed classes are smaller than regular classes, and the people who choose to work with kids who have learning difficulties usually have a strong desire to help others. They work with the parents, too, and get involved not only in teaching the students but also in helping them cope with life in and outside of school.

But while some students may find that special ed gives them psychological support, there's also a cost. One of my college students spent the day in an elementary school observing students in special education. When she ate lunch with these kids, who sat at a separate table, one of them said, "Other kids call us retarded because we are in a special ed room, but we're not. The other kids are for calling us that!" My student wrote, "It made me feel kind of sad, but it's also something I expected. . . . Kids are so cruel, and they're not blind to the fact that certain kids are singled out as 'special' in some way. My elementary and high schools were the same way." Earlier in the day Anna noted that even when a special student was mainstreamed into an art class, she was still separated from the regular kids. Her desk was outside the U-shaped arrangement of the rest of the desks in the room, near the teacher's desk. The label may be invisible, but it's always there.

Because special attention from a caring teacher isn't always enough to compensate for the difficulties these students face when they leave the security of the special ed classroom, sometimes the consequences are much more serious than hurt feelings. A North Carolina policeman and his wife started a non-profit organization called Parents Against Teen Suicide after their teenaged daughter killed herself with her father's service revolver. Among the families for whom they have provided support was that of a thirteen-year-old girl with a learning disability, who wrote that her classmates were making fun of her. The girl's mother found her on the bathroom floor after an overdose of a painkiller.

Given large classes and traditional instruction methods that depersonalize learning, regular classroom teachers get to know few students well enough to reach them, unless they overcome the institutional requirements imposed on them. And students in regular classes don't get to know and appreciate their handicapped classmates when they are taught in separate classes.

Henry M. Levin, a professor at Stanford University, believes that elementary special ed students, who have been given slow-paced remedial instruction in pull-out programs, actually learn better with a fast-paced curriculum normally reserved for gifted students. Gains in student achievement have been reported after the first eighteen months in classes where teachers replaced a drill-and-practice repetitive approach with techniques that actively engage students. Students maintain a higher level of interest with the faster pace.

And similar results have been found in the Higher Order Thinking Skills (HOTS) project, which began in California several years ago and has now been adopted by schools across the nation. Teachers have given up traditional remedial work for the disadvantaged students who are in the program because they are behind their classmates in reading, language, or math. Students instead learn higher-order thinking skills by working on intellectually challenging activities not directly tied to the school curriculum. As author Stanley Pogrow describes it, the program is "purely a general thinking – even a gifted – approach for at-risk learners." There are no remedial services, yet students have made gains in their scores on standardized tests. "The Detroit Public Schools found that HOTS students who did *not* receive supplementary remediation in math achieved a level of mastery on their math tests that was three times higher than that achieved by students who received extra drill in the specific objectives measured," Pogrow wrote.

The French immersion school in Prince George's County, Maryland, is an example of an approach that works for all students. While special ed students in some schools don't even take foreign language classes, in this school they learn some of their regular subjects in the foreign language. Teachers like the fact that students are generally more motivated to learn, but they "also discovered that the approach had kind of an equalizing effect. In the second language, they found students considered 'at-risk' . . . tended to perform as well as their peers."

If teaching methods and curriculum normally reserved for gifted students work for the less able students, perhaps we should consider using these methods in the regular classrooms. Then we could eliminate special education for all except the most mentally handicapped youngsters, who even today are usually isolated in self-contained classes.

The resource rooms that serve the largest number of students with special needs accommodate kids with a variety of problems —everything from dyslexia to emotional instability—that up to now have prevented them from learning in regular classrooms. While resource rooms serve kids with legitimate needs, they are often also dumping grounds for kids whom teachers can't or don't want to deal with. These special ed kids know when the teachers don't want them around, but they often don't realize they are being cheated out of the opportunity to develop positive relationships with their peers in the mainstream.

When I was the principal of a small middle school (grades six through eight), I was shocked by the large percentage of students who had been classified as having special needs. Soon I knew why. Whenever teachers had students who disrupted the class or continually failed to do assigned work, they would fill out a referral form for special ed placement. The pupil evaluation team would meet and recommend further testing or a psychological assessment. I can't remember one situation where a student didn't come up short enough on one scale or another. Thus, placement in the resource room became routine.

School-wide discipline problems decreased, because now these students had someone who cared about them (the resource room teacher) to help them when things got rough. But the difference in achievement was negligible. And while these at-risk students stayed in school through grade eight, they usually dropped out after they got to high school. That many of them developed neither the self-esteem nor the skills and knowledge they needed to succeed in the real world became evident later. Two of these students with whom I worked burned down the old middle school building, and both would have served prison terms had one not been killed in an auto accident before the trial. The police reports are filled with the names of others who were special ed students when they were in school. We don't need formal research statistics to tell us that something is very wrong.

Because students can't work to achieve academically until their more basic needs—physical and emotional—have been satisfied, and since placement in special education classes can lower students' self-esteem, we should focus on finding ways to create school and classroom environments that foster personal as well as academic growth for all students.

In the late Sixties and early Seventies the schools did attempt to deal with students more personally, but society rejected the "touchy-feely" methods and general lack of intellectual standards, and eventually pushed hard for a back-to-basics approach that often neglected the personal aspects of education. Neither extreme makes sense. What we've needed all along is balance. At the same time teachers cover the subjects they're assigned to teach, they can work to help students believe that they have value as individuals, that they can learn, and that they do have a future.

When students believe that teachers and other students care about them, they begin to believe in themselves. Each small success makes them hungry for the good feeling that comes when something goes well, so they're motivated to risk more and try again. When classroom activities require only that they listen or read to get information, which then must be spat back on a test, there are too few opportunities for students to figure out how they learn best, and to discover and demonstrate their talents and abilities.

If success breeds success, then knowledge breeds knowledge. When we know nothing about a topic it can seem boring. But every subject is fascinating once we get into it. And once we're hooked by knowing a little, we discover we want to know more. Someone once said that a good teacher can make the dullest subject interesting. Unfortunately the reverse is also true: a poor teacher can make the most exciting subject dull. The trick for teachers is to find ways to get students to make personal connections with what they're learning, and they can do that more easily if they first make personal connections with the students they teach. Even if the subject seems boring at first, students are willing to do what teachers ask when they feel teachers care about them. Then, if what teachers have given them to do makes sense and engages them, they will end up learning because the learning itself is pleasurable.

Many elementary schools have begun ungraded or multigraded programs so that children who develop more slowly can learn at their own pace without getting behind. If schools continue to group children by age and ability, some students will suffer lifelong negative consequences. When one mother discovered quite by accident that her child had been placed in a lower classroom math group than she had been in the previous year, she was upset and immediately contacted the school. What she didn't realize was that had she done nothing, her daughter, although only in second grade at this time, was effectively being assigned to low groups in high school math. Why? If in December of second grade the child is sixty pages behind the top group, she will be even further behind in June. When placement tests are given the next September, she won't be able to answer questions based on concepts she hasn't studied yet and thus will be placed in a lower group again. Once a child gets behind in a system like this, there is no way to catch up. The situation isn't fair to anyone, but it's especially harmful to the young child who is not less able but simply developing more slowly than other children. Once a child is labeled by the system, the label is difficult—if not impossible—to change.

So what can teachers do to get students to take the first step? Consider how you would respond if you were a student after your introduction to two different sophomore English teachers on the first day of school. In whose class would you want to be? Which teacher will help students develop self-confidence and self-esteem?

You walk into Mr. Worden's class two minutes before the bell, but he's nowhere in sight. The teacher's desk, centered in front of the chalkboard, commands five neat rows of student desks, seven to a row. The walls, a pale shade of institutional green, are bare, as is the top of the book shelves built along the wall under the windows. The shelves beneath, however, are filled with several sets of literature anthologies and paperback copies of novels, poetry, and short story collections.

You and your classmates have already taken seats when Mr. Worden comes in as the late bell rings. He stops two students who were right on his heels, shakes his finger at them, and says, "I expect you to be on time for this class. Next time you're not in your seat when the bell rings, you've got detention after school." Before the victims can get to a seat, Mr. Worden tells everyone to get up so he can assign seats. Reading from a seating chart he has already prepared, he puts everyone in alphabetical order. You hear a timid young girl complain to her friend that she'll never be able to see from the back of the room, but she's too afraid to say anything to Mr. Worden.

While Mr. Worden fills out the attendance slip, he directs two students to pass out books, heavy hardcover copies of *Adventures in American Literature*, and book cards. For a few minutes the room is silent while everyone fills out book cards.

Then Mr. Worden begins, "You're in the tenth grade now, so you'll have to get used to being treated like adults. Plan to do homework every night, but if you cooperate in class, I may give you the weekend off. The word 'sophomore' means wise and foolish, but I expect you to leave the foolish part outside when you come in here. Don't bother to ask me for passes to your locker or the bathroom. Take care of everything before class begins. And as I said to those two young men earlier, if you come late to class, you'll have time to make up after school. You're late if you're not in your seat when the bell rings. Also, I don't expect anyone to talk or be out of their seat without permission from me first. Raise your hands if you have a problem and I'll come to you. I shouldn't have to mention that this is English class so if you try to finish up your math homework in here and I catch you, I'll rip it up. That, by the way, is also what I do on tests if I find anyone cheating. Any questions?"

Seeing that there are none, Mr. Worden continues, "Homework counts 30 percent of your grade, essays and tests are 35 percent each. I don't take late work, so if it isn't done on time you take a zero. I'm here on Monday and Wednesday after school for make-up and extra help. You should be adult enough to know when you need help and come and get it. I won't hold your hand in here the way your teacher probably did last year. If you're absent, it's your responsibility to find out from me what you need to make up. But you'd better be careful about those absences. I'll take points off your final grade if you have too many."

"Now open your book to page two." Mr. Worden glances at his seating chart. "Mr. Smith, begin reading the first paragraph. In a good loud voice so everyone can hear you." But before the student begins, Mr. Worden notices some whispering in the last row. He marches over, looms over the offenders, and shouts, "I thought I said no talking without permission! Didn't you hear me?" The two girls are shrinking down into their seats, but one says very quietly, "I'm sorry. I just needed to know what page." Mr. Worden softens slightly and replies, "Well, next time raise your hand and ask me. Otherwise you'll be staying after school."

The remaining thirty minutes in the period pass slowly with students each taking a turn reading from the first selection in the book. Just before the bell rings, Mr. Worden says, "For tomorrow read the next story and write out the answers to all the questions at the end. Better have them done when you get in here because I'll check your papers first thing." The bell rings, but a stern look from Mr. Worden lets students know they better not move. "You're dismissed," he finally says, and everyone hurries to get out of the room.

Unlike Mr. Worden, Ms. Jacobs is at her classroom door. She smiles and says hello as you walk by into the room. The walls are painted the same sickly green as the room next door, but you don't notice it at first glance because they are covered with colorful posters. Some are obviously the work of previous students – they must have written and illustrated the poems they wrote.

The top shelf by the window is lined with healthy plants, several still in flower. The shelves underneath contain some sets of books similar to the ones in Mr. Worden's room, but there are also stacks of magazines, and one section has been reserved for a variety of single copies of paperback novels. The teacher's desk and file cabinet create a kind of little office in the corner of the room nearest the back door. The student desks are arranged in a big circle with an opening close to the front classroom door.

Ms. Jacobs comes in from the hall and stands by the opening in the circle. The bell rings and just as she is about to speak, two students come through the door. "Grab a seat anywhere. It's tough getting to all your classes the first day, but I know you'll be here before the bell rings tomorrow," she says in a friendly, understanding voice. "If you don't like the seats you've chosen, better switch now. I'm going to pass a sheet around for you to sign, and you'll have to keep the same seats until I learn all of your names. Once I do, you can sit anywhere—although I reserve the right to move you to a seat of my choice if you engage in private conversations while the rest of us are talking as a class."

Ms. Jacobs continues talking as she moves around the circle passing out a questionnaire to each student. "I'd like you to take a few minutes to fill this out, and then on the back just write and tell me about yourself. Include anything you think I should know about you that might have some bearing on how you'll do in the class. If you have a job, for example, that might interfere with getting your homework done, I'd like to know what you do and how many hours you work. Maybe you're a procrastinator. If so, tell me. Then I'll know that you might need an extra push from me or a classmate now and then to get you going."

You look at the questionnaire and begin responding to the questions there: What school subjects do you like best? Least? How do you feel about English? What kinds of books and magazines do you like to read? What's the best book you ever read? What are your hobbies? What kinds of writing have you done in school? On your own? And so on.

When everyone finishes writing, Ms. Jacobs collects the papers. "These will help me get to know you, but some of you may not know each other. I'd like you each to find a partner—

someone you don't know at all, if possible. If not, then someone you don't know very well. I'll give you ten minutes to interview each other and take notes. Then we'll come back together as a group, and each of you will introduce the person you interviewed to the rest of the class. Questions?" Since there are none, the students quickly find partners and settle down. The classroom hums with conversation.

When ten minutes are up, Ms. Jacobs calls everyone back together. "Before we begin the introductions, let me explain just a little about my expectations for you in this course and give you tonight's homework assignment." One student groans. "I know the idea of homework isn't pleasant, but I hope in this class you'll find that usually it's interesting, and sometimes even fun to do. Tonight, for example, I want you to write about yourself as a reader and a writer. Think back to your earliest experiences with books and tell me what you remember. Don't just write about what you did in school. If your parents read you stories when you very little, write down as much as you can remember. Don't worry about spelling, punctuation, or correct usage. Just make your handwriting legible enough for someone else to read it without needing you to translate. I want you to write a lot, so I don't want you to waste time looking words up in the dictionary on first drafts—although spelling will count on final drafts. Just pretend you're talking to us on paper, telling us everything you can recall about what you've done up to now with reading and writing and how you felt about those experiences."

One girl raises her hand, and Ms. Jacobs says, "You don't have to raise your hand if no one else is talking in here. Just go ahead and say what you have to say. If two people do start talking at once, just say, 'Excuse me. Go ahead.' That's what happens in real life, isn't it?" The students nod in affirmation. Then the girl says, "Is it O.K. if we cross out on this paper or can we use pencil?"

"Crossing out is O.K. Pencil is O.K. Your choice. I just want you to get your memories recorded on paper so we can talk about them. O.K.?" The girl smiles and shakes her head.

"Your grade in here will be more than just an average of your graded papers and projects. Class participation—remember, you have to be in class to participate, so attendance counts—and effort are important, too. I won't fail anyone who's making an honest effort to do the best he or she can. But that means you have to show me you really are trying by doing the best you can on *every* assignment. You won't necessarily earn an A, but you'll pass. However, I have no patience for anyone who doesn't care, so I'll fail anyone who misses an assignment." At that point a student says, "You mean we flunk if we don't do one little homework assignment?" "That's right," Ms. Jacobs replies. "That's not fair," a few students protest in unison.

"Well, remember that I said you were guaranteed to pass if you showed me you were trying. I'll remind you when you owe me work, so I figure anyone who doesn't make it up by the deadline at the end of the quarter doesn't care about passing. Besides, I won't give you homework that's just busy work, and since what we'll do in class will be based on what you read or write for homework, you won't be able to participate if yours isn't done. But I should also tell you that you all have an A right now for a homework/classwork grade. It counts 20 percent of your quarter grade and you get to keep it just by having your work done when you come into class. If you're absent, you can make it up. One day's extension for each day you're out. And tomorrow I'll give you a calendar with all the assignments for the quarter, so if you know you'll be out late for a meeting or practice, you can get your assignment done ahead of time."

The students all look comfortable again. Ms. Jacobs continues, "This is a lot to cover in one day. I'll spend some time over the next few days helping you understand what you need to do to be successful in this course. You will be able to make up low grades on graded tests and papers if you wish. I also want you to evaluate yourself. I'll explain the details of the process tomorrow, but I don't believe your final grade is something I should decide by myself. I'll set up the criteria, of course, but we both should agree on how well you meet them. We'll talk more about this tomorrow. I don't want you to worry about grades. Do your best, and your grades will take care of themselves. I'd like to think that you're in school to learn because you enjoy learning. Even though I know grades are important to you, I'd like us all to focus on learning."

The rest of the period passes quickly as students introduce

each other to the rest of the class. Ms. Jacobs says a little about herself, too. Everyone seems surprised to find out that she loves beachcombing and has written a book about making crafts from the driftwood and beach glass she's collected. When the bell rings, the students are chatting easily with each other, some with newfound friends, as they walk out of the room.

It's easy to see the difference a teacher's style and philosophy of teaching can make in how students respond, even on the first day of class. Consider what we might expect would happen to students' self-esteem and motivation depending on whether they end up taking Sophomore English from Mr. Worden or Ms. Jacobs. In whose class do you think students will exert the most effort? If students invest more time and energy in a course, they are certain to learn more. But even more important, if they believe that they can succeed, they'll be more likely to do so. If students are put down and turned off to learning by a teacher's style and methods, they'll do as little as possible and not feel very good about the whole experience.

But students aren't the only ones who need a supportive and encouraging environment. When principals act like dictators and use their power to control teachers, teachers expend less time and energy on their teaching. Linda McNeil, in a book called *Contradictions of Control*, explains that the more administrators concern themselves with rules, regulations, and procedures, the more teachers will hold back their knowledge from students. In one school she studied, she traced what happened to classroom instruction when a district moved from being a less-controlling environment under one administration to a more-controlling one under new leadership. Teachers who had previously involved students in a variety of exciting and innovative learning activities now cover the textbook material in dull, routine ways. As teachers feel they are valued less by administrators, they in turn value their students less. Everyone loses.

Moreover, school districts are not immune to the effects of self-esteem. One suburban Maine district enjoys above-average financial support for schools, in large measure because it encompasses an area where well-paid and highly educated professionals live. When Maine introduced a statewide assessment program, students in this school district came out on top and have remained there every year. In fact, officials think they need to use other tests to find out how well their students are doing, because there's nothing they can learn from the Maine assessment except that their students are the best in the state.

On the other hand, students in a small school district in Northern Maine continue to earn the lowest scores on the statewide assessment. Because many of the students come from Franco-American families, they are bilingual–and the test is given only in English. Money is tight both for families and school support. This district spends much less per pupil than does the suburban district mentioned above. Attracting good teachers to an area that is geographically remote and where salaries are low is difficult. The assessment has been in place only a few years, but this district will always be in a "lose-lose" situation. Even if students do earn higher scores each year, this district will still be at the bottom of the heap if the state average continues to increase as it has in the past. While the suburban school district has every reason to feel good about itself, this little district has none. How long will anyone care about improving if it doesn't matter what they do? No system that rewards the same winners and demoralizes the same losers year after year can accomplish much. Maintaining the status quo, even in relative terms, is not progress. Consider that on norm-referenced standardized tests, 50 percent of the students will always be below average.

If we must continue placing so much emphasis on test scores, then at least we could change the way statewide scores are reported. The school districts with the lower scores might show the greatest amount of improvement–theoretically, the lower their scores, the greater their potential for improvement. By listing results so that the school or district with the greatest improvement appears in first place, rather than the one with the highest average score, we could reward progress where it most needs to be rewarded. Self-esteem for an individual student or a community is a prerequisite for success.

In conducting interviews for their book, *Women and Self-Esteem*, Linda T. Sanford and Mary Ellen Donovan found that "a single positive experience could have had an enormous impact on the outlook of a small child from a troubled family. Sometimes one affectionate, encouraging, and supportive teacher made the difference between self-hate and the start of self-acceptance for a child."

Apparently John Joubert, convicted murderer of young boys, wasn't lucky enough to have had such an experience in his life. If we change the way we think about teaching and learning, we can make many more positive experiences possible for the kids who are in our schools today. And there may be another John Joubert sitting there whose life will be different as a result.

Suggestions for Parents

Remember the Four C's for self-esteem: caring, competence, confidence, and control. If your children feel cared for, capable, and confident, they'll also have a sense that they have some control over what happens to them. They'll be able to confront the routine challenges of life rather than be overwhelmed or paralyzed by them.

Let your children know you care: hug them, listen to them, spend time with them. Children who feel loved by others find it easier to love themselves.

Whenever possible, give options rather than orders. When children have the opportunity to make choices, they have a sense of control. They'll care more about outcomes when they have some ownership of a task or project.

Make sure you keep negative statements directed at children's actions or words. Children need to know that they are not "bad people" even when they make bad choices. Repeatedly being told "You're dumb!" or "You're clumsy!" will cause children to believe that they are dumb or clumsy. Better to say, "You aren't dumb, but what you did wasn't smart" or, even better, "I love you, but I didn't like what you did."

Tell children that bad feelings aren't wrong, but they must choose appropriate ways to deal with them. Punching a pillow when you are angry with a brother or sister is a good thing to do, but punching the other person is never O.K.

Compliment children often and try to catch them being good, but direct comments to what they did, not their person, just as you would when criticizing. "I like the way you helped your sister." "That's a wonderful idea." "You handled that situation very well." These are good ways to compliment children because by identifying the specific action, you make it more likely that they will repeat it. Avoid saying, "You're a good boy." or "What a smart girl you are!" because at a later time children will have to believe that they are bad or dumb when they do something that warrants a negative comment. Also be careful not to give "yes-but" compliments: "You did a good job on that paper, but your handwriting could be a little neater."

Give children a chance to display their talents and build on their strengths. Post drawings and schoolwork on the refrigerator. When they're feeling down because they couldn't do something as well as they wanted to, suggest a task you know they can do so they can focus on their strengths. Tell them no one can do everything well, but anyone can improve with time and practice.

Maintain high expectations for children, but make sure that goals are within their reach. It's better for them to set and work for their own goals rather than yours. Encourage them always to do the best they can, but don't expect perfection. Getting all A's in school isn't possible for every child, and grades are not the best reason for working hard anyway. Remember that younger children develop at different rates. One five-year-old may be able to color and stay within the lines while another lacks the muscle control to do the same. Discourage children from trying to do everything perfectly. They need to feel comfortable making mistakes; that's often the best way to learn. Help them realize that a positive attitude and persistence are more important than perfection.

Give children responsibilities for chores that contribute to the family's well-being and acknowledge their contributions. Chores can be changed as children grow older. Younger children can serve as assistants to older children on tasks they aren't yet ready to assume on their own.

Suggest that children keep records of their accomplishments: charts, journals, and scrapbooks. Don't forget to tell them that you're proud, too. Sometimes parents "brag" to relatives and friends when children aren't around to hear, forgetting they haven't said anything to the children themselves. All children need to know that they are lovable and capable.

Finally, attend school, community, and church activities in which your children participate or perform: choral and band concerts, baseball and soccer games, exhibits, plays, and talent shows. Your presence not only indicates that you care, it also shows that you value the skills your children are developing.

Chapter Five

Writing for Learning, Communicating, and Motivating

WHY DO MY CHILDREN bring home papers filled with spelling errors the teacher hasn't marked? If the teacher doesn't make students correct the mistakes they make in writing, how will they ever learn what's right?"

"Why do teachers have students help each other with their writing? Children will just reinforce each other's mistakes! Teachers are trained to teach, shouldn't they be the ones to help students improve their work?"

If teachers want to engage students in making personal connections with what they learn, thereby motivating them to learn and do more, they must also deemphasize such traditional methods as lectures, worksheets, and study guides. These direct students to memorize bits and pieces of knowledge rather than lead them to a holistic understanding of basic concepts, of which these little fragments are only part.

Through informal writing and collaborative learning activities, students develop the skills they'll need to function on their own at the same time they learn the subject matter called for by the school's curriculum. Moreover, with these approaches teachers can accommodate students of varying abilities in the same class, a much more democratic and realistic way of teaching because it simulates life in the real world. Because these methods also help teachers get to know students as individuals, they can help make the classroom a place where all students feel valued and meet with some success.

As classes become more student-centered, the teacher's job changes. Teachers must work to create supportive and challenging environments, and design a variety of structures wherein students can experience and explore knowledge both on their own and with their classmates. Students then can learn how to function in situations where the material they have to learn hasn't been artificially simplified by someone else. They learn to think and solve problems. They develop confidence and discover their own strategies for making sense out of complex matters, enabling them to continue functioning effectively when they are out of school.

Writing no longer belongs only in the English and language arts classrooms. Students do writing assignments in every grade and in every subject, because many teachers now use writing not only as a way to check on what students have or have not learned, but also as a method for *helping* them learn.

Like discussion and reading, writing can be a tool for learning and understanding a chapter in a history book or a new concept in math. Teachers don't have to correct or grade these sorts of writing assignments, just as they don't usually assign letter grades to class discussions, or stop a class discussion to correct every student who makes a usage error. Writing can also be useful when teachers want to vary the activities during the class period, when they want to solve problems with a class or an individual student, or when they'd like feedback from students on classroom activities or assignments.

You are probably familiar with writing used only as a means of evaluation. Your teachers read, corrected, and graded your writing in many classes. They determined what you learned in science or social studies by giving you essay tests; in English class, they evaluated how well you understood a poem or novel by having you write a critical essay. Most of the writing you did when you were in school was probably assigned in order for the teacher to evaluate what you knew or didn't know about a subject. But there are many other ways teachers can and do use writing today.

Even the way students work on writing in English or language arts classrooms these days is different from the way it used to be. Few teachers assign an essay topic and leave the students to complete the assignment on their own, to be handed in as a final copy on the due date.

Instead teachers try to guide students through the writing process. Students often choose their own topics and spend time in class on prewriting activities, such as brainstorming ideas for their papers, talking about their ideas with other students in small groups, role playing, watching a film, or making "clusters" —a kind of visual brainstorming. Beginning with the topic written in a circle in the middle of a page, students list related ideas in circles, connecting them to each other with lines. [See the cluster on the next page, which covers the material presented in this chapter, for an example.]

Encouraging students to develop ideas by talking and role playing rather than first writing them down on paper accommodates students' differing learning styles—some students find it easier to talk than to write. Clustering works better than outlining for students who favor right-brain activities. In the old days, when all teachers required preliminary outlines, many students had difficulty getting started on a writing assignment. In fact, the late poet John Ciardi said he always had to write his essays early because he couldn't do an outline until he knew what he had written!

After students have a good sense of what they plan to include, they write rough drafts either at home or in class. Sometimes the teacher collects and reads these drafts, but more often students read them to each other in pairs or small groups. As the other students comment and ask questions on a draft that's been read aloud, the writer makes notes of changes to make. The teacher may hold individual conferences with students. In the drafting and revising stage, students focus on getting their ideas down on paper, developing them in some depth, making them clear, and presenting them in an organized fashion.

While the students work on drafts, neither they nor the teacher worry about spelling, mechanics, and other surface features of the writing. Until their pieces are shaped and developed, it would be a waste of time for them to look up words they don't know how to spell. As they revise their work, they will add and delete sentences and paragraphs. When teachers emphasize cor-

Example of a cluster or map based on material in this chapter. Making a cluster is helpful for getting ideas down on paper before beginning to write the first draft.

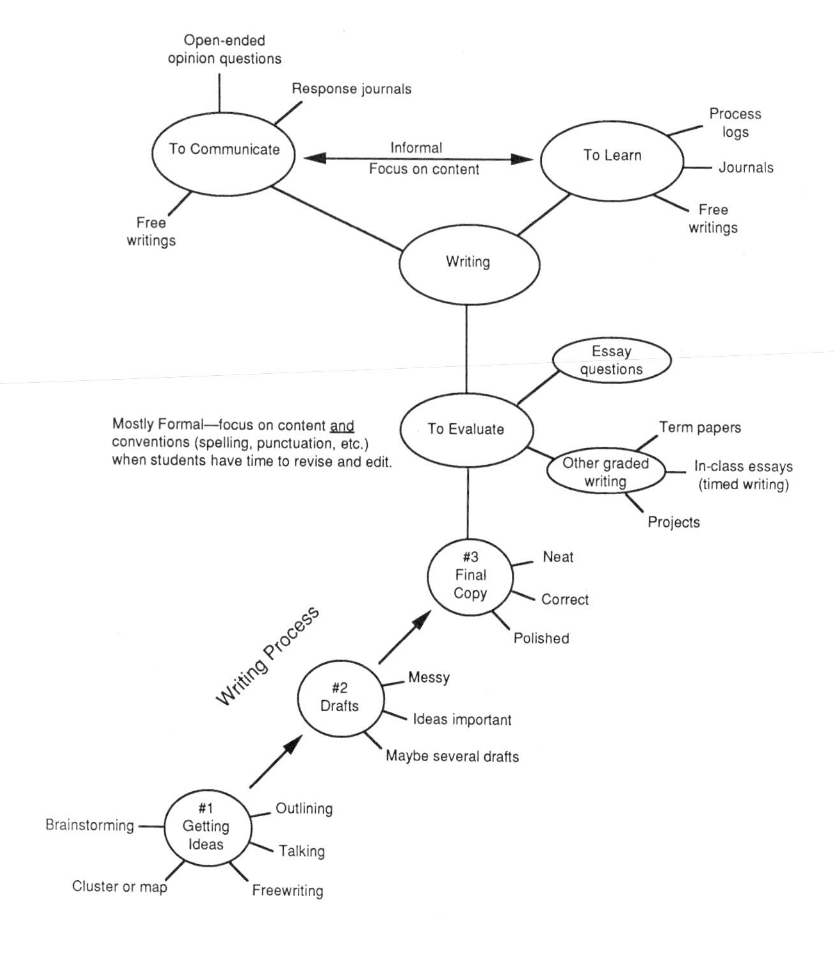

rect spelling on all work, they inadvertently discourage students from writing well. People who have difficulty with spelling have told me that they often changed their wording—not for the better—in order to use words they knew how to spell. Worrying about spelling or where to put commas and semicolons prevents students from concentrating on the ideas they're trying to communicate. In the worst cases, such concerns can cause students to get severe cases of writer's block. Correct spelling, punctuation, and usage are important—but later in the writing process, as you will see.

While their writing is in the drafting stage, students work with the teacher and with each other. The classroom becomes a writing workshop. Every child is a reader; every child is a writer. When students read their drafts to each other, they find out from the questions and comments of classmates which parts work and which ones need more work. Once students learn how to help each other in writing groups, student feedback can be as effective as teacher feedback. But there's another benefit as well. Teachers foster students' self-esteem when they allow them to "own" their writing; when a teacher becomes too directive about the changes students should make, many students become less interested in rewriting because the work is no longer "theirs." One eighth grader let her teacher know just how she felt about a piece her teacher had taken over. Instead of writing her own name on the finished copy, she put the teacher's name!

When the pieces have been revised—expanded, cut, clarified, or otherwise reworked—they are ready for editing. Students again work with each other to check spelling, punctuation, sentence structure, and usage, correcting errors they discover. Then they make neat final copies of their pieces to hand in to the teacher to be graded or published. At this point correct spelling and punctuation *do* count—I take off a letter grade, for example, for each spelling or sentence error. Teachers can expect these final copies to be as error-free as possible since students can get help from a number of sources, including other students or the teacher, as they proofread their work and make corrections. Both computers and white-out make correcting errors much easier than it used to be. Computers have also made penmanship less important. While teachers still insist that students write legible papers, many allow students to print instead of using cursive writing. Most teachers wisely allocate more class time to the process of writing than to practice in the formation of letters.

And many teachers today do something else teachers didn't do very often in "the good old days." Because they understand the motivational and instructional benefits of having students write for other audiences in addition to the teacher, students may write pieces that they "publish" on the bulletin board, in a class magazine, or newsletter; send to the local newspaper; or enter in a writing contest.

In the primary grades, students may dictate their stories to an adult or write them with "invented spelling," sounding a word out and writing down the letters they think it has. At first children often mix pictures with "words" in their writing. Primary teachers become experts at deciphering the individualistic spellings of the words, which are made up almost entirely of consonants (Those are the letter sounds children can hear; vowel sounds are more difficult to detect so they come later).

Of course, these young students are not yet able to edit their own work, although they do revise what they write and often write several drafts. Thus, parent volunteers or classroom aides type their final pieces with conventional spelling, capitalization, and punctuation. Then the stories are bound into books and added to the classroom library for other students to read. As they do more reading and writing, the children gradually begin to use standard spelling. It's perfectly natural for them to notice how words in books are written and to make the words they write look just the same.

In many classrooms you'll probably find charts that list the steps of the writing process as described above: *Prewriting, Drafting, Revising, Editing,* and *Publishing*. In classes where you find these charts posted in the room, you'll know that the teacher probably spends a lot of class time helping students with their writing, and the students are encouraged to help each other. The writing process parallels the way spoken language develops naturally: first fluency, then clarity, and finally correctness. Isn't that the way children learn to talk? Do you know parents who begin correcting the grammar of children who were just saying their first words? Most parents are so delighted that they heap praise on a child for saying anything that even resembles a word. Someone once told me, "If parents used the old methods of teaching writing in order to teach kids to talk, we'd have a lot of adults walking around who'd never want to say anything!"

Many states now require students at several grade levels to write essays as part of a statewide testing program. The English Composition Test, which many students take for college admission, requires an essay, and ETS (Educational Testing Service) is developing a new SAT that will include an essay. Generally these essays are read by two readers and given holistic scores—that is, the essay is evaluated as a whole and assigned points based on how well it was written. While the best essays have few surface mistakes, it's possible for a student to earn a top score even with a few errors, because the organization and development of the essay get the most emphasis when it is read through quickly by each reader. (A third reader may read an essay if the scores of the first two readers are more than one point apart.)

Students can prepare for these essay tests by practicing timed writings. Some teachers of college-bound high school students assign in-class writings several times a year to get students used to writing on an unannounced topic in a limited period of time. If their teachers don't include practice essays as part of the course work, students who take such tests can do them on their own. Studies have shown that the best writers are those students who do both the most writing and the most reading. Students who write and read a great deal, in school and at home, will always do better on standardized writing tests than those who do less.

Writing that is more casual, such as "talking" on paper, can help students process new information. When students summarize new information in their own words, they remember it longer. It's been estimated that we remember 10 percent of what we read, 20 percent of what we hear, 30 percent of what we see, and 70 percent of what we ourselves say. There's no way a teacher can have everyone talk through all of the new material in a typical class. There just wouldn't be time, given the number of students in most classes. Writing can then be used as a way of "talking" on paper.

Consider how such a writing-to-learn activity can increase the amount of learning that occurs when students read a chapter in a social studies text. A typical traditional assignment would be to write out the answers to the questions at the end of the chapter. What usually happens? Many students don't even read the chapter. Instead they read the question, flip back through the chapter, check the topic headings or paragraph beginnings until they find the one they need, and then copy the textbook words onto their papers. I was guilty of doing assignments this way, and perhaps you were, too. It's possible for a student to write complete answers to all of the questions without ever *thinking* about one idea in the chapter. Even when answering questions about a story in a foreign language, students can look at the question in French and then search the story for the sentence with the same French words, copy it, and complete the question accurately without ever knowing what the words mean! The student has the assignment ready the next day, the teacher is pleased, but the student has learned nothing.

On the other hand, if the teacher asks students to write chapter summaries in their own words (in the foreign language if the reading assignment was not in English), students are forced to think about the material, process it, and decide what information has the greatest importance. For a literature assignment students might be asked to summarize a story in their own words or write about an experience they've had that was similar to the main character's. In class the next day the teacher may ask students to read their summaries to classmates in small groups, discuss them, and then choose the best one. All of this processing of the information will help students understand and remember it in ways traditional assignments will not. Of course, there's an additional benefit, too: students are also developing their language skills *while* they are studying a particular topic.

Because writing-to-learn is considered a means of comprehending and remembering information and not a "learning-to-write" assignment, teachers tell students not to worry about spelling, mechanics, and sentence structure. Their purpose is to get their ideas down on paper. Of course, a teacher may ask that students revise and polish a piece that was originally done as a writing-to-learn activity and turn it in for a grade. Usually, however, this kind of writing is for the students' benefit in learning content. Teachers may check to see that papers have been done, but they won't correct or grade them (although they may write comments or questions on them).

Because teachers can get a great deal of information from these papers to help them do a better job of teaching, they often do quick readings as a means of checking on their own teaching. If students spend the last five minutes of the class summarizing what they have learned in a learning log, the teachers can tell by skim-reading the logs how well each student understood the new material, what confusion still exists, and what, if anything, needs to be retaught the next day. Because every student does a learning log, they know how *every student* is doing. Although it may appear that the whole class understands the new material when the teacher questions students orally, only a few students may actually understand. What's more, teachers can discover that students haven't mastered new material long before they fail a test. They can give students the additional help they need, and prevent failed tests. Every time any student succeeds rather than fails, he or she gains a little self-esteem and is motivated to continue learning.

When teachers ask students to write, they tell them not to worry about spelling and mechanics because the exercises are for "thinking (or talking) on paper." If your child brings home a paper with a written comment from the teacher but no grade and no marks on misspelled words, you have more cause to celebrate than to worry. That teacher may motivate your child to work harder and learn more than he or she ever would in a class where a teacher pounced on every tiny error. Teachers who focus on mechanical errors too often ignore students' ideas.

After students finish writing, teachers have several options: they can collect the papers to read later; ask volunteers to share what they wrote and then collect; have students share with one other student or in small groups and then collect; or let students keep papers for themselves after sharing them, the way they would keep any notes they took in class.

The sample list of writing-to-learn activities below can be adapted for use in any class at any level in any subject.

• *Write down everything you know about [topic which has been studied or is about to be studied].* When students write all they know about a subject before they study it, teachers can clear up prior misunderstandings that could hinder new learning if they went uncorrected.

• *Write down what you think will happen next.* When students write what they think a character in a story will do next, or where a particular event they've been studying in history might lead, they can then read on to see how accurate their predictions were.

• *Paraphrase the text [or lecture], or write a summary in your own words.*

• *Write down all the questions you'd like answered about this chapter.*

• *Write a summary of today's lesson for a student who was absent.* If a new math concept is taught, students can explain how that concept works.

• *Write your reactions to [the film, lecture, class activity, or reading assignment].*

• *Write how you think this [chapter, story, concept] applies to your life.*

• *Write a dialogue between two characters in the story or from two different stories, two historical characters, two math symbols].*

• *Write a letter to the author of your textbook.*

• *Summarize what you have learned in this class [today, this week, this month, this semester].* This kind of writing is sometimes called a learning log.

• *Write out the process you went through to find the solution to a problem.* If students end up with an incorrect solution, teachers can see where in the process they took a wrong turn.

• *Respond to situations.* Students explain what they would do if they were put in a situation like one confronted by a particular fictional character or historical figure.

When teachers ask students to do this kind of writing, they often call it "free writing," in that students are free from worrying about mechanics and form. Free writings are a good way to use the few minutes of wasted or dead time at the beginning or end of the class. Such writing also gives teachers a way of finding out what students think. By giving students an opportunity to talk to them on paper, they can learn more about individual students and get valuable information to help them do a better job as teachers. Writing as a means of communication between the teacher and students is a powerful means of motivating students and making them feel the teacher cares. Teachers too find it very enjoyable to get to know individual students, something that's very difficult when they teach 100 or more students a day.

Free writing does involve some risk, however. Some students will tell teachers things they don't want to know. Teachers must learn to refer students who have personal or family problems that are beyond their professional training to guidance counselors or others who can help. Of course, some students will use the free writings to complain, so teachers must be prepared to accept what they have to say and not take their comments too personally. Even negative, hostile students get some benefit: writing out their feelings is a catharsis, and can actually prevent some overt disruptive behavior in the classroom. Sometimes these students will reveal enough of themselves in their writing for teachers to discover ways to change their attitudes and behavior.

Here are some other free writing topics teachers can use to communicate privately with each student.

• *Tell me about yourself and what you'd like to learn in this class.* This is a good topic for the first day with a new class.

• *What did you think of today's activity? What changes should I make when I do it the next time?* This information is very useful when teachers try out a new activity. Even if students write only about what was wrong with the activity, teachers may be able to figure out how to avoid the problem the next time.

• *Tell me what you think of this class so far (or today).* Students generally will be thoughtful and honest in their responses. Teachers should not get upset with the totally negative and insensitive ones. They may be surprised, however, at how much positive feedback they get. They'll also discover problems developing that they can solve before they're too big to manage, and they'll find ways to improve their teaching when they cover the same topic again with another class

• *Tell me why you were late to class.* The student has a chance to speak without disrupting the routine of the class, and the teacher will be able to handle each case in the most appropriate way.

• *Tell me why you weren't able to finish your homework today.* The teacher can deal differently with a student whose pet died unexpectedly and another who chose to watch TV all evening.

• *We can't continue with the discussion if everyone is going to talk at once. Tell me how you think we might solve this problem.* Having students all write will quiet the class down. If they then share their ideas, the problem may be solved without the teacher's doing anything else.

• *I'd like each of you to write down what happened.* This technique is very useful when two students are squabbling with each other or there has been some other problem between two students. When they finish, the teacher has each listen while the other reads what was written. Then they both discuss how they might resolve the issue or what they might have done differently to avoid the difficulty in the first place.

Teachers often ask students to evaluate the class and their teaching at the end of year, but by then it's too late to change anything for that group of students. It makes much more sense to get feedback on a continuing basis, so that teachers can make adjustments and deal with situations as they come up. Even if teachers don't feel comfortable asking students directly to tell them how they feel about the class, they'll get valuable information when they use writing-to-learn activities.

When I taught a modern novel course to high school students, I used to give them five-question reading quizzes to see if they had read the book when it was due. I made the questions specific but easy enough so that students who read the book would get them right while those who hadn't wouldn't be able to answer them. But now I ask students in my introductory education class to do a free writing on what they learned from the reading instead of giving them a quiz. If someone hasn't read the assignment, then he or she must write and tell me why it wasn't done. What I've discovered is remarkable.

First of all, I can easily tell by reading what the students write whether they've read the chapter, so my original purpose is fulfilled. But I also discover what they've misunderstood, so I know what I need to clarify in the class discussion. Even more useful, however, is what I've found out about the students who didn't do the assignment. One student wrote a very entertaining and lengthy narrative filled with details about boy friend-roommate problems—a college-student soap opera—but in her last paragraph she promised that she'd get the reading done that night and swore she'd never come to class unprepared again.

In fact, no matter what reason students give for not having the work done, they invariably tell me when they will make it up without my ever saying a word about it. The writing accomplishes much more than the reading quiz ever did because I get insights into the lives of my students outside of the classroom. Sometimes the problems are serious and real. Sometimes I can suggest a way they might be resolved, but even when I can't, I can empathize. The writing assignments actually make it possible for students and me to value and respect each other as people—powerful motivation for learning and achievement, and no small way to increase everyone's self-esteem.

Free writings also have shown me how so much of what happens in a class goes unnoticed by the teacher, and may lead to problems that later cannot be easily solved. One day my college students spent the class session enthusiastically discussing the question of whether a teacher should be held responsible if students don't learn. The realists argued that once a student reached high school, it was his own fault if the student didn't learn, but the idealists felt that if teachers tried hard enough and really wanted to, they could reach every student. I was pleased that everyone was so involved in the discussion, and at the end of the class I had a good feeling inside. As one student left the room, she stopped to ask me about an upcoming assignment. Very routine, I thought, and collected their free writings to take home to read.

Imagine my surprise when I picked up that student's paper and read, "Never have I been so humiliated as to be put down so rudely by a classmate. I don't care how much class participation counts, I'll never say anything in this class ever again. I'll participate in my own private way." I had listened to the whole discussion and had not thought anyone put anyone down. Sure, the discussion was lively and students disagreed, but it was all good-natured. But what I thought didn't matter if the student felt so badly. Here was a situation I had to deal with right away. I wrote her a long note on the free writing and then made arrangements to speak with her privately after class. She said she had been having a bad day and had overreacted. Everything would be fine now. I didn't have to worry.

Later, though, I thought about what might happen in a slightly different situation. Suppose, for example, the student was an eighth-grade girl in the throes of a turbulent adolescence, who hadn't yet developed the self-confidence to deal with bumps in life. Imagine that she ended up feeling the way my student had, but the teacher never found out. How long would it be before the teacher noticed that the girl no longer spoke in class? And when she asked her about it, suppose the girl replied, "There's nothing wrong," and refused to say anything further. I've learned that students, even those who don't write very well, feel much freer to say what they think on paper. Carried to extremes, I could see how this eighth-grader, who may have been a fairly good student, could go from not saying anything in class to losing interest in the subject altogether. And by the time the teacher realized her grades were going down, it might be too late to do anything about it.

Informal writing has so many benefits—with every class I teach I discover more—that it's hard to imagine why teachers everywhere haven't discovered its power to motivate students and improve their own teaching. Some teachers think that they won't be able to keep up with the paperwork. The irony is that the time they'd spend reading and writing a brief response would save them hours of dealing with discipline problems and hassles over grades and assignments. Sometimes, when students are upset, all they really need to do is get it out.

I remember one student who wrote two pages to me complaining that she was only getting B's on her papers when she deserved A's. I read her free writing and wrote, "If you'd like to come in and go over your papers with me, we can talk about how you can improve them." She never came in. I didn't expect her to. The free writing was merely a catharsis. She was frustrated with her own inability to take the necessary steps to get the A's. The free writing didn't change anything, but writing it made her feel better—temporarily, at least. The responsibility for doing what was needed was still hers, but the free writings provided her with a useful means of relieving tension—something of use to all of us at various times.

Last year I expanded the idea of occasional free writings by asking students to keep a journal throughout the semester. They were to include entries on reading assignments, class sessions, team meetings, and visits to the school where each was doing a field experience as part of the course. The first class I tried this approach with turned out to be one of the most motivated and engaging group of students I had ever worked with, and I'm convinced the course journal had a great deal to do with it.

At the end of the semester I asked each student to reread the entire journal and write a final entry summarizing what they had learned during the semester. I've excerpted the work of a student I'll call "Helen." Helen's entry shows what journals can do to increase both learning and motivation. As you read what she wrote, you'll see how journals provide a vehicle for thinking about content, and how they can be adapted for use in any subject. Helen did her field work in high school English classes for two periods a day. She was student teaching under the supervision of one teacher and observing the class of another.

"I thought the journal was basically a lot of work. Especially at first, I wasn't really sure the effort would be worth the experience. Now that I'm looking back, I really learned a lot from doing a journal. The time was worth the result for me. I think I remember much more about my reading when I write about it, (this is probably true in general) and it's nice to have a record to go back to. I liked being able to connect reading with observing and teaching—I don't think I could have done this as well in my head (I also probably would've skipped some reading). Anyway, these are some thoughts on what I gained. . . .

"In general, I think writing down my questions enabled me to answer them myself—it was also easy to see my own flawed thinking when I had it written in front of me. Sometimes I would write some idea I thought to be true and realize I didn't believe it any more. My journal enabled me to question many things—I questioned my observed teacher's methods a lot. Before I kept a record of the class I think I might have missed many of her flaws—some of which are large. I also became more skeptical of some of her methods. Neither of these teachers is bad, but I would have been more inclined to see both as totally wonderful teachers. When you write down things you see in a class each day, it's easier to get the whole picture. For example, when [the teacher] suggested using 'assertive discipline,' I was very glad—it seemed like an easy way to 'control' the class. Then I experienced and wrote about it. Now, I don't think I would use it all—'control' is not my goal at all. If I hadn't reflected (by writing) about assertive discipline, I probably would have just used it based on her success with it. So, I guess, in general, I learned to question my own ideas by writing a journal.

"Specifically, I learned many positive teaching ideas from writing about my reading and my observations. I see the importance of teaching beyond the 'knowledge level' as even more crucial than I did before. I also like the emphasis being placed on writing skills. Of course, I am biased since that is my area. Journals based on themes sound great for any class. I guess many positive things I learned are more 'non-negative' things. The major example of this is that by writing about my own teaching, I have a clearer idea of what I won't do in my own classroom, than if I hadn't written anything down. I'm really looking for new vocabulary techniques—just writing about traditional vocabulary . . . is boring. I definitely won't accept mediocrity from any level of students I teach—I have seen that trend in all of my writings about [the high school], and I think it stinks. Learning should be valuable, but it should also be as fun as possible too. Kids should like to come to school."

When students use writing to learn, they also learn to write—even without direct instruction on writing skills. A consultant with the Maine Educational Assessment reports that 11th grade students who said they wrote in their social studies, science, or other classes earned scores 101 points higher on the 11th grade writing assessment than students who said they wrote only for English classes.

Suggestions for Parents

There are many ways parents can help children become more successful as writers. Because you are the most important role model in your children's lives, let them see you writing. But you should also encourage children to do more writing themselves.

Use letters and notes as reminders and for praise. Make note writing a family affair: messages posted by the phone or on the refrigerator, a surprise note slipped in with children's lunches, and congratulatory notes when children accomplish small tasks and large.

Encourage children to be letter-writers. And be one yourself! Get the family into the habit of sending letters to friends and relatives instead of simply calling them on the phone. Children can write letters to companies and organizations for information or to express opinions to the editor of the local newspaper.

Write stories and make books for children. Special occasions can be celebrated with a handmade book. Make up a story or write down a bit of your family history. Collect photos, and write a story about a family vacation (or whatever) to go with them, rather than just putting them in a photo album uncaptioned. When you make your own book or buy and write in a blank book, you have created a personalized, one-of-a-kind gift that will be treasured for years to come.

Have children make their own books. Children can write original stories and illustrate them using either handmade or store-bought blank books. They can add their books to their own libraries or give them as gifts to younger children or relatives.

Begin a family journal. Buy a notebook or blank book to use as a family journal. Invite family members to write in it on a regular basis. Entries might be short (an unusual bird observed in the yard, extreme weather conditions, something nice that should be remembered) or long (a funny family incident, thoughts at Christmas or Thanksgiving, a special visitor or event). Everyone can contribute to the family journal. Younger children can draw pictures instead of writing.

Over time you'll have an invaluable collection of your family's thoughts and observations. If on New Year's each person shares his or her own highlights of the past year, the journal will document the family history for future generations. A few years ago I was thrilled to receive a diary written by my great-grandfather over a hundred years ago. Even though the entries were sketchy, I was excited by the picture of life that emerged as I read his penciled words.

Write the family's history. The family can collaborate to write their history before the elder members are gone and their memories are lost. Children can interview their grandparents and others and write their stories down. The whole family might wish to join together in researching genealogical records to construct a family tree that goes even further back in time.

Encourage children to begin their own personal journals. Journals are a good place to reflect, sort out feelings, and record private thoughts. If someone is upset or angry, writing feelings down can be a catharsis. This is an especially good strategy for keeping one psychologically healthy when nothing can be done to change the situation that caused bad feelings. Even three- and four-year-olds can begin to keep journals. They'll draw pictures at first and gradually begin to combine words with images as they develop.

Suggest that children keep a reading notebook. When they finish reading a book, children can write a brief summary in their own words. They may find this notebook a good resource for future school or family projects, but they'll also have a concrete example of their progress in reading.

Keep logs for family vacations and trips. Ask everyone to contribute. The details of the event will remain clear in the future, and you'll have useful information when you finally get around to labeling your many photos or slides.

Encourage everyone in the family to make their own greeting cards. This idea is a great way to encourage self-expression. Such a card will be a wonderful gift because of the time and thought represented, and the messages will be very personal.

Ask children to write for the family's holiday letter. If you send a photocopied letter once a year with holiday cards, as many people do, let your children write their own message to add to yours. Very young children can draw a picture or perhaps just print their names.

Encourage children to publish their writing. There are many writing contests for children and magazines which publish children's work. (See list of magazines in the appendix.) There's no greater thrill for writers of any age than seeing their names in print. Look for these opportunities and encourage your children to make submissions.

Again, don't focus on correctness when your children begin to write. Beginning writers should be encouraged to develop fluency. They'll spell words the way they think they are written, and you may not be able to interpret them. Instead of correcting everything they write, have them read their stories to you. It's O.K. to point out the correct way to write some words, but if you emphasize correctness, you'll discourage them from expressing themselves.

If children read widely, they'll begin to notice the discrepancies between what they write and printed versions. They'll naturally begin to change their own spelling and punctuation to standard forms. If a young child asks you how to write something, let them try it first before you provide them with the correct word. Remember that children need to learn to do things on their own.

You'll be best able to help your children with school assignments if you know what their teachers' expectations and goals are. At the beginning of the year, take time to find out what kinds of writing your children will be doing, and how their teachers think parents can help. Here's a list of general tips to guide you when your children ask you to help them with their writing at home.

Don't type children's papers for them. Keyboarding skills are becoming increasingly necessary in the world today. Children learn by doing, so you're not helping them if you do their typing. If they waited until the last minute to get an assignment done, they need to suffer the consequences. Otherwise the same thing will happen again. If their typing is slow, it won't get any faster if you're the one who gets the practice.

Don't correct spelling and punctuation errors. Point out the places that need correction and help them find words in the dictionary or rules in the handbook. But let them do the work themselves. That's how they'll learn. You might suggest that they begin to keep a list of words they have trouble spelling and another of the punctuation or capitalization rules. These lists are good references to check when they're writing a final copy. Gradually they'll need the references less often because the information they need will be in their heads.

Don't tell children what to write. When children are faced with writer's block and can't get started, they won't benefit from your ideas. What they need are strategies that will open up some possibilities. Suggest that they try some of the methods described in this chapter, such as clustering, brainstorming, and free writing.

Help children plan for long-term projects. I've known many high school students whose parents allowed them to miss school to finish a term paper or project because they didn't want them to be graded down. These parents were doing more harm than good. Stay informed about your children's assignments. When they have a long-range assignment due, help them set up a schedule to get it done, a little at a time. Once the plan is written on a calendar, check with them to make sure they're keeping up. When children understand how to develop and follow a schedule, they'll be able to do it on their own. And they are also more likely to realize the value of planning ahead—a useful habit.

Encourage them to read drafts aloud. There's no better way to see where revision is needed than to read a piece aloud. Oral reading also helps children get punctuation marks in the right places. If they read aloud to you, say more than "That's good." Comment on the ideas they've expressed. Ask questions to help them see where the piece isn't clear or needs more development. As they answer your questions, they'll usually know what they need to add or change.

Discuss written assignments with children after they've been graded. When your children bring home writing that teachers felt could have been done better, talk with your children about changes they could make to improve their work. Even if their teachers don't accept rewrites, encourage your children to do them anyway.

Encourage children to save their writing in folders. Keeping papers for the whole school year is useful for two reasons. First, children can learn from looking over their previous work. Second, and perhaps even more important, they'll get a sense of how much they've accomplished when they see all of the work they've done. Their confidence and self-esteem will grow.

Your children will benefit from anything you can do to get them to write more. Despite the many recent technological developments, no one can argue that good writing skills aren't crucial. According to one estimate, nine out of ten blue-collar jobs require a worker to read and write one-and-a-half hours per day. Of the projected U.S. workforce in the year 2000, 30 million people will not have the basic skills they need to do their jobs. We must change this sad state of affairs for today's students, and we can—by replacing teaching methods that haven't worked with those that will. Writing as a tool for learning and communicating is one example. The next chapter explains how collaborative and cooperative learning can make a difference.

Chapter Six

The Classroom as Community

LIKE WRITING-TO-LEARN and writing-to-communicate activities, collaborative and cooperative learning methods motivate and involve students. Considering how much of our lives depends on our ability to work cooperatively with other people—in the home or on the job—it's hard to understand why schools spend so little time teaching this skill. Getting along with others does not usually come naturally. When schools fail to help students develop interpersonal skills, many must learn them on their own, often through painful and costly experiences such as lost jobs and divorces. Many people never learn. Child abuse, wife beating, and other forms of physical violence persist because many adults have no other way of handling their problems and frustrations.

But there is yet another reason teachers should adopt collaborative and cooperative learning methods: students can learn as much—if not more—from each other as they can from the teacher. Working together forces them to be active rather than passive learners. They learn to take responsibility and to think for themselves instead of depending on the teacher to tell them what they need to do. The more they practice working with others, the more effective they'll be—as students, workers, and responsible adults.

That children do benefit and learn from participation in groups is exemplified by 4-H, the Boy and Girl Scouts, church youth groups, and school-related extracurricular activities such as music, drama, debate, and sports programs. Even when academic learning is not the focus, children can learn a great deal while at the same time enjoying interaction with other children.

In a speech at a conference for English language arts teachers, Shirley Brice Heath described a new model of learning based on her study of neighborhood-based organizations. In these groups, which were activity-focused, adult-sponsored (but not "taught"), and cross-age, Heath found that children were learning even when no one was teaching. She also reported that studies have shown such organizations can be important to later success. Many minority individuals who became successful share common characteristics: a feeling that they were responsible for control over their own destinies, and an involvement in a neighborhood-based organization with an adult or older children who pulled them along.

It is important to consider the reasons why children are motivated to commit time and energy to the activities of such groups. They participate voluntarily because what they are doing is personally meaningful. As they earn badges, win games, and enter projects in competitions, they are rewarded for their achievements and motivated to set further goals and work to meet them.

If children will try so hard and learn so much as a result while working cooperatively outside the classroom, why then don't teachers use more group activities in the classroom? Partly it is because teachers fear losing control. The teacher next door may complain because the students are too noisy. The principal may think the teacher has poor discipline. And they would be right. Students have to be taught how to work productively in small groups, and few teachers have been trained in how to do this. When I've done workshops for teachers on small-group training, I always meet several who tell me, "I tried small groups once, and they didn't work. The kids just fooled around. I had a hard time getting them under control. I don't want that to happen again!"

In my workshops I try to give teachers the experience of working in small groups themselves, by having them do some of the same activities they can later use with their own students. In her book *Writing Groups: History, Theory, and Implications,* Anne Ruggles Gere says that teachers without firsthand experience as *members* of small groups are not likely to be successful in using small groups with students. Since most teachers are products of schools that depended primarily on lecture/test methods of teaching, they have not had the opportunity to understand from the inside how small groups function.

I first used small groups with my own students after I participated in a small group while taking a graduate English course. As a high school and college student, I rarely participated in class discussions and never asked questions. I can remember sitting in a class, trying to get my nerve up to say something. My face would redden, my palms would sweat, and something would do cartwheels in my stomach. More often than not, I would let the moment pass and say nothing.

Taking a graduate English course was frightening for me, as I had majored in history and government. I had little background in English and had depended on Cliffs Notes to point out and interpret the symbols I never could find in the books I read. Unfortunately, Cliffs Notes weren't available for the novels we had to read for this course, and the class was filled with English majors—all expert symbol hunters. I kept my mouth shut and took careful notes until one night the professor divided us up into small groups to discuss the current novel. After only a few minutes I felt comfortable enough with the other four students to ask a question, then later to venture an opinion. Soon I was participating in the discussion as actively as everyone else. It was exciting and fun.

As I drove home from class, I continued to think about the points raised in the small-group discussion. Then suddenly it occurred to me that some of my students must share my fear of speaking up in class. I could picture several bright students whose written work was excellent but who remained as silent as stones unless I tugged responses from them. Maybe small groups would help them gain confidence, too.

Even though I tried small groups the next week, I found that it took time to figure out ways to run them best. Effective small groups don't just happen—the teacher must make them work. Through trial and error I developed training activities to introduce students to the idea of learning with and from each other. Such training is essential to the success of cooperative or collaborative learning.

Students can begin to understand their responsibilities as members of a learning group by doing a series of short activities, such as calculating the average height and weight of group members or solving a logic problem, followed by discussion and evaluation of how their groups functioned. For instance, my students enjoyed and learned from playing mystery games. The solutions required input from everyone, even shy students who are usually afraid to speak up. Because the clues were written on separate, evenly distributed cards and couldn't be passed physically from one person to another, everyone in each small group had to share information and focus on solving the problem. When several groups competed against one another to see which group could correctly identify the guilty parties first, students were very motivated. Afterward we talked about the process each group used, identifying the strategies of the most successful group so that the others might improve their effectiveness next time.

Teachers need first to create good group assignments, and then they must constantly monitor—and help students learn to monitor—their own progress. Both the teacher and the students have to give as much attention to the *process* of working in a group as they do to the intended group product or outcome. Otherwise the groups will not be successful. Recently, for example, I've begun asking students to write individual responses to the group work. I discovered that the group as a whole may think everything is going well, but one student may feel left out or put down. When there is a hidden problem in a small group, I can help the group work toward a solution without directly revealing what one member shared on an individual evaluation.

Teachers often fail to realize that top students may be as much of a deterrent to successful small-group work as the kids who disrupt the class by behaving inappropriately. When students who get all A's do most of the work, for fear of getting a lower grade if others can't carry their weight, they prevent everyone from learning. Moreover, because the best students are not always the most effective leaders, they may not shine on group work the way they do on individual assignments. Thus, small groups can give different students an opportunity to do something well and thereby increase their self-esteem.

Contrary to what some may think, bright students are not held back when they work in groups with their less able classmates. In fact, they often learn more rather than less, because as Roger Johnson, a leading proponent on cooperative learning, points out, "The behavior that correlates most highly with achievement in groups is giving explanations, not getting them."

Small groups can take many forms. Cooperative learning groups can function in any subject to help students learn regular course content. Because the small group has the responsibility of making sure each one of its members understands the material, small groups actually have the effect of increasing the number of teachers in the room. In *The Caring Classroom*, Dewey J. Carducci and Judith B. Carducci explain how they use "triads" to improve the behavior and academic achievement of problem students—the ones most teachers find impossible to handle. Groups of three students form a unit, the triad. When one student has an off day, the other two can often help him or her remain in control—friends helping a friend who's in trouble, rather than a teacher coming down hard and possibly increasing the problem.

That's one advantage the Carduccis cite. They also describe an interesting approach to teaching. Their goal when introducing a new concept is to make sure at least one person in each triad understands it, so that he or she can teach the others. Of course, they circulate around the room while the students work with each other; but now, in a class of eighteen students, there are effectively seven teachers instead of just one. And sometimes peers can find better ways to clear up the confusion of fellow students than the teacher can.

William Glasser, a psychiatrist, also believes that small groups can motivate students who have been turned off to school. His recent book, *Control Theory in the Classroom*, explains how and why small groups work when most other teaching methods have failed. To show that students work best when they feel they have some control, Glasser points out the motivation of students to do well in band, drama, and athletics. "Control theory," he says, "is based on the fact that we're internally motivated and driven by needs that are built into our biological structure. . . . From birth to death we *must* struggle—we have no choice—to try to survive and to try to find some love, some power, some fun, and some freedom. To the extent that we can satisfy these needs on a regular basis, we gain effective control of our lives."

When students work with each other in small classroom groups, they are able to meet these personal needs in the same way they do in extracurricular activities or in the neighborhood-based organizations Shirley Brice Heath speaks about. Put another way, small-group participation allows students to develop two of the basic needs Maslow identified—self-esteem and belonging.

Just as the writing teacher who takes over a student's paper can snuff out student initiative, teachers find that giving students more—rather than less—control on group projects is necessary if they are to succeed. One high school teacher designed an interesting activity that involved a small group of students writing a story. She carefully planned and listed each step and described the final product on a handout. She was very disappointed and discouraged when many students came to class without having done their individual pieces. The whole project bombed, and she didn't know why.

The problem was that she did too much. Her directions made the activity little more than a group worksheet. Had she merely outlined the overall goal for the project, given some general guidelines, and then left the students free to decide how and what they might do to meet that goal, the project would have been theirs, not hers. Just as many renters won't take as good care of a home as owners will, students won't commit as much effort to an assignment "owned" by the teacher as they will to one they themselves create and develop. Moreover, in figuring out what they need to do to accomplish a general goal, they must think for themselves and assume greater responsibility for the result.

When a teacher does students' thinking and planning for them, they can always say, "We didn't understand what we were supposed to do," or "Your directions didn't make that clear." But when teachers allow students to think and plan for themselves, they often produce even better projects than the teacher expects. Instead of rationalizing why they fail, students get to feel proud of what they accomplish. And the teacher's and classmates' praise for their work further increases their self-esteem.

Even when students learn cooperatively in small groups, they most often have to take tests individually. Group work does not go unrewarded, though, because teachers can award bonus points when each student in the group earns a passing grade or a certain predetermined score. Students then have more incentive to make sure their classmates do well. Because many businesses operate in this manner, students get valuable practice for real-world jobs. When individuals compete, there are more losers than winners. When students work cooperatively, they can all win.

Small groups can also work collaboratively: students work together on a project to which they all contribute, such as an oral or written report, a skit based on historical or fictional events, or a summary of issues the group has discussed. They can help each other on individual assignments by working in writing groups or as partners in a classroom "buddy system," not unlike that used by swimming instructors at a summer camp.

The kinds of projects and assignments small groups can do are limited only by the teacher's imagination. Teachers often give both group and individual grades on this type of work. I tell my own students that what they learn about working with each other may be even more beneficial to them than the subject area information they learn. In addition, the students who end up in groups with interpersonal conflicts that prevent the group from working well together are the ones who most strongly recommend that I continue using small groups. They learn from an unhappy experience what they can do differently the next time they're stuck dealing with difficult individuals.

Although some teachers use small-group activities randomly, so that students do not work with the same classmates for any length of time, I prefer to set up small groups that will stay together for an entire semester. It takes time to establish relationships, and the longer students work together, the better they get at resolving differences, creating a comfortable and effective working relationship, and developing a team spirit. Rather than let students work only with their friends, I assign them to groups that are balanced in terms of abilities and personalities. When teachers don't do this, they often find that the troublemakers band together in one group and the bright, teacher-pleasing students in another. A sure-fire formula for trouble!

Students have told me that small groups enabled them to become friends with people they wouldn't otherwise have met, and that sometimes those friendships continued long after the class was over. In one of my classes, a female who ended up in a group of male athletes said, "I never would have gotten to know these guys if it hadn't been for the group. I always had the stereotyped idea that jocks only cared about sports, but in our group they worked very hard. I'm glad I made some new friends I would never have met otherwise."

It's easy for students to remain anonymous and unconnected if all they do is come in, sit down, and take notes while the teacher lectures. If they're just a square on a seating chart or a line in a gradebook, they may not exert much effort to learn beyond the minimum required to earn the grades they want. But when students are part of a small group they start to feel a sense of belonging—someone really misses them when they're not there, and they become more enthusiastic about the material as well.

Along with the sense of belonging, students realize that others depend on them to do their part in a small group. If you don't care about your grades and you're the only one who's affected if you don't do your work, it's easy to slack off. In a small group, however, it's not the teacher but rather fellow classmates who will be hurt and resentful if you don't do your share. Peer pressure, especially for teenagers, is strong motivation for keeping up.

Beyond the increases in belonging, self-esteem, and motivation, students in small groups actively engage in developing higher-level thinking skills as they work on group projects. If the teacher hasn't overcontrolled the assignment and parceled it out in bits and pieces, students must brainstorm possibilities, discuss alternatives, seek information, make decisions, solve problems, evaluate results, and accept responsibility for how everything turns out. Small groups force students to be active learners, and active learners are interested in what they do. If the project will later be shared with the whole class rather than being seen and graded only by the teacher, they'll want to do their best work. When I've compared the projects completed by individuals with those done by small groups, I've found that more students do better work when they work together than they do when they work by themselves. Everybody wins.

Teachers can easily transform traditional assignments into group learning experiences. One way of doing this is the "jigsaw" method of sharing information, so named because it resembles a jigsaw puzzle. Instead of asking students to read the whole chapter in a textbook, for instance, the teacher gives each person in the small group the responsibility for learning one part of it and teaching that section to the rest of the group. Students still have to know the information in the whole chapter because everyone is tested on everything, not just the individual part they were assigned.

Because students spend class time in active discussion, they are active rather than passive. The jigsaw method also accomplishes another important goal. As students talk through the information they teach to the rest of the small group, they clarify and reinforce it for themselves. Like talking on paper in writing-to-learn assignments, the jigsaw method helps students process what they read so they'll remember it longer.

Another traditional assignment, the research project, can also be done as a group investigation. Instead of working alone to research a large topic, students in a small group choose the topic they wish to investigate and divide up the responsibilities for gathering information on it. As they work on their specific parts, they can share articles and books with teammates who are researching other aspects. As a group they plan and develop the final product—a panel discussion, paper, or other means of demonstrating what they learned.

Yael Sharan and Shlomo Sharan, who have spent twelve years researching the effectiveness of group investigation, found that among both elementary and secondary students, "Group investigation classes generally demonstrated a higher level of achievement than did their peers taught with the whole-class method. Moreover, students who experienced group investigation did better on questions assessing high-level learning, although on occasion they did only just as well as students from the traditional method on questions evaluating the acquisition of information."

Sharan and Sharan also discovered that group investigation promoted positive social interaction among classmates from different ethnic groups. And teachers expressed more positive attitudes toward their work following participation in group investigation projects. In line with Glasser's beliefs, the teachers in these studies also felt "less need to control their students' behavior all the time." When students have more control over their learning, both they and their teachers benefit.

My students share my enthusiasm for small groups. The students whose comments are included below met outside of class throughout the semester to plan a lesson they would teach to the whole class, as well as to discuss course reading material.

One student wrote in her personal log, "I just came back from our team meeting. I think it went well and turned out to be fun. Groups can be very rewarding—I never realized that before. When everyone has something to say and then we keep on building with new input, it brings us closer as we agree enthusiastically with each other. Our meeting lasted an hour. . . . It was a very productive hour and the questions we came up with seem very philosophical."

Even a member of a group that had serious problems, because of one student who wouldn't attend meetings and didn't do his share, felt positive about group work. "I realize that we didn't have the ideal group and that our meetings have gotten more difficult as the year wound down, but in a weird way I'm going to miss them. I looked forward to our meetings. They were a break from routine and I liked discussing "academic" things in a non-academic setting. I liked hearing others' points of view and being able to kind of challenge them and vice versa in a close setting. It's a more immediate thing than having to wait your turn in a large group. They *did* help."

Here's what another student wrote when she was asked to describe a positive experience she had observed or experienced in a classroom. "While observing a second-grade class engaged in a group activity, I was really impressed by the interaction that was taking place between the students. Children were helping and encouraging each other and everyone was enjoying the class. The activity was fun, for it involved cutting and pasting and pretty pictures, but the activity was also encouraging learning and interaction among the students. I can look back and remember a similar learning experience from my own second grade. My teacher divided and arranged the classroom by putting the two desks of team members next to each other. My partner was a boy of low level, and I am sure my teacher put us together so that I could help the boy. The teacher's hopes were met. I was able to explain things to my partner when he needed more explanation, and I even understood things better myself after explaining them. Sometimes my partner helped me. We made a great team. After many years I still remember this second-grade teaching technique, and I am able to associate it with the positive interaction I recently observed in the second-grade class."

Because collaborative and cooperative learning activities can lead to new friendships, their use in the classroom may help to resolve larger societal problems. A recent report on National Public Radio pointed out that because cooperative learning reduces racism, prejudice, and stereotyping, it is being used in schools to reduce tensions in Israel between Arab and Israeli students, and in Canada between French-speaking and English-speaking youngsters. Studies in American schools reveal that students who engaged in cooperative learning are more likely to list friends who have different racial and ethnic backgrounds.

When cooperative learning gives students a chance to get to know others whom they've considered different, they begin to see how much they are alike. Differences, no matter what they are—race, religion, or ability—begin to disappear. A San Francisco State University study found that pairing learning-disabled fifth- and sixth-graders with non-handicapped classmates resulted in students liking their partners better when they worked on activities designed to uncover their mutual interests. C. Lynn Fox, the researcher who conducted the study, said, "If we want to help learning-disabled students become better accepted by their peers, then it is important that we provide opportunities for them and their non-handicapped classmates to learn, in a social sense, what they have in common."

While students who work in small groups develop skill in resolving conflicts, some schools have established programs that involve students in a more formal process for resolving disputes. Elementary students who have been trained as peer mediators actually handle playground problems normally treated as discipline problems by teachers. Not only are these students learning a useful lifetime skill, the students they help begin to see that there are alternative ways to handle disagreements.

Research studies on conflict resolution and mediation are underway in a variety of schools, including an alternative high school. There are several organizations involved in training teachers and developing curriculum conflict resolution. The International Center for Cooperation and Conflict Resolution at Teachers College, Columbia University, has been setting up a network of people who can provide training. Others who offer resources and assistance to schools starting conflict management programs include Educators for Social Responsibility, Cambridge, Massachusetts; National Association for Mediation in Education, Amherst, Massachusetts; and the Community Based Program in San Francisco.

Cooperation and teamwork have worked on a much larger scale at the 2,000-student Holweide School in Cologne, Germany, where teachers as well as students work in teams. The school is divided into smaller units that function like independent schools within the larger framework. Teams of six to eight teachers work with groups of about ninety students (three classes). Because the same students and teachers stay together for six years, they get to know each other very well.

Anne Ratzki, the headmistress and teacher in grade six, and Angela Fisher, a grade seven teacher, wrote that the small-group plan was developed "to diminish the anonymity of a big school . . . and to design a way of teaching in which students of very different abilities and backgrounds could reach their potential by working together." The teachers work together to teach all the subjects, plan the schedules, and supervise the overall education of the students in their charge—a team effort. But the team idea also extends to the way students are taught.

Students are organized into heterogeneous "table-groups" of five or six students who generally work together for a year, sometimes longer. "The table-group concept has become the school's core instructional idea," according to Ratzki and Fisher. The table-groups are together for every subject and hold weekly meetings to suggest improvements in their everyday working situations. Many checks are built into the plan so that students will succeed. A teacher, for example, takes one group out of the regular lesson once a week to help students learn how to work more effectively as a group. Parent activities are also very important, and they, too, work on a team—each class elects five parents to form a council that serves as a link between the teachers and the other parents.

The school has been operating with the small-group concept since the mid-Seventies. Recently educators from the United States have become interested in finding out how and why the system works so well in a country where students of different abilities have traditionally been—and often still are—separated in the educational system. Ratzki and Fisher admit that a democratically run school, where every group in the school community—teachers, students, parents—is actively involved in decision making, takes a great deal of time and effort. At the same time, they say, "It is more enjoyable to work in an atmosphere where you are involved in decision making. . . . Being a student at our school is more rewarding and more fun, too. . . . Students can get special help when they need it. Their self-confidence increases, which leads to other positive outcomes." The dropout rate is under 1 percent, and about 60 percent (in comparison with the German average of 27 percent) of the students score high enough to win admission to the three-year college that leads to the university. Holweide School may provide a good model for schools in America. And cooperative learning also may offer us a chance to live in a better world, one in which collaboration and tolerance can replace conflict and prejudice. We have nothing to lose—and no time to waste.

Suggestions for Parents

Encourage cooperation in your own home. Ask your children to help each other with chores, with homework, on family projects, or in the community. Show children that you value cooperation by letting them see you work with your spouse, other family members, and friends. Point out the benefits that come from helping others. Share real-life and fictional stories of people helping each other.

Stress cooperation more than competition. Get children more interested in competing with themselves rather than with other children: they can strive to do better than they did before, rather than doing better than someone else, such as a sibling or friend. Even in competitive sports, children can usually achieve more by cooperating with teammates. Their own skills will improve and they can contribute more to the team effort. Encourage them to set goals they can achieve on their own: increasing their scores on the next math test, running a mile a minute faster than they did the year before, selling more boxes of Girl Scout cookies this year than they did last year.

You can also help your own children learn to use conflict resolution to settle disputes. When you're faced with a situation in which both children blame the other for something that happened, try the following. First, let each child take a turn to tell his or her side of the story. Children should describe the events as they think they happened, without including any statements blaming the other person. At first children will probably need your help in learning to state the events as objectively as possible. The other child should listen without interrupting and then tells his or her version of the events. After listening to each other's points of view, the children themselves will often settle the problems with no help from you.

If that doesn't happen, ask each child to state how the situation made him or her feel. If at this point you don't think the children listened to each other, ask them to repeat in their own words what they heard the other person say. Alternatively, ask children how they think the other person must have felt. Next, ask the children to say what they could have done differently to avoid the problem in the first place. Finally, ask them what they think they should do now. Often mutual apologies will end the matter, but before they go back to whatever they were doing, you also may ask them what they plan to do the next time they encounter a similar situation.

In most cases, you won't need to think about penalties because the children will have solved the problem. If one child was clearly a victim and the other refuses to acknowledge what he or she did, or perhaps even twists the facts, you'll probably be able to get a good sense of what really happened by listening to their stories. If further action on your part is warranted, you can explain why, for example, you have chosen to discipline one of the children.

As children gradually become aware of others' points of view, they will become more sensitive to the feelings of others and will try harder not to hurt them. As they grow older, they will learn to say to someone else, "Tell me what you think happened here," listen carefully, and then say, "Here's what I thought." They'll be able to initiate calm, reasoned discussions of issues and differences rather than being trapped in pointless, endless arguments. Spouses might want to consider this method for discussing adult problems. The process allows everyone to learn.

If a problem proves to be so highly emotional that discussion is impossible, ask the children involved to write down what happened. Writing usually has a way of taming any "savage beast." If they are calm enough when they finish writing, ask them to read what they have written and then follow the rest of the steps outlined above. If not, wait until later in the day or the next day to follow up. If the problem is an ongoing one, consider having children develop written contracts that specify consequences in the case of default.

Children who learn the values of cooperation and the benefits of conflict resolution develop lifetime habits that will make their school and home lives happier, and increase their chances of success with others on the job or in their own homes.

Chapter Seven

The Call for Change

ON NOVEMBER 7, 1989, *USA Today* published a good summary of the differences between the old and new ideas about learning. "The Old Way," which some people refer to as "passive learning," may be familiar to many of you because that's what you experienced when you were in school. By contrast, the "The New Way" engages students in active or real learning—the kind of learning this book describes. The following summary expands on the list published in *USA Today* and makes use of some of the issues discussed in this book.

OLD WAY: Students are passive. Teachers are experts who "fill the empty jugs" by telling and showing students what they need to know.

NEW WAY: Students are active. Teachers are guides or coaches who design activities from which students learn new information, process it, and develop skills to add to the knowledge and skills they already possess.

OLD WAY: Knowledge is broken down into smaller parts. Students understand the whole by mastering each of the smaller parts.

NEW WAY: Students must have a sense of the whole in order to see how the parts relate to each other and to the whole. They master the parts as they work with the whole.

OLD WAY: Students should avoid making mistakes. Teachers determine what students know or don't know by counting the errors they make.

NEW WAY: Students learn from their mistakes. Teachers view errors as indicators of developmental levels and analyze them to find out what students don't yet understand.

OLD WAY: Educational products (essays, exams, or homework)

are more important than the educational process. Teachers evaluate students primarily on the basis of these products.
NEW WAY: The process students use to solve a problem or complete a task is as important as the final product. Teachers are interested in finding out how students arrive at a particular answer so they can deal with students' misconceptions and misunderstandings. Students generally produce better products when teachers work with them during the process.
OLD WAY: Teachers focus on the content to be taught and tend to think of students as part of a group. Students learn by doing the same assignments in the same way.
NEW WAY: Teachers view students as individuals and adapt content to their needs and interests. Students can learn the same information in different ways or different information in the same way.
OLD WAY: When teachers vary classroom activities, they do so to maintain student interest.
NEW WAY: Teachers vary classroom activities to accommodate students' differing learning styles and interests.
OLD WAY: Students who have difficulty learning should be taught in separate groups or classes.
NEW WAY: Students with a wide range of abilities can learn in the same class.
OLD WAY: Students generally do their work alone. When a more able and a less able student work together, one person will usually do all the work.
NEW WAY: Students can learn as much from each other as from the teacher. More able students learn as they help less able students do what they couldn't do alone.
OLD WAY: Students learn some things that aren't meaningful to them now but will be in the future. It isn't always necessary to explain to students why they are learning something.
NEW WAY: Students must have a personal investment in what they learn. They need to know why they are learning what teachers expect them to learn.
OLD WAY: Teachers don't need to pay much attention to students' backgrounds because the curriculum is planned for all students.
NEW WAY: Teachers recognize that social, economic, cultural,

and ethnic backgrounds affect both the ways students learn and their chances for success in school.

OLD WAY: Extrinsic rewards–grades, prizes, awards, stickers–are good ways to motivate students to learn. Students are unlikely to do work that isn't graded or given specific credit toward a grade.

NEW WAY: Because students develop self-esteem and a commitment to learning when they do work in which they have a personal interest, external rewards are nice but not necessary.

OLD WAY: The teacher makes all the decisions about classroom rules and what students will learn.

NEW WAY: Students share in developing classroom rules and sometimes decide what they will learn.

OLD WAY: Students study each subject separately.

NEW WAY: Students see connections that cut across subject areas by doing interdisciplinary units and taking courses, such as American Studies (instead of history and English separately).

It was ironic, however, that the same issue of *USA Today* included the first in a series of short tests in different subject areas that readers could take to test their own knowledge. These tests were wonderful models of the old ideas about learning with which we are all too familiar. The public would have been better served if the newspaper had instead given examples of activities that reflected the newer approaches some schools and teachers are using.

All too often, textbooks reinforce the old way of learning. Many teachers use textbooks to determine what they will teach. They ask students to read the text, memorize the material in a chapter, and then take a test on it. For some teachers, getting through the textbook by the end of the year is more important than making sure students understand the material that has been covered. There are many reasons to question both the use of textbooks in school and the textbooks themselves.

What image comes to your mind when you hear the word *textbook*? When I think of high school or college classes, I remember the books–thick hardcover volumes with glossy pages, too heavy to carry more than two at once or curl up comfortably with on a couch. Despite the colorful graphs, pictures, and diagrams in many of them, they were boring to read. Every chapter was chopped into smaller and smaller pieces with headings, subheadings, and italicized vocabulary we were supposed to memorize.

Thus, when I was a high school senior in the Fifties, I was thrilled beyond words when my English teacher passed out paperback copies of *The Old Man and the Sea* by Ernest Hemingway. It's hard to imagine how radical a move that was because paperbacks abound today, but up to that point all the literature I'd read in school came packaged in hardbound anthologies. My classmates and I had never thought paperback books were respectable enough for school. Since "quality" writing was always published in hard covers, paperback publishers were left to titillate the buying public with stories of mystery, romance, and adventure.

There was another reason that *The Old Man and the Sea* was such a delightful surprise as a school assignment: the author wasn't dead! Suddenly literature wasn't just deciphering archaic language and memorizing old poems. Now I could read a book by an author in school, and then read articles about the same living author in *Time* magazine. Literature had immediacy and relevance. It even helped me see long-dead authors through new eyes. It became possible for me to think about the *act* of writing, not just the words that had been written.

Others share my preference for paperbacks. Bill Stonebarger, the editor of *Hawkhill Science Newsletter*, reported a survey showing that, given the choice, students prefer paperbacks over hardcovers more than two to one. For older students and boys, the percentage is even greater. Stonebarger's own preference for paperbacks goes back to his Navy days, when he first really began to enjoy reading. "What better companion," he wrote, "than an interesting small paperback book that you could stick in your back pocket and whip out at a moment's notice. A simple, effective way to banish boredom as well as light up your life with new meanings."

Stonebarger's company, Hawkhill Associates, publishes small, easy-to-carry, and well-written paper booklets on a variety of science topics. A biology teacher who experimented with using one of the booklets said that her students not only understood the assignment better than they usually did after covering similar material in regular textbooks, but many of them also asked, "Why aren't all our textbooks like this?" As Stonebarger points out, the small books are "emotionally less formidable" than reading an assignment in a hardcover text.

Too many teachers continue to use only the heavy hardcover texts, and these textbooks are one major obstacle to getting teachers to adopt more effective teaching methods. Harriet Tyson and Arthur Woodward, in an article called "Why Students Aren't Learning Very Much from Textbooks," write, "In most subject areas, textbooks define the scope and sequence of instruction, and the accompanying teacher guides . . . provide a road map from which few teachers make major detours."

In fact, teachers in some school districts construct their written curriculum guides by editing together the tables of contents of their textbooks. When teachers become addicted to textbooks, they are often unhappy about the adoption of a new one, because then they must re-do all of their lessons. Even though teachers should serve as models of experienced learners (which the best ones do), many teachers are so resistant to change that planning how to use a different textbook is very painful.

On the first day of school some teachers already know exactly what page they will be on come January 10, and have tests and quizzes for the whole year ready to distribute to students. Instead of viewing a new text as a chance to add excitement and zest to their classroom, a chance to learn along with their students, they complain and make new lesson plans that reflect their lack of involvement with the ideas they are teaching. Their negative attitudes can't help but be communicated to their students, who then view their assignments with the same feeling of dread their teachers felt in planning them.

If textbooks were better, the fact that so many teachers base so much of their teaching on them wouldn't be a problem. Unfortunately, most textbooks in the major subject areas do not do a good job of presenting information in ways students can understand. First, because publishers must meet the curriculum requirements of the states and districts to which they wish to sell books, they cover too many topics in too little depth. Tyson and Woodward comment that in such books the information is "compressed to the point of incomprehensibility." They point out that it's not surprising only 60 percent of American students who took a national assessment on American history understood the Constitutional system of checks and balances: "This important concept is usually 'covered' in a drab paragraph or two, which does not allow the author to tell a story that would vivify the principle and fix it in the student's memory."

Not only have "market pressures . . . produced encyclopedic textbooks that purport to fulfill every curriculum content requirement," they also contain far too much new vocabulary. In a study of science textbooks for grades six through nine, the textbooks contained "as many as 2,500 new and unfamiliar words—double what could be expected in a foreign language text for the same grades." A high school biology text contained 9,900 such words!

Sometimes, though, textbooks don't include *enough* new material at first, and that can cause problems later. Tyson criticizes math textbook series, for example, because they "often repeat basic skills again and again until algebra, at which point students are overwhelmed with new material."

Textbooks with so much information and so many unfamiliar terms force teachers who depend on them to view teaching as the transmission of information. The books themselves focus on products rather than processes. Thus, students who get their knowledge of science from them do not learn the fundamentals of scientific inquiry. They never learn to think like scientists—a skill useful in many real-life situations.

Publishers of history and geography texts often have difficulty keeping up with knowledge in the field. Tyson and Woodward write that "it can take as long as 25 years" for new knowledge in geography to be incorporated into textbooks. Students' lack of historical knowledge can be attributed mainly to "inaccuracies caused by excessive compression of text and by misconceptions fostered through the avoidance of controversial issues." It's no wonder students don't find history exciting when so many are forced to read books that present it in such stilted prose. They never get a sense of the overall development of important concepts, nor a feeling that the events covered happened to people who once lived and breathed in the world they now occupy.

Tyson and Woodward believe that better textbooks are possible if selection committee members "know enough about a subject to reject books with gross errors and significant omissions," and if they judge the quality of the writing, not just the "readability formula score." At a recent symposium on textbooks, Tyson told the audience that textbooks are improving–"they're better than they were ten to fifteen years ago." She mentioned that unabridged literature has been included in literature books and that readability formulas are being used less "heavy-handedly." New guidelines for literature textbooks in California–a large state that uses state-adopted texts, which means big sales for the winning publishers–may have helped in this area. But Tyson and others agree that much more needs to be done to improve the books students use in schools.

At least one publisher has plans to use new technology to make books tailored to specific needs. According to a recent article in *Education Week,* McGraw-Hill is testing the use of a new procedure, "which allows educators to select a book's contents from an array of materials on a computerized data base." They are beginning with a college-level accounting book, but if the system works, teachers or local school districts will eventually be able to custom-design their own classroom materials. This process might also make it easier for publishers to update books more quickly.

Making sure that textbook information is current won't solve the whole problem, however. Schools must purchase the new editions and use them. One of my students commented recently that the books she used in her elementary classes were so old that they made no mention of men landing on the moon.

Even if students have access to better textbooks, they still are better off learning from teachers for whom the textbook is only a starting point. The opening of the Berlin Wall and the dramatic changes in other Eastern European countries came quickly and caught the rest of the world by surprise. Although students everywhere were interested in what they were seeing on TV and reading in newspapers, many sat through history classes where teachers took only a few minutes to discuss the news at the beginning of the class and then said, "Let's get back to work. Turn to page 233." Some teachers felt they had too much to cover in the regular curriculum and didn't have time to add anything new. Others, unsure of themselves, didn't see how they could "teach" these developments without a textbook to follow.

The heavy dependence on textbooks and the idea that teachers must be experts on a topic before they teach it reinforces a very narrow view of learning. Even though the decline of communism in 1989 and 1990 presented the sort of "teachable moment" good teachers dream of but never expect, too many teachers let the moment pass almost unnoticed, and missed a golden opportunity. Not only did teachers fail to take advantage of students' heightened interest in current issues, they failed to let their students see them functioning as model learners. We know that actions speak louder than words. Think what students could have learned about the process of learning as they watched their teachers explore and consider with them the meaning of events everyone in the world–including the most noted scholars–was struggling to put into perspective.

Because many children had parents or relatives who were directly involved in the Persian Gulf War, schools did pay more attention to that event. But few teachers were prepared to teach in-depth lessons on the background of the war. Teachers who believe in the new way of viewing teaching and learning are usually comfortable teaching without textbooks. They are more flexible when current events suggest changes in the planned curriculum. Moreover, because they see themselves not as experts but as coaches, or guides, they don't hesitate to tackle a new subject with the students. The teachers who weren't afraid to learn about the Middle East along with their students during the Gulf War not only helped the children learn history and current affairs, they also modeled the process of learning. When children see adults as lifelong learners, they are more likely to view themselves that way.

While many teachers resist these new ways of teaching, some teachers in almost every discipline are adopting interactive, small-group-oriented methods. What follows is an overview of the kinds of support teachers' professional organizations and other groups are giving classroom reform.

English

Teachers of English language arts from all levels, kindergarten through college, presented their common goals for teaching English in a report entitled, *The English Coalition Conference: Democracy through Language*. The Coalition believes that "only if teaching is transformed from fact-feeding and fact-testing to an interactive process will today's students be induced to participate more fully in their own learning. It calls for a major effort to break with narrow conceptions of learning in which isolated bits of information are fed to passive students and testing focuses on memory rather than on analyzing information to make meaning."

Classrooms at all levels should become "interactive communities of learners" where teachers "coach" students in problem-solving and exploratory tasks that are linked to their own lives. The teacher won't be an information-giver or judge of "right answers" but a role model from whom students can learn how to ask questions, find answers, and think through problems to find solutions. "At all levels, constant practice of reading, writing, and discussion would develop language abilities."

English language arts teachers also advocate other reforms. For example, instead of being forced to read stories with controlled vocabulary (as they appear in many basal reading books), students should learn to read from real books and stories—the "whole language" approach described earlier in this book. Literature for older students should include works by minority, third world, and female authors as well as the classics, most of which were written by authors one of my college students called "the great white males." The teaching of literature should be based on the idea that students must learn to construct their own meaning from the texts they read, rather than depend on the teacher to present them with academic interpretations to be memorized and given back on tests and essays.

Science

In a report called *Science for All Americans*, the American Association of Science outlines "a blueprint" representing "a shared vision of what Americans want their schools to achieve" in science, mathematics, and technology. The plan stresses "the connections among scientific disciplines, rather than the boundaries between them."

Because many teachers are inadequately prepared to teach science, and textbooks and current methods "actually impede progress toward scientific literacy," the report says teachers "emphasize the learning of answers more than the exploration of questions . . . memory at the expense of critical thought, bits and pieces of information instead of understandings in context, recitation over argument, reading in lieu of doing." Given agreement on a definition of scientific literacy, a clear statement of goals, the right resources, and good teaching for the thirteen years they're in school, "essentially all students would be able to reach the recommended goals by the time they graduate from high school." Science teachers should "start with questions about nature, engage students actively, allow them to work in teams, and deemphasize the memorization of technical vocabulary."

In an anthology for educators titled *Toward the Thinking Curriculum*, James A. Minstrell, who contributed a piece on teaching science, acknowledges that students come to school not as "blank slates," but with many concepts about science. However, these concepts are "often very different from what we want them to learn." Thus, it's important for teachers "to encourage students to seek, identify, and resolve inconsistencies between their ideas and what actually happens in the laboratory or demonstration activity." Many science teachers now begin a new unit by using informal writing, or other means, to discover what misconceptions students might have that would interfere with learning the new material. Identifying and dealing with misconceptions is usually not part of the plan in classes based on the old ideas about learning.

Minstrell also advises teachers to make sure "that what students learn in the formal learning context is transferred to life and everyday situations." Many good teachers are doing just that. Their students learn to think like scientists by doing projects, both in school and in the community, that have real-life connections.

Mathematics

Everybody Counts, a report by the National Research Council of the National Academy of Sciences, includes the controversial recommendation that "teachers make greater use of hand-held calculators as a way of helping their students keep pace with a 'mathematical revolution' that favors the logic of problem-solving over purely computational skills."

Shirley A. Hill, the chair of the academy's math-education board, says that "the 'lecture-and-listen' format" used in most classrooms is one reason so many students turn off to math early on. "We recommend that teachers serve more as class facilitators, moderators, questioners, and coaches than as lecturers. The basic goals should be to encourage students to think mathematically, rather than simply to memorize mathematical skills without understanding."

The report also suggests the need for a campaign to overcome both the mistaken notion that "it takes some innate ability, rather than effort, to succeed in math," and the "student peer pressure which has branded math ability as socially unacceptable." Many math teachers have already begun to change the way they teach math. Having students work cooperatively on teams, for example, gets students thinking and depending on themselves and each other, instead of relying on the teacher to figure out how to solve math problems.

Another report, this one published by the National Council of Teachers of Mathematics, recommends that the curriculum provide for student participation in "*constructing* their own conception of mathematics." Students should be involved in "doing mathematics," by manipulating objects, "discussing the results of their investigations, and writing the results of their experiences." Students would then be able to build on their knowledge "by inventing new methods of assaulting problems." These approaches will also develop students' confidence in their ability to succeed in mathematics. "Teachers will need to become co-investigators in the process of learning and structuring mathematics and in creating rich environments that allow for investigation and growth." The report also recommends that "calculators and computers must be integrated into the curriculum as 'fast pencils,'" but their primary use should be "to support the overall growth of concepts and processes, not just to quickly check answers or serve as objects to teach programming skills."

Math educators now recognize that students must make personal connections with what they study in school as well as understand its purpose and application in the world outside. To this end, the National Council of Teachers of Mathematics has developed a model curriculum for mathematics that many schools are now beginning to implement. There's help, too, from private sources. The Ford Foundation, for example, has funded a $10 million project to boost math education for middle school children in poor communities. The goal of Project QUASAR (Quantitative Understanding: Amplifying Student Achievement and Reasoning) is to help schools "go beyond drills and rote memorization and get pupils to see real-life meaning in numbers. The project hopes to find ways to combine the teaching of basic skills with higher-order math reasoning and problem-solving."

Social Studies

Social studies educators are calling for clearer statements of goals, as well as better textbooks and teaching methods. In her article, "Improving History in the Schools," Charlotte Crabtree writes: "students must understand that the nation's democratic ideas . . . are *moral values* . . . that history is the study of continuity and change and that every problem of the present or future can be understood in terms of some version of the past." She calls history "a casebook of dramatic events that can help these students build these essential understandings as well as the understandings they must acquire to cope with an increasingly interdependent world."

According to Crabtree, a carefully articulated curriculum is needed, "because high school students must be able to build on a strong grounding in history, pleasurably acquired during their elementary and middle school years." While there has been much debate about returning history to the elementary school, "the preponderance of the evidence . . . supports those who endorse introducing children to the whole universe of space and time and not limiting them to 'near to far' or 'expanding environments' models." Teachers should include biographies, myths, legends, folktales, and historical narratives "to capture the imagination of the children and to hold their interest."

How to sequence offerings in American and world history in high school has always been a problem. Social studies educators agree that students are not spending enough time on twentieth-century European and world history and current issues, but many students don't know much about recent American history either. Because many teachers teach chronologically, they find they run out of time at the end of the year. As one California educator remarked, "We used to yell out the door, 'The United States won World War II!' as the students left the eleventh grade."

To deal with this problem, the National Commission on Social Studies in the Schools recommends that high schools teach a three-year sequence that combines United States and world history and geography. California has done this in its new curriculum framework, and similar requirements have been adopted or are under consideration in other states.

Geography comes under the general heading of social studies, and is rarely ever taught anymore as a separate course. Recently many people have become very concerned about students' lack of knowledge in that area. The National Geographic Society has helped bolster our commitment to better geography teaching by funding projects that instruct teachers in innovative strategies, and developing high-impact materials and technologies so that students will become more active learners. The National Geographic Kids Network, for example, will eventually link students in grades four through six in 10,000 schools across the country and around the world via computer. They will be able to work together on scientific and geographic research and share the results. Team learning within the classroom, simulation games—playing the stock market, for example—and role playing are other ways teachers are making social studies learning more personal and meaningful to students.

Some social studies teachers are working with teachers in other disciplines to develop interdisciplinary programs, such as American Studies courses, that dissolve traditional subject area boundaries. This more integrated approach allows students to see connections they might otherwise miss. Because the interdisciplinary approach to middle school education involves teachers from each major subject working as a team with specific groups of students in the same grade level, teachers are more frequently planning their lessons so that students can study general topics by doing related activities in every subject. Students in one school worked to help build a nature trail near the school and write a guidebook for it. This project, like an earlier one on whales, combined math, science, history, and language arts.

Even though an integrated approach makes sense, teachers and parents are often resistant to such changes. The barriers separating the different subject areas have been in place much longer than the Berlin Wall was, and will be much more difficult to tear down. An interdisciplinary approach involves more than a curriculum change; it requires changes in the way people think, behave, and interact with others.

One controversial aspect of curriculum reform in social studies has been the effort to make the curriculum multicultural. Textbooks and teachers, the critics charge, have always presented a white, European perspective of world history. Native Americans, blacks, and other ethnic and minority groups want students to learn about people and events from a much wider perspective. It is not within the scope of this book to present an in-depth consideration of this issue. However, as the earlier chapter on self-esteem suggests, to do well in school all students must feel valued. If certain groups are not represented in the curriculum, children from those backgrounds are likely to feel less worthy than other children. But if teachers allow students to have more options about what topics they study, no child should feel excluded. In fact, by doing independent or small-group projects, students who investigate their own cultural heritage and history can enrich the curriculum for everyone, by sharing what they learn with the whole class.

The debate over multiculturalism isn't going to end soon, but we can all learn by listening to and trying to understand the perspectives of those with whom we disagree. Here again is a situation from which children can learn, as they watch how adults behave when there seems to be no easy resolution to an issue.

Other Subjects

It isn't only in the "big four" academic areas – English, math, science, and social studies – where the calls for change are being heard. If you glance through back issues of your local newspaper from the past year, you'll probably find stories describing new ways of approaching the teaching of fine arts, health, physical education, and home economics.

A headline in a Portland (Maine) newspaper, for example, proclaimed "Industrial arts to get retooling." The reporter explained that IA is now called "technology education," but that's not the only difference: "The technology education method is to present a problem, such as how to reach a high shelf, and have students brainstorm solutions, which could include more than simply building a footstool. Students . . . would then build a model of the solution using whatever tools are necessary." Students will still use table saws and other tools, but "they will use them to learn about technological systems—construction, communications, manufacturing and energy, power and transportation—instead of simply learning to use the tool itself." The new curriculum, which involves students in a series of shorter problem-solving projects instead of a single project that might take several weeks, has been designed for all students. In one high school, students combined science and technology as they worked with teachers of both subjects to build and race paper cars.

The teaching of foreign languages is also changing. While more students are studying foreign languages than ever, and doing so at younger ages, the traditional audio-lingual and grammar-based programs are out of favor. As Rebecca Oxford of the University of Alabama said, "Neither one of them really added up to any kind of free communication." Current approaches emphasize proficiency in the language and what the learner can *do* with language rather than what the learner *knows* about language. Grammatical accuracy is still important, but teachers are giving students more opportunities to talk and write informally in the language. They practice communicating meaning, in order to develop fluency without worrying unduly about correctness. Teachers believe that as students develop more proficiency, they will also develop more accuracy and sophistication in the language. New foreign language teaching methods parallel those that teachers employ with younger students learning to read and write in English. Students, for example, do free writings or write daily journal entries, stories, and poems in the language they are learning.

Physical education, music, art, and home economics have always involved students more in doing than in memorizing, but even they are changing in important ways. Because many teachers no longer believe it's enough to have students learn a subject for its own sake, they work to help students see how school learning connects with real life. In physical education, for example, teachers want students to see fitness not as just a lesson but also as a way of life, and they focus more on teaching students lifetime fitness activities rather than team sports. Home economics students in many schools are running day-care centers to practice interacting with young children, not just reading about child development in books.

Art and music teachers have enriched the classroom environment by bringing artists into the schools to work with students and by taking students on more field trips—to museums, concerts, plays, and art exhibits. No matter what the subject, many teachers have realized the importance of connecting what they teach to the real world.

The American Library Association (ALA) also recommends a restructuring away from textbooks, workbooks, and lectures and toward another sort of "literacy" needed for life in the technological age. ALA President F. William Summers described "information literacy" as "the ability to find, analyze, and use information. . . . Information-literate people are those who have learned how to learn." Teachers need to work with librarians and other media specialists to help students learn how to use the wide variety of information that is available now but too often underused. The ALA joins the "growing chorus of groups calling for teachers to shift from the role of 'presenter of ready-made information' to that of facilitator of student learning."

Of course, when teachers change their view of learning and teaching, the traditional classroom organization no longer works. As students work on varied assignments and projects, the teacher functions more as a guide, or facilitator. This kind of classroom structure is also necessary if students are to learn to use computers in meaningful ways while in school.

Few, if any, schools will ever be able to afford one computer per student, and technological advances have come so fast in recent years that models quickly become obsolete. If students are to work on computers, they can't all do so at the same time. If a classroom has two or three computers, the teacher who depends on traditional teaching methods is not likely to let students have access to them, except during occasional study periods when the whole class isn't involved in some activity. But in a class where teachers allow students to work on different assignments in different ways, computers can be used frequently as a matter of course.

One obstacle to more extensive use of computers in schools has been teachers' lack of knowledge about them. Teachers who have been trained to think of themselves as experts often fear introducing anything into the curriculum unless they know a great deal about it and feel comfortable with it. These feelings prevent many teachers from doing anything with computers in their classes. If, however, they already have changed their classroom structure to a more informal kind of workshop format, and encourage students to learn from and with each other, then students can help teach each other how to use computers. In almost every class there's usually at least one kid who has a computer at home and has learned an enormous amount about its capabilities. These students can also teach the teachers—if teachers can perceive of themselves as co-learners rather than experts.

The power of computers in educational terms hasn't yet been realized in most schools. Hypercard, for example, is a software package that can be used for writing high-tech term papers. Developed by Apple Computer, Inc., for use on its Macintosh line, Hypercard now has been joined by similar software packages made by other companies. Even people with little technical knowledge can use this user-friendly computer software language to "create programs with a powerful capacity for cross-referencing and for merging different media." Its backers claim that its use actually boosts thinking skills.

Using Hypercard, a ninth-grader at Cincinnati Country Day School (the son of Joseph Hofmeister, the school's computer teacher) wrote a history paper on Hannibal's crossing of the Alps in which the text was complemented with graphs, sound effects, and animated maps. Hofmeister was quoted in *Education Week* as saying, "The adoption of Hypercard . . . has changed the emphasis in many classes from a 'transmission model' of education —in which students sit through traditional lectures, take notes, and then spit their notes back—to a 'student-centered' learning environment." History teacher Nancy Fogelson said that since her students have begun using Hypercard, "I get much more enthusiasm about history and much more productivity. It's exciting because the kids can make their own discoveries."

Unfortunately, because they cannot envision how to fit these tools into their traditional classrooms, many teachers will not be as quick as Hofmeister and Fogelson were to embrace technological advances that have implications for school use. Thus, administrators who purchase enough computers so that every classroom has one or two, and then set up training sessions so that teachers can learn to use them, may be disappointed when they don't later see students using them in many classes. Greater use of computers in schools may depend on teachers changing the way they structure and organize their classroom learning environments. That change won't come unless they move away from the traditional views of teaching and learning.

Classrooms where kids work with each other in groups or pairs, where they write and talk informally, where computer use is as natural as reading and writing, and where the teacher functions as co-learner signal a fundamental change in education. When more teachers begin to adopt methods that focus more on process than product, and more on coming to understand how the parts fit into the whole than on the parts themselves, then students will learn more, and enjoy learning more.

Still more work needs to be done to develop standardized tests that measure the outcomes of process-oriented teaching. But, given more motivation and a greater personal investment in learning, students should do better even on the tests we're using today. Just as early cultures remembered the details of what their ancestors passed on to them in the context of stories and legends, so too will students remember more about literature or history when they learn it through activities that are interesting and personally relevant. It's time to stop forcing our schools to teach for tests, as if life required nothing more than knowing answers to TV game show questions.

Suggestions for Parents

Become familiar with the curriculum and textbooks used in your children's schools. Make sure children have up-to-date materials available. When financial resources are tight, encourage the school to consider buying a few copies of several different titles, because that is more cost effective than purchasing one copy of an expensive hardcover textbook for each student. Students don't all need copies of the same book if they are working on small group or independent projects and later sharing what they learn with the whole class.

Ask teachers and administrators what the latest research studies indicate and how this information is being used in the school. Suggest that they conduct sessions to inform parents. Try reading yourself some of the many reports that have been issued in the last few years by organizations representing teachers of various disciplines, as well as by foundations and special commissions. Compare these recommendations to what is being done in local schools. If nothing is being done, ask the school or a parent group to sponsor sessions where those who are interested can get together to read and discuss the reports.

Find out what computer equipment is available in the school and how much time students regularly have opportunities to use it. If funds for purchasing new equipment are limited, consider working with a parent group to raise or solicit funds to buy more. In this day and age, no classroom should be without at least one computer.

Consider purchasing a computer for your children if they do not already have one. You can get good buys on used equipment, because many people replace computers for updated models. Children don't need state-of-the-art technology to learn the basics. No one who has discovered the advantages of word processing will ever consider using a typewriter again. And some studies show that learning-disabled students can learn to write much better with a computer than they can by hand.

Invest in computer games that teach as well as entertain. Children get hooked on games that may not add much to their knowledge and skills (other than manual dexterity), but there are many games and programs available that can help children learn everything from keyboarding to geography.

Write to the teachers' professional discipline organizations for a copy of their current catalogs. (Names and addresses appear in the appendix.) Although their publications are directed to teachers, most offer a few that are addressed to parents. Some of those not intended for parents may provide you with useful information as well.

Whenever possible, call your children's attention to the way what they are studying in school is being used in the real world. Encourage your children to connect the specific knowledge they learn in school to their lives outside.

Chapter Eight

Homework Kids Like

EVEN THOUGH THE WORD "thinking" isn't always mentioned in recommendations for teaching reform, most such recommendations make it clear that teaching students to think–and giving them *opportunities* to think–should be school's central focus. What's surprising is that some administrators reflect their own inability to think when they decide that the best way to teach students to think is to institute a "thinking skills" program.

Thinking is not something we should teach in isolation. One can't think about nothing. By having students do thinking exercises for a few weeks every year, or take mini-courses in thinking, schools inadvertently teach students that thinking is unconnected to anything else. It's almost like telling them, "You'll need to think to do these exercises, but next period we'll do math or English. You won't need to think then." In reality, of course, students need to think to do well in anything.

No matter what subjects they teach, teachers have a responsibility for teaching thinking–and reading, writing, speaking, and study skills–as they cover the content in their respective subjects. Perhaps some administrators think special units and courses are needed because teachers often give students assignments that don't require much thinking. But if teachers did a little more thinking themselves, they could design assignments that would require students to think more. When assignments and projects require higher-order thinking skills, students are less likely to view them as "busy work." Thus, they are more likely to get them done and do them well.

Unfortunately, too much of what students are asked to do, in class and for homework, is busy work: answering questions or filling in blanks on worksheets, or completing sentences with the correct words for English usage exercises. The assignments themselves are boring. If students already understand the material, they become more bored dealing with it in such a perfunctory way. If students don't get the principles being taught, boring assignments quickly cause them to lose interest or get discouraged.

I can remember how I felt about such homework assignments in my high school English classes, and the strategy I devised to cut corners and still get credit. Even when the handbook exercise only required us to choose one word to show that we understood subject-verb agreement, for example, my teachers felt that we would benefit from writing out the whole sentence. I did well in English and usually understood the rule or principle right away. I didn't need the homework exercise to reinforce what I already knew. Writing out all those sentences seemed like an incredible waste of time, but I didn't want to jeopardize my grade by not doing the assignment. So in large handwriting I would fill one side of one sheet of paper with sentences completely and correctly done and then write on the bottom of the sheet, "continued on next page." There never was a next page, and no teacher ever noticed that it was missing! They collected and checked off the homework, but I suspect they didn't look at it because we spent most of the class period going over it.

Today's students are more resistant to authority than kids were when I went to school. Unless they are motivated by grades, many of them just won't do busy-work assignments at all. That means that the large numbers of students who aren't aiming for admission to selective colleges often don't do assigned work or do it carelessly. And teachers, especially when they have non-college-bound students, often respond to students' failure to do the homework by assigning less of it. A homework study in Illinois, for example, found that while only sixty teachers of college prep students said they gave no homework, 508 teachers of general-track students gave no homework.

Yet, according to *What Works*, a report published by the U.S. Department of Education, "Student achievement rises significantly when teachers regularly assign homework and students conscientiously do it." Quality, though, as well as quantity, makes a difference. "Students are more willing to do homework when it is useful, when teachers treat it as an integral part of instruction, when it is evaluated by the teacher, and when it counts as part of the grade. . . . Assignments that require students to think, and are therefore more interesting, foster their desire to learn both in and out of school."

Discussing the findings in the National Assessment of Education Progress (NAEP) report that compiled data on student achievement for the first twenty years of testing, NAEP executive director Archie Lapointe said that while students' basic skills have improved, there are "deficits in higher-order thinking skills, which means that large proportions of American students do not appear to be adequately prepared for college work, career mobility, and thoughtful citizenship." He went on to say that "students who report participatory and varied instructional practices in science and literature tend to have higher proficiency levels than their peers in less exploratory classrooms."

Even college-bound students often find out later that high school did not prepare them well for the kind of work they had to do in college. In a letter Sylvia Fraser wrote while she was in college and later included in her book, *My Father's House,* she reflects on the inadequacies of her high school preparation: "It really burns me when I think about all that time we spent in high school dissecting frogs and counting metaphors. Everything was analysis, analysis, analysis. No synthesis. No ideas. No awareness of the connectedness of things in time and space. Prissy sonnets about clouds and daffodils because that's what poets wrote in the nineteenth century. Remember the day I asked Mr. Hutton what algebra was for? His answer is indelibly printed on my mind: 'Sit down. You've always been a troublemaker!' "

Some teachers give busy-work assignments because it's a useful way of controlling students. The authors of *The Shopping Mall High School* describe the treaty teachers and students sometimes make: if the students behave themselves, the teachers won't push them. If you've ever sat in a class where the teacher has lost control, you'll realize that maintaining control, by whatever means necessary, is a matter of survival for many teachers. Many are afraid to try new methods because they're simply afraid such measures might create chaos. Busy work that doesn't require much of students is part of the unspoken agreement they have with their students. The issue of whether students learn very much is usually ignored.

But the safe haven teachers and students create often seems like a prison. A fourteen-year-old girl named Vita Wallace, who has been home-schooled, wrote a letter to the editor of the Portland (Maine) *Press Herald* protesting proposed legislation that would prevent dropouts from getting drivers' licenses, because until she could take and pass the high school equivalency test, she too would be ineligible for a license. The last sentence of her letter shows that, even though she doesn't attend one, she understands the attitude that too often pervades public schools: "I would recommend that legislators and educators put their energy into making schools places where people can learn skills which they need, rather than places where children are imprisoned in the hope they will become better citizens."

Homework should not be the punishment students get for misbehaving in school. You probably remember a teacher who said, "If you'll behave and get right to work today, you won't have homework tonight," or, "If you can't pay attention in class, you'll get twice as much work to take home." As an assistant high school principal, I talked to several angry students whose teachers had given the whole class double the usual number of math problems for homework when a few kids disrupted the class. These kinds of efforts to get students to do homework are obviously counterproductive.

Making the assignments students are required to do more meaningful would be an important step in the right direction. If students are challenged to think, and engaged in activities that make sense and have some value, they'll do the work and learn from doing it.

Parents often get involved when their children have term papers or projects to do for school – usually because kids wait until the last minute or feel helpless (or feign helplessness) about what they have to do to get the job done. Parents often don't stop to think that when they bail their children out because of an impending deadline, they are fostering poor planning and teaching their children that they can be irresponsible without suffering any consequences. Teachers inadvertently make it easy for parents to do students' work because of the way they structure assignments.

Some friends of mine will never forget an assignment their eighth-grader son, Chris, had to do for his English class – his mother spent several hours typing the twenty-two poems he included in his report on three poets. Some of you may recall similar experiences, and wish teachers didn't assign projects kids couldn't or wouldn't do by themselves. Of course, one problem with this assignment was the fact that the mother rather than the student did much of the work; but more importantly, it didn't require the use of higher-order thinking skills – the kind of thinking Sylvia Fraser found missing in her high school education, and which the NAEP results show our students unable to do.

The poetry project is a fairly typical research assignment, not unlike those given in other subjects where students do reports on subjects like Napoleon, India, or pollution. Not only are most such topics too broad, but they have no focus. The English teacher in this case asked the students to research and report on three poets. They dutifully went to the library and looked up biographical information on the poets and found some poems they had written. Most students wrote three-part papers – really three separate papers. And "wrote" is probably not the best word to describe what the students did because most simply copied information from books and collected sample poems. I call these kinds of papers "collages of quotations." Students, having been warned not to plagiarize, are generally very careful to use quotation marks and footnote what they copy from other sources. Because they often don't internalize or think about what they read and copy, their finished papers are crazy quilts of information from other people, some more carefully sewn together than others.

I don't know whether Chris had his mom type all the poems without ever reading them himself, but I'm sure some students didn't read the poems. For an assignment of this kind, they didn't need to. If their written reports are carefully and neatly done, they could earn top grades without knowing much of anything about any three poets. Students who care about their grades but aren't particularly interested in the subject matter will choose to do the least amount of work possible to get the grade they desire. They won't, however, remember much of the material they worked on very far into the future. If an eighth-grader approached a unit on the Civil War in this manner, he'd likely forget the years the war took place by the time he was in college. Without a personal investment in what they do in school, students don't remember what they study. That children will spend time doing what they consider important or interesting is clear from the beautiful covers some students make for reports they didn't want to do. I've seen students spend many hours illustrating a cover for a report that took them only an hour to copy from an encyclopedia or book.

Chris' teacher could have made the poetry assignment more meaningful by making only slight changes in its design. Had she done so, Chris's mother wouldn't have wasted her time typing all of those poems in order to make his project appear to be more than it was. The teacher could have said, "I want you to look up information on three poets and read several of their poems. Then choose one poem by each poet and write a paper showing how these poets and/or their poems are similar or connected in some way." Not only would Chris have had to carefully read several poems by each poet (maybe more than twenty-two to find three he could use), he also would have had to think about what the poems meant individually and how they were similar to or different from each other.

Even if Chris wasn't thrilled about analyzing poems, he might have become interested in the intellectual challenge such an assignment presented. Those students who favor math and science over literature would find that they could use thinking and problem-solving skills in much the same way they would on a math problem or science project. Since the assignment was no longer so much busy work–copying and recording–students could make it personally meaningful. And the teacher could tell from their essays how much the students themselves had invested–whether they copied from one another, claimed someone else's ideas as their own, or finagled their parents into doing too much of the work. Having completed such an assignment, students would also be much more likely to remember what they learned.

In assigning research projects like this one, teachers need to consider the process of completing the work as well as the final result. When teachers assign a project, give students a due date, and leave them on their own to do it, they risk being dissatisfied with the finished work. Because students have a more difficult and challenging job to do, some may get discouraged without help along the way. Others may try to fool teachers by handing in a paper for which someone else—a friend or a parent—did much of the work.

To avoid these problems, teachers can ask students to keep a process log, where they note when they work, what they do, and what problems they encounter. If help from parents or others is permissible, students can indicate who helped and how. By collecting these logs every so often, teachers can identify students who need more help. They can take steps to encourage students by scheduling help sessions or by assigning students to help each other. Before the final papers are due, perhaps students can bring their drafts to class and share them in small groups.

All of these strategies will help students do a better job and become more interested in what they are doing. Of course, the benefit for teachers is seeing students produce better assignments, work that will reflect their ability to think and write (rather than rearrange, restate, or misstate someone else's words). And if parents are enlisted to type the final copy, they'll get to see how well—or how poorly—their children can think and write.

Teachers and students benefit from reflecting on what they are doing, both while they are doing it and after it is over. Students who stop in the middle of a research project to consider what they've done, what they have left to do, and how all the pieces will fit together in the final product, will likely spend their time more efficiently. As they consider the steps they have taken to reach a goal, they reinforce the process in their own minds so that the next time they face a similar task, they will be able to do it more easily. After the process is complete and the project has been evaluated by the teacher, students should be able to see what they might have done differently to achieve a better result, and can file this information away for use on similar projects in the future.

Teachers can reflect on their teaching—the directions they gave students, the design of the assignment—so that the next time they make a similar assignment, they can improve the way they present it and help students with it. Many teachers routinely evaluate and reflect on their own teaching by keeping journals. As they describe in a journal entry what happened in a particular class or with a certain student, they often discover ways to solve the problems they encountered or see how they can avoid similar ones in the future. Taking the time to stop and think about what we're doing makes us more aware of the little things that often go unnoticed as we hurry from one task to another, but which can cause big problems later on.

Many teachers have begun to realize the benefit of having students share their thinking processes as they solve a math problem, or the strategies they use to make sense of a reading assignment. Metacognition, or thinking about thinking, is useful for everyone. When students verbalize what's in their minds as they solve a problem, for example, teachers are able to spot where the process breaks down—there's more than one way to arrive at the same wrong answer. When successful students model good strategies for solving problems, the students who are having a tough time see other approaches they might try. Often students who just don't "get" a concept may be unable to explain what they don't understand, but by listening to other students think out loud, they may be able to follow in their steps and suddenly catch on.

The educator James Alvino has identified several learning-to-learn skills that will prepare students for the more complex metacognitive skills—planning, monitoring, assessing—they will need to be successful in school and in life. Both parents and teachers can help students develop these skills as they assist them in working on school assignments. Adapted from Alvino's original list, the following are questions children should consider when working on a task.

What does this assignment require? What are you expected to do? Ask children to tell you or do a free writing in which they explain what they understand the task to be.

How long do you think it will take to complete it? Help children plan and then record an estimate. Afterward check to see how close it was, and talk about the reasons the assignment took more or less time than the children estimated. With practice children will get a better sense of time and will be able to plan better on future assignments.

What books, materials, and supplies will you need? Get children to answer this question and actually gather the things they need before they begin to work. Otherwise they are likely to waste time when something isn't available, or use the lack of supplies as an excuse for not working.

What have you learned before that might help you now? Can you remember an assignment you did before that was something like this one? Ask children to recall similar tasks or situations encountered in the past, how they went, how they are like this one, how they are different, and how they can apply their prior knowledge to this task.

Can you break this task down into smaller parts? Big projects can overwhelm us if we think of the whole thing as one unit. But there is no large undertaking that can't be divided into smaller pieces. It's the same principle Alcoholics Anonymous teaches: one day at a time. Children need to figure out what steps they must take to reach their goal and then do them, one at a time.

How many ways can you think of to do this task? Can you guess at an answer? Too many children worry so much about the "right" way or the "right" answer that they won't risk trying something new. I ask my students to write down the questions they have as they do a reading assignment and then speculate about the answers. Sometimes they can answer their own questions when they think about them and don't worry whether they're right. One strategy successful readers employ is reading to find the answer to a question they've posed. The search for an answer helps them focus on the assignment.

Who could help you with this task? How? Even if children must do all of the actual work on a project, talking through what has to be done with a friend, parent, or sibling is very helpful in clarifying the task and exploring ways to complete it. Getting feedback from someone on a draft of a paper almost always results in a better finished paper. When your children ask you to read a draft, don't point out errors or omissions. Ask questions instead, so they can consider what might be changed or reworked. Tell children that when they ask for someone's advice, they should listen carefully and show respect and understanding for different points of view. In the end, though, they must make the final decision about following any advice they have been given. They have the choice to ignore it if they wish, but they shouldn't argue with the person who's making a suggestion. This point is usually emphasized when teachers have students working in writing groups, giving each other feedback on their work.

What will you get from finishing this task? Help children realize that doing something for a grade or to please the teacher or parent is not the best reason for doing anything. Help them see what skills they're developing when doing a particular task. Encourage them to become "intrinsically" rather than "extrinsically" motivated by helping them view work done well as its own reward. As one teacher I know has commented, "There aren't enough M&M's in the world to get everyone to do what they should on the basis of external rewards."

What can you do if you get stuck? Advise children to stop if they feel frustrated before their frustration paralyzes them. The feeling is normal and it will pass. Sometimes ideas and problems need time to "incubate." Our subconscious can work on them while we're doing something else. If children plan far enough ahead, they can take time off to do something else when they get stuck. Often the difficulty will solve itself if they take a break to go for a walk or sleep on it overnight. It may also help to recall similar past experiences and think about what worked in those situations. It's important that children don't see temporary frustration as an indication of their lack of ability. Because situations like this can occur, it's a good idea when planning assignments to allow for time away from the task. If an assignment is done at that last minute, children don't have that option.

What options do you have? When children do get stuck, ask them to consider their options. Alvino says, "Make . . . [them] aware that they have three options when they face an obstacle: they can run away from it; they can go around it; or they can go through it, do their best, and learn from the experience. Help them assess which obstacles are worth going through and which are not, as well as the consequences of their choices. But give them permission to *make* those choices."

Finally, it's important for parents and children to remember that no matter how well or how poorly children do on any task, they must believe that they have value apart from that. Help them to realize that a task is something they *do*, but that tasks do not define who they are. Help them to accept suggestions and criticism as possible sources of help, not attacks on them personally. A low grade on an assignment or test does not mean they are stupid, but that they have further work to do. No one is successful 100 percent of the time. Everyone has strengths and weaknesses. With time and effort anyone can improve at anything.

As in the case of projects, students can learn spelling and vocabulary more effectively if teachers modify the assignments they give. Traditionally students get a new list of words each week. They write definitions for the words and use them in sentences before being tested on them at the end of the week. I observed a junior high class in which the teacher spent the first half of the period having students read their definitions and sentences aloud as they corrected their own homework papers. When they finished the random words on the spelling list, the teacher told them to put away their papers and take out their vocabulary words. The rest of the period was spent doing exactly the same thing with another list of words! The students were well behaved but not excited about learning, and I could see why. Some probably wondered, as I did, what the difference was between the two lists and why one list couldn't serve both purposes. One list certainly would have been more efficient, but not necessarily better.

First, consider that after we get out of school, we never have to spell a list of words correctly. What we have to do is recognize which words we write are spelled wrong and look them up or ask someone how to spell them. (With computer spell-check programs the task is even easier, although such programs won't pick up on homonyms that are used incorrectly, such as "there" and "their.") When I was required by California state law to use the state-adopted spelling books with my students, I was appalled by the number of times students spelled words correctly for tests and then misspelled the same words in their own writing. They might have learned to think of spelling more realistically if I had asked them to find and correct misspelled words that were buried in a piece of writing, instead of reproducing a list I dictated orally.

I have since taken a more thoughtful approach to spelling with my basic writing students. Most students have problems with only a few words—often little ones, such as "there," "their," and "they're," or "two," "too," and "to"—and the words they misspell are usually ones they use frequently. Instead of giving the whole class a list to memorize, I require that students keep personal spelling dictionaries. One student discovered that a small address book was the handiest place to write down troublesome words along with definitions and, if necessary, sample sentences. Another student in the class, an older woman learning English as a fourth or fifth language, was delighted with the idea. She used her address book/dictionary more often than anyone else. Whenever any of us used an English word with which she was not familiar, she would ask that we write or spell the word and define it for her dictionary. Because the little book was so easy to carry, she kept it with her wherever she went.

Students add to their own dictionaries throughout the semester and then use them when they edit the writing they do. Because the words listed are meaningful to them, and the personal dictionary can be more easily used and carried around than a standard dictionary, they often learn to spell words very quickly even though I don't test them on their lists. There's no reason teachers couldn't let students give each other tests on their own lists of words—a practice that makes more sense than using arbitrary lists created by textbook authors.

Some students, especially those with learning disabilities, find spelling difficult, and they misspell so many words that they can't even begin to imagine how they'll ever learn to spell correctly. Two students in my basic writing class were extreme cases. One, a Franco-American woman, grew up speaking French and learned English as a second language. The other was a man who had recently been diagnosed as a dyslexic. Because they both misspelled about every fourth word in any writing they did, they were overwhelmed by the idea of learning each word, one by one, and didn't make much of an effort to do anything about their problem. One night I sat down and listed all the misspelled words I could find in journal entries they had written—about twenty-five for each student. Then I analyzed the misspellings and discovered something surprising: learning five spelling "rules" would take care of 80 percent of their errors. When I showed them the lists and explained what I had found, they were able to develop workable plans to improve their spelling. Of course, they didn't become champion spellers, but they were motivated to make an effort to improve after already having given up.

A more thoughtful approach to vocabulary study would improve student performance as well. Most of the words we know weren't learned from lists we memorized in school. The vocabulary exercises we might have done in preparation for the SAT probably helped our scores, but most of those words didn't stick. We learn words by hearing them used and coming upon them in what we read. We internalize their meanings by repeated contact with them in a variety of situations. Some new words we'll begin using in our own sentences, in talking or writing. We'll know the meanings of others when we read them in context, but because speech is more informal than writing, and many of us don't do much writing, we may not have the occasion to use them ourselves. Our reading vocabularies are usually much larger than our spoken ones.

The best way to learn new words is to pay attention to the words we see and hear and to make them our own by trying them out. Slang words spread fast, and everybody understands what they mean and when it's appropriate to use them. Even though no one can look up a slang word in the dictionary, and there's no test to make sure it has been learned, people use these new words willingly, naturally, and very quickly.

Teachers and parents who want children to develop their vocabularies would do well to forget about lists and get students to do more thinking and reading. Although a dictionary can be helpful, students should practice figuring out the meanings of words by considering the parts of the words they do know (roots, prefixes, and suffixes) and the contexts in which they appear. Like personal spelling dictionaries, personal vocabulary dictionaries are another way to aid vocabulary development. The most effective way to increase vocabulary, however, is wide reading. Studies show that the more students read, the more words they know, and, perhaps even more important, the better they write. Get kids hooked on reading and curious about words, and vocabulary and writing skills will almost take care of themselves.

Perhaps you can remember "Current Events Day" from elementary school. In my school it was usually scheduled on Friday—the day of the week when we got to do enjoyable rather than "serious" work. I'm not sure the teachers intended to send an unspoken message that currents events were not as important as the events we studied in our history books, but that's what many of us thought.

Current events study took one of two forms: either we read stories and did the puzzles in *Weekly Reader*, or we all brought in clippings from the local newspaper and reported on them in front of the class. I don't remember ever spending much time discussing the articles, and we made few (if any) connections between current world events and their historical background. This was true even if we happened to be studying the earlier history of a country currently in the news. I did well in school, but until I took college history and government courses, I never saw how present situations were rooted in the past. I'm sure some of my classmates never got that insight.

This way of looking at current events in isolation is just one more example of busy work. It's an approach that fails to promote understanding about the global society in which we all live. There are many ways teachers can incorporate current events in meaningful contexts; "The Ambassadors' Report" is one example of an ongoing project that promotes long-term, in-depth learning as it helps students become more responsible. At the beginning of the year each student chooses or is assigned a country to follow for the whole year. They become "ambassadors" to these countries. (Everyone follows the United States.) At first the whole class does some initial background study of such organizations as The United Nations; some basic geography; a look at current world leaders; and other general information. Then individual students do background research on the history, geography, politics, and economic and social concerns of the countries they represent. By dividing the class into five or six small groups, which roughly correspond to the countries in a given geographical area, such as Europe or the Middle East, the teacher can schedule panels once a week on a rotating basis.

Students take notes and collect clippings and keep these in notebooks. These are due every time they are scheduled for a panel presentation to the rest of the class, about once every five weeks. In their first panel presentation students summarize what they've learned about the background of their countries; thereafter they report the current events they've followed, making connections whenever possible to background information that clarifies or explains what's happening in the countries now. During the last few minutes of the class period, panel members respond to questions from classmates.

The process is a collaborative one because as students read the daily newspapers or *Time,* they get into the habit of noticing articles on other students' countries and sharing what they find. The project gives students a fair-to-good general knowledge of world affairs and an in-depth knowledge of one country, all in a meaningful context. Students become the "experts" on their countries—often knowing more than the teacher—and they are motivated to become active learners who recognize that they have an obligation to share what they know with their classmates.

Earlier I discussed the importance of reaching students with different learning styles. Many of us studied Shakespeare in high school by reading one of his plays, participating in teacher-led question-and-answer sessions, and then writing an essay or taking a test on it. This kind of teaching favors only one learning style. It's possible, however, for a teacher to plan a unit on a Shakespeare play in which students with varying interests and talents can become meaningfully involved.

There are any number of different activities teachers could introduce. Students could view a live professional production of the play, or, if one is not available, they could watch the film or videotape of a production. Students could perform a scene from the play in class. (If they do see a professional version, they should do their own first so they can compare their interpretation with the professional production.) A group of students could research some aspect of life during Shakespeare's time or some other topic related to the play or Shakespeare's life, and then share it with the rest of the class. In one of my classes a small group told us what they'd found about Elizabethan food and served a meal they had prepared. Students can be as creative as they wish in figuring out interesting ways to report the research they did. Note that none of these activities replace the reading of the play, but rather enrich and expand it.

More students are likely to experience success when some of the unit assignments play to their strengths. No single teacher could provide the rich background for studying a play that results from students of varying interests and talents sharing with everyone the special areas they investigated.

This approach can be used in classes dealing with almost any subject matter. Think about the differences in student engagement involved in the pairs of assignments listed below. Which approaches are likely to work more effectively and encourage more learning?

Math: 1) Students can do twenty examples from the book, all of which test their understanding of the same principle. 2) Students can do three examples, write out the process they went through to find the answers, and then choose from a page of twenty problems covering several principles the ones that require them to apply the principle they are presently working with.

Science: 1) Students can read about photosynthesis from the text, discuss it, and have a quiz. 2) Students can read the text and then design and conduct an experiment that will test the concept–in this case, they might log what happens to plants that have been subjected to different environments: sunny window sill, corner of the room with no direct light, and dark closet.

Social studies: 1) Students can watch a movie about Watergate, such as *All the President's Men,* and in the follow-up discussion the teacher can ask them to recall specific details from the film.

2) After watching *All the President's Men*, students can write about and then discuss issues connected with Watergate, such as whether the reporters or other characters in the movie did the right thing, whether they would have made other choices, or how situations like Watergate might be avoided in the future.

This last example is interesting to me because a student teacher I once observed used the first approach. When the movie ended, the students didn't write. Instead the student teacher quizzed them on the details of the movie. Because the students responded to his questions with only a word or two, he ended up doing most of the talking. The students looked bored and anxious for the period to end. Before the class began, the host teacher had told me this particular group of seniors was not in the least curious about learning anything. It was difficult to get them to participate in any class discussions even when he, for example, tried to make them angry enough to get involved by playing devil's advocate.

What the host teacher told me was borne out by what I saw when I observed the class. Perhaps you're thinking now, as I did then, that the student teacher reinforced the students' lack of involvement. Imagine how a different approach might have increased student participation. For example, if the teacher wanted to make sure students knew the facts from the movie, he could have asked them to write individual summaries. He could collect the summaries and see how much students understood, or, better yet, he could ask students to read summaries in small groups and share in developing an improved group summary that he could collect, or which the groups could report to the rest of the class.

If the teacher wanted students to extend and apply what they learned from the movie, he could have had them write and then discuss, either in small groups or as a whole class, issues and questions that the movie raised. Other possibilities for getting the students more actively involved in thinking and talking about what they learned could include such activities as role playing characters from the movie, holding a debate on the issues, or writing diary entries the characters might have written at different points in the film.

Many of the complaints students have about school center around the fact that what they're learning has little to do with real life. If teachers plan assignments more creatively, however, they can involve students in projects that both reinforce their learning and get them out into the community. Some examples follow. I'm sure you can think of others.

- Researching local history by interviewing senior citizens.
- Surveying community attitudes about environmental, political, or social issues.
- Tutoring younger students.
- Researching pricing in grocery stories or housing costs in the community.
- Investigating what cultural, social, or educational resources are available in the community.

These kinds of projects mean that the whole class won't always be doing the same assignments at the same time. Because students will have to do much of the work outside of school, teachers will have to enlist the help of parents and others. That's a benefit for everyone, because education is everyone's business. We need closer cooperation between the home and the school, as well as between businesses and community agencies and the school. When students extend the classroom into the community, they are more likely to become lifetime learners because they see that learning can take place anywhere, and they have the opportunity to come in contact with many different possible role models.

By meeting adults who have various kinds of jobs in the community, students may discover career paths they had never thought about. The awareness of such a possibility can lead them to set future goals. If school makes more sense to them, they will work harder and be much less likely to drop out.

In an article entitled, "When Teaching Thinking Does Not Work, What Goes Wrong?" Robert Sternberg lists ten ways in which the problems students often are given to do in school differ from everyday problems.

1. "In the everyday world, the first and sometimes most difficult step in problem solving is the recognition that a problem exists."

2. "In everyday problem solving, it is often harder to figure out just what the problem is than to figure out how to solve it."
3. "Everyday problems tend to be ill-structured."
4. "In everyday problem solving, it is not usually clear just what information will be needed to solve a given problem, nor is it always clear where the requisite information can be found."
5. "The solutions to everyday problems depend on and interact with the contexts in which the problems are presented."
6. "Everyday problems generally have no one right solution, and even the criteria for what constitutes a best solution are often not clear."
7. "The solutions to everyday problems depend at least as much on informal knowledge as on formal knowledge."
8. "Solutions to important everyday problems have consequences that matter."
9. "Everyday problem solving often occurs in groups."
10. "Everyday problems can be complicated, messy, and stubbornly persistent."

By contrast, school and textbook problems are clearly presented and easily understood, because they relate directly to a limited amount of material recently covered in class or included in a textbook chapter. Students usually have all the information they need to solve the problems right at hand. Moreover, these "dummy problems" have been constructed to have one right solution. Students get little practice for real life because too much already has been done for them.

Students working together on a project, however, do have to deal with issues in much the same way they would in confronting everyday problems. The group process itself has most of the characteristics Sternberg assigns to everyday problems. Students probably will be frustrated in their attempts to get information, they will have interpersonal problems within the group to identify and solve, and they will have to figure out what resources are available to help solve them. Unlike artificial and easily solved textbook problems, group projects, even when the teacher is available to assist and advise, closely simulate real-life problems.

Independent and group projects that require students themselves to be responsible for most of the planning also help them develop the ability to think creatively. Psychologist Dr. Perry Buffington, who believes that the idea that creativity is linked to intelligence is a myth, identifies five stages of creative thought: "1) orientation–to define a problem and identify its dimensions; 2) overpreparation–to flood oneself with information related to the problem; 3) incubation–to forget the problem for a while, to let it simmer; 4) illumination–the 'aha experience'; and 5) verification–the testing period." He says that creativity is "a combination of intuitiveness, enthusiasm, flexibility, independence, initiative, and intelligence." Buffington's five steps, and the qualities he assigns to creativity, are all necessary for the successful completion of student-designed projects. Giving students practice in honing their abilities to think creatively is important to their future success. As futurist Marvin Cetron points out, "these are the same characteristics desired of the ideal worker by most employers," and the stages Buffington describes also closely describe "the way most people learn."

The examples of assignments and projects included here should give you an idea of the ways teachers can make learning more meaningful for students. Teachers in classrooms across the country have engaged students in innovative ways–your own children may be fortunate enough to have such a teacher–but too many students are stuck in classes with teachers who, without intending to, turn them off to learning. We need to work to make sure that all teachers find ways to get students to think and to learn every day in every subject. Changing the status quo doesn't mean that teachers have to give up the old methods; but it does mean they need to add new strategies to their repertoire and to be more thoughtful about what they are doing and why.

Suggestions for Parents

Don't be tempted to do your children's work for them. When you do, they miss a good opportunity to develop their own skills. Parents can help best by listening to children's concerns, discussing their plans and problems with them, and monitoring their progress.

Encourage your children to begin their own personal spelling and vocabulary dictionaries and to read widely. (Limiting time for TV may help in this regard.) Make current events part of the family's conversations. Read newspapers and magazines. Share interesting articles with each other.

If your children are given an assignment that doesn't require them to think, try to provide a meaningful context for it: tell them how the information or skill might be useful in the real world, or extend the assignment by talking about it with them.

Help your children learn to plan, complete, and reflect on school assignments by using the ten-question guide that appears in this chapter. Also, the ten tips that follow should help any student become more successful in school:

1. Designate a special study area at home and use it consistently.
2. Collect needed reference books and supplies. If you don't have your own desk, put them in a box that you can get out when you sit down to do your work at the table in the kitchen after dinner.
3. Schedule a regular homework time and stick to it.
4. Use a calendar and plan ahead. Record regular commitments, such as athletics practice and dancing lessons, as well as holidays and special events. When you have a big project to do, begin work early so you can take time off if something unexpected comes up. Being ahead is better than being behind, and staying caught up is easier than getting caught up.
5. Organize your notebook(s). Use a looseleaf-binder with separate sections for each subject. Include a few pocket pages to hold small sheets of paper and other materials that can't be hole-punched.
6. Get a tote bag or backpack for carrying things to and from school and keep everything you'll need in it. Put it where you can't miss it in the morning.
7. Listen carefully in class.
8. Ask questions immediately when you don't understand. Get help when you need it.
9. Use writing to help you learn in every subject.
10. Spend more time reading than watching TV.

Chapter Nine

New Ways of Evaluating What Students Learn

NEARLY EVERYONE has an interest in knowing how students are doing in school. Taxpayers want to know what they're getting for their money, and how well local schools measure up against schools in other communities. Parents want to know how their children compare with others and if they're doing well enough to meet the standards for college admission. Students themselves want to know where they stand. Test scores and grades traditionally have been used to provide this kind of information.

Critics view lower scores on standardized tests as an indication that schools are failing to do a good job of teaching. They demand that schools get back to emphasizing "the basics." But what is "basic?" Will our students be prepared to live in the twenty-first century if they know enough to get higher scores on standardized tests—tests that require only that students choose one answer from the five provided? The answer is probably no, unless we redesign tests to measure a wider variety of knowledge and skills. Efforts are already underway by the NAEP to add a performance-based component to the multiple-choice questions typically found on national tests. Students will respond to open-ended questions and write essays, but the cost of having people score these responses is much greater than that for the multiple-choice questions, which can be machine-scored. We must be willing to spend the money it will take to develop and administer better tests. Even more expensive and more difficult to standardize are "assessment strategies," which attempt to evaluate what students know by having them discuss their work with an evaluator.

It is estimated that the cost of standardized testing in U.S. schools is close to $900 million a year. The National Commission on Testing and Public Policy says that some students in some grade levels take as many as twelve tests per year. All told, students from kindergarten through twelfth grade take about 127 million tests annually. Despite all this there is no true national test, so several groups are now working to develop national standards and assessment proposals. The idea of a national test linked to national standards for curriculum and instruction has provoked a great deal of debate, because there is still a very strong feeling that states and local communities should maintain control. Meanwhile, as everyone works to develop new forms of assessment or argues about the wisdom of setting national standards, students continue to take traditional standardized tests, and parents should consider what these tests don't do.

Even with tests that measure students' ability to think and solve complex problems, there is much we can't learn from them. Test scores show what students actually do at one moment in time with a particular set of questions and tasks. A test is more like a snapshot than a motion picture. Tests don't show what students are capable of doing at other times or in other contexts. Whether scores are high or low, they don't indicate why students scored the way they did. We have no way of knowing, for example, how much the scores reflect the teaching methods and textbooks students were exposed to, students' home lives or personal situations, or students' own personal motivation. In reporting the results of many state and national tests, the media usually fail to point out that students have little incentive for doing well on them. Unlike the SAT score, which may make a difference about college admission, the NAEP does not "count" for anything. Students may not take these tests as seriously as they would a teacher-made test that will be figured into their grades.

Even when students do their best to answer test questions correctly, they may be penalized for not sharing the background of the testmaker. Critics, maintaining that standardized tests are biased against minority children, have forced testmakers to revise tests, but it's probably impossible to make tests fair for everyone. When an elementary child in a Franco-American community read the name "Jose" on a test (chosen, no doubt, to make the test more friendly for a Hispanic child), he had no idea that Jose was a boy's first name. No one he ever knew was named Jose!

No test requiring students to give one right answer to a question can ever be made totally fair for every child. One mother I know discovered that her older daughter had incorrectly answered the question, "Where does bacon come from?" on a standardized test. She began playing a game with the nine-year-old and her twin sisters, who are five. "Where does milk come from?" "Where does ham come from?" As they were playing the game one day, someone asked the twins, "Where does hamburger come from?" One answered, "Elk," and the other said, "Deer." Of course, the correct response on a standardized test would be "cattle or cow," but these children didn't respond as expected because the hamburger they ate did come from deer and elk–their father was an avid hunter. How much can we rely on test results when they are scored by machines and no one asks children how they arrived at their answers? How many times might your children have marked the wrong choices on a standardized test because they interpreted items differently from the testmaker?

Another fact that often goes unmentioned is that only a small percentage of students in individual states actually take the sorts of tests on which the national media report. Thus, even if the results do reflect the performance of students in general, they are not based on the actual scores of all students. In the case of the SAT, only students who plan to go on to college take the test. The number of students who further their education after high school is much greater now than it was thirty years ago, and that may account in part for the drop in scores. Even the experts don't agree on the reasons for the decline in SAT scores. The debate continues.

If the public knew more about the tests, more people might question the usefulness of the results. Several years ago, when I was a high school teacher, Maine did a one-time assessment of all high school juniors. The test included questions that were very basic, even simplistic, such as one designed to find out whether students could read road signs. Students were also asked to write a short essay explaining how an accident diagrammed in the test booklet occurred. I'll never forget the test day. We herded all of the juniors—about 300 students—into the armory next door to the school for the three-hour test. What I witnessed during that test session has made me forever skeptical about standardized test results.

The bright students found the test ridiculously easy and breezed through it with hours to spare. Motivated to do well, they tried to answer the questions correctly. The students who didn't like school and rarely did their best on any school task treated the test as a big joke. Some students later told me they purposely answered questions wrong—a way of rebelling against a system they felt treated them like prisoners. They, too, finished early. Yet everyone had to stay for the full three hours because the principal, never anticipating that students might not need that much time, had no alternate plan. So we teachers were trapped in that armory for what seemed like years with a very restless group of teenagers who had nothing to do.

When the test results were made public, many people believed that they had useful information about student performance. Without seeing the test itself and the way it was administered in many schools, and without knowing the students' attitudes toward it, they had no way of knowing how little those test results meant. Now that Maine has instituted an annual assessment of fourth-, eighth-, and eleventh-graders, and test results for individual schools are published in the newspaper, test administration has improved considerably. Students are pressured to do well even though the tests don't count in their grades. Nevertheless, other factors that may not be apparent even to the people who collect and report the scores still influence test results.

In announcing an NAEP report that showed little or no improvement in student writing skills since testing began in the early Seventies, a television reporter read one student's essay as an example of the poor performance of students in general. Students had been asked to write a letter applying for a summer job.

The piece the reporter read went something like this: "I want a summer job where I can earn lots of money and don't have to work hard." Viewers, no doubt, were appalled to think this essay was typical of many eleventh-grade students. I might have felt the same way had I not scored hundreds of essays on this same topic for a state writing assessment.

The reporter did not show viewers how this task was presented in the test booklet. If the student whose essay he read had used the same form of the question as the students whose essays *I* read, he or she might have been confused about the task. The test booklet for the exam I scored included an application form to make the writing task seem more real. Unfortunately, students didn't know that they would be scored only on the letter they wrote beneath the form. Many students filled in the form and listed a specific job there but neglected to mention that position in the letter below. They assumed, and rightly so for a real job application, that someone would read both the form *and* their letter. But the people who scored the essays were directed to base their evaluation only on the information as it appeared in the letter.

The essay the reporter used also illustrates another problem. The NAEP essay was scored as a writing task, and the reporter used it as an example of a student's inability to write. But the essay was perhaps a better indication of this teenager's values as they were formed by the society in which he or she lives, or as an impulsive, less-than-serious response to a test that has no personal meaning or consequences.

Furthermore, some students don't test well. A student named Pauline was assigned to my adult developmental reading course because she scored very low on the placement test. She also had done poorly on the writing test. Until I talked with her, I couldn't figure out why she had been placed in my class. She read and wrote so much better than the other students that she didn't seem to belong in a remedial class. I later learned that she never had tested well. Even when she was in elementary school she got low scores on standardized tests. It was no surprise that her score on the reading test was low even after a whole semester of work–she worked so slowly on the test that she didn't finish. The test score didn't reflect what she could do. I intervened on her behalf and got the college to waive the requirement that she waste another semester in a remedial writing course she didn't need. Other students earn low scores because they freeze on standardized tests, but there isn't any way this fact can be noted in the results.

Typical standardized tests cannot measure the full range of student accomplishments. How then can teachers determine how well students do? By what standards can teachers, students, parents, and others evaluate student progress? How can this information be collected and shared?

Classroom learning will probably always be translated into some form of letter grading, but the letter grade can reflect a variety of assessments in addition to scores on tests. And test scores themselves can reflect something other than the percentage of questions answered correctly out of the total asked. Holistic scoring, for example, which was developed as a way of standardizing the scoring of written essays for national exams, can be used in the classroom.

Holistic scoring can take a variety of forms, but, as the name suggests, the score is based on the "whole" product, not an evaluation of its individual parts. Score ranges might be 1–4, 1–6, or 1–9—the highest number usually designating the best work. Sample responses that reflect the whole range of scores are chosen and established as "rangefinders." The people who are to score the essays use the rangefinders and score sample papers until there is a consensus in the group about the scores particular papers should be given. Readers, as the scorers are usually called, do not correct the papers (though they do rate them), but rather take into account all features of the writing as they read the papers they are given to score. Thus, for example, they do not count spelling errors, but they consider misspelled words along with organization, development, and other features of the essay to determine a score that reflects how successful the piece of writing is as a whole. Holistically scored papers are usually scored by two readers, and, if there is a discrepancy of two or more points, the essay is read by a third person.

Another form of scoring that provides more specific information is called analytic scoring. Writing done for the Maine Educational Assessment used to be scored in much the same way as described above, except that readers scored essays in six categories rather than one: topic development, organization, details, sentences, wording, and mechanics. The readers did not correct papers or count the number of errors. They determined a score for each area by reading through the paper and comparing it to the sample essays used as rangefinders. (The Maine Assessment now notes strengths and weaknesses in the six categories but does not assign points for them. The change in scoring was made because of cost. By eliminating the category scores, readers could finish the job faster and thus reduce the expense for scoring.)

After reading hundreds of student essays both for state and national assessments, I have come to realize that more often than not the whole is greater or less than the sum of the parts; rarely is there a match. For example, I've read some powerfully written essays that were outstanding pieces of writing despite a number of spelling and punctuation errors, and, on the other hand, I've seen just as many papers with nearly perfect surface features that said nothing. Classroom teachers can easily work with students in the first category to improve their ability to use standard punctuation, usage, and spelling, but it's a much more difficult task to help students develop ideas, to put words together that say something worth saying. Writing is thinking, and thinking is more than knowing how to apply rules.

Teachers can adapt the technique of holistic scoring to grade projects and group activities that do not easily lend themselves to standard grading practices. They can, for example, develop a list of criteria by which a project or activity will be evaluated, share it with students before they begin work, and then "score" the final products themselves. They also can ask students to score each other's work, or invite other teachers, the principal, or even parents to help.

Some states and many teachers have begun to use portfolios as a means of assessing student progress. Unlike tests, which are snapshots of what students can do at a particular moment in time, portfolios show what students have done over a long period of time. Like artists who collect representative samples of their work to show to an editor or ad agency, students gather samples that document their learning.

Many writing teachers have used portfolio assessment for a long time, although they may not use that term to describe it. Rather than grade each individual piece of writing students do, they ask students to collect their work in folders, which include not only some finished pieces but also notes, previous drafts, journal entries, and unfinished pieces as well. Several times during the quarter and again just before grades are due, teachers may ask students to go through their folders and assess what they have accomplished. Sometimes students choose their best work, which teachers will grade in a standard way. Other times they may be asked to evaluate their work as a whole against previously established criteria.

Students and teachers get a much better idea of what individuals have accomplished by looking at a wide range of work at one time. The folders also show how much effort students have exerted—something teachers often want to count in course grades, but can't usually document when they grade in a traditional way. For example, the student who's a gifted writer can often earn high grades without putting in a great deal of time, while a struggling student can put in many more hours and end up with a lower grade. The portfolio-folder approach, used along with graded papers, takes both into account. Folders themselves can be given a letter grade if the teacher sets up criteria and uses a holistic method for scoring them. Statewide assessment of portfolios involves a similar scoring process based on preestablished criteria.

The portfolio concept can be extended with the use of technology. At the Key School in Indianapolis, for example, students' projects, activities, and personal observations are documented on videotape. The tapes, which can be reviewed later by parents, allow a much wider range of accomplishment to be demonstrated. And students, too, can see concrete evidence of how much they've grown and learned.

When students get out of school, they'll have to assess their own progress toward goals they set for themselves. Many of the newer teaching methods give students an opportunity to set their own goals in ways that traditional teacher-directed learning do not. It makes sense, then, to ask them to assess their own progress toward meeting them.

On long-term individual or group projects, students can focus on their progress as they go along by keeping a process log, in which they document what they did and how it went. When the project or activity is finished, they have a running record of what went into the final product (as well as the product itself), which they can use to evaluate their own learning. By looking at the process as a whole, they can examine in some detail how they could do a better job on a similar project in the future. This kind of self-evaluation gets students to look at the skills necessary for success on many real-world projects: planning, organizing, cooperating with others, and developing a sense of what constitutes quality in a given context.

The pre-test/post-test writing assignments described in Chapter Three are another example of student self-evaluation. When students write what they know about a topic as they begin a course or unit, and then again at the end, they have clear evidence of how much they learned. By reflecting on these two pieces of writing, they can analyze what they learned and how. This kind of self-reflection is much more meaningful to students than any grades teachers could assign to their work. In addition to gaining a sense of their own accomplishments, students learn to evaluate how well they did—exactly what they'll have to do in the real world, where teachers and parents won't be around to tell them.

Teacher-student conferences are yet another way of assessing student learning. Both teachers and students can write narratives describing what students have done during a given time period, and then meet to discuss them. A joint conference is also the best way to consider the work a student has collected in a portfolio, even when it may also be assigned a letter grade. Narrative statements with or without samples of the students' work can be shared with parents or put into students' permanent folders and passed on to future teachers.

Peer evaluation is also effective, and doesn't mean that students "grade" each other. Peer evaluation may be as informal as one student commenting on a piece of writing another read aloud in a small group, or writing a note to the author after reading it silently. Group projects that students present to the whole class can be evaluated by the rest of the students. They can complete an evaluation checklist or write comments on the strengths and weaknesses of the presentation. Sharing and discussing responses in a supportive classroom climate helps students realize that getting feedback on what they do is useful, and that it's possible to consider comments from others as suggestions or other points of view rather than as criticism.

Surprisingly, the introduction of a statewide writing assessment in Maine spawned more peer evaluation of writing. Several teachers who learned to use the analytic scoring process as readers for Maine Educational Assessment took the scoring guide back to their classrooms. They taught students to score essays in the same manner used for the statewide assessment. Some teachers regularly asked students to score each other's classroom writing using this process. Not only did students improve their writing, but they also were better prepared to take the test in the future because they understood how their writing would be evaluated. A chemistry teacher even adapted the scoring guide to use with lab reports. Two high school English teachers in separate communities had their students score each other's essays throughout the year. At the end of the year, the students (who had not met each other previously) got together for a day-long writing workshop at an area college.

Most people generally operate on the assumption that an A on a test or in a course means that a student has learned well. Yet we all know that letter grades aren't really a reliable measure of anything. Students taking a course from one teacher can get A's very easily, while students enrolled in the same course taught by another teacher have to work very hard to earn the same grades. The A's look the same on report cards and will be counted equally when used to figure class standing or honor roll status, but grades are not a good reflection of student performance. Thus, along with grades, we should consider other ways students can demonstrate what they have accomplished. Teachers can make grades more meaningful by including students in the process of determining them.

Students often forego responsibility for not having done well by blaming the teacher for their low grades: "She doesn't like me," "He wouldn't give me a chance to take the test again even though I told him I had been sick and couldn't study for it," "I turned my homework in, but the teacher said I didn't." Teachers can avoid such comments and get students to focus on evaluating what *they* have done by making self-evaluation part of the grading process.

At the beginning of the course, teachers can let students know the criteria on which their grades will be based, and ask them to keep their own records of what they do in the class. In a science class, for example, the teacher may state that the quarter grades will be based on the following: homework 20 percent, classwork and class participation 20 percent, lab reports 15 percent, term project 15 percent, and tests and quizzes 30 percent. She may tell students that they have the option of redoing any graded assignment for extra credit, so that students are encouraged to improve their standing throughout the grading period. They keep a list of what they do, the grades they receive, and the extra work they do. No category is weighted so heavily that a student who does poorly in only one area will fail, and the extra-credit option gives every student the chance to recoup losses when they don't do well.

The week before the quarter ends, the teacher asks students to complete a self-evaluation of their work and determine the grades they should get based on the preestablished criteria. They turn in their quarter gradesheets along with information justifying the grades they feel they have earned. In their written statements they have the opportunity to remind teachers of their individual contributions to class discussions, and to explain any extra work they might have done—areas where the teacher may not have specific information documented. The teacher, having first evaluated students based on records she has kept and penciled in tentative quarter grades, reviews the students' self-evaluations and compares their grades to hers. When she and the student are not in agreement, she can then meet with the student privately to discuss their differing perceptions and arrive at a grade both can support.

This process encourages students to assume responsibility for themselves; the grade is not something teachers "do" to students but a reflection of their own effort and achievement. Although the grades themselves still don't tell the full story, the grading process enables students to realize that how well they do is within their control, and motivates them to work harder.

People often comment that kids work harder playing basketball or football than they do in the classroom. Of course, playing sports is voluntary while taking a school subject is often a requirement, but there's another important difference as well. Other people get to see the results of the time and effort students spend learning and practicing skills on the basketball court, while what these students usually do in social studies or English is a private affair. Because no one wants to look foolish in public, students want to do well. When they have a good game, they also get recognition – their names are mentioned in newspaper or TV stories, words of praise come from parents, friends, and others. The positive feedback feels good, so they work even harder to get more of it.

In the last few years, academic competitions such as the Olympics of the Mind have been expanded so that intellectual achievement can be fostered in the same manner as athletic accomplishment. Writing teachers, however, have discovered that they can increase student motivation with public performance in less organized ways. When students write for audiences outside the classroom, they work harder to make their writing interesting, understandable, and correct. When their work reaches a wider audience, students get the same kind of feedback that basketball players get when they play a game.

The work students do in any subject can be made public, and doing so not only benefits the students. The general public gets a real understanding of what students know, which they cannot get from a mere reporting of test scores or grades. Public displays also make it possible for students to demonstrate a wider range of ability and accomplishment. Standardized tests, for example, don't give students who are artistically talented or very creative a chance to show their stuff–in fact, creative thinkers are often penalized on such tests, because they interpret questions in ways the testmakers never anticipated and thus choose the wrong answers.

Public display may also make standardized test results more useful and understandable. When the tests include essay responses, for instance, the general public might be better served if, along with the numbers, they are also given sample essays that represent the range of scores. Even if the tests are limited in what they measure, the ordinary citizen will have a better sense of what the numbers mean if they have some context in which to consider them.

There's been a great deal of talk about issuing state and school "report cards," which show how a state or school stacks up against other states or school districts. Maine, for example, has already been issuing annual report cards for school districts that compare statistics, such as the dropout rate, standardized test scores, and the like. Proponents of report cards believe that the information is useful in determining how much progress local districts make and where they need to make improvements. But although the idea of report cards sounds good in theory, there are problems with it in practice.

Chester E. Finn, Jr., writing in *Education Week,* says we need to collect better data on education: "It is a near certainty that those annual education 'report cards' the White House and governors have vowed to issue will have a lot of 'incompletes' on them unless urgent efforts are made to gather data nobody now has." Finn points out, for example, that there are no uniform definitions of "dropout," "high school equivalency," or "grade level." Obviously the numbers on report cards will mean little if one district supplies numbers based on one definition and others use different criteria: apples and oranges can't be compared.

Likewise Finn disputes comparisons among states and between the U.S. and other countries. Nobody gives international tests on a regular basis, and because the NAEP doesn't provide information at the state or local level, state data comes from a variety of commercial tests and state assessment programs. In 1990, thirty-seven states voluntarily participated in a project to assess eighth-grade math, but Finn says, "As late as 1993, we will have *no* state-level achievement data in science, history, or writing, nor any for twelfth-graders in any subject, nor for youngsters who have dropped out."

Even with better data in the form of test scores, and agreement on common definitions of "dropout" and "grade level," something important will be missing: some sense of how well students feel their schools are working for them. Numbers can't accurately reflect all of the learning that takes place in a school, but we'd have a better idea of where to make improvements if we also collected and published the results of student attitude surveys. Many state and some national testing programs do include supplemental questionnaires to accompany the tests. Students are asked questions, such as how much homework they're assigned, how much writing they're required to do, and whether they have part-time jobs. But even though this information is collected, it is not reported in a systematic way to the general public.

People often say we can't evaluate schools like businesses because they don't have profits and losses. That may be true in dollars-and-cents terms, but it's not true in terms of customer satisfaction. And we can measure that by asking students how they feel about their schools and teachers, and whether they think what they're learning is meaningful. If test scores were reported along with student attitudes, we could look, for example, at individual schools to determine what might account for positive student attitudes, or what correlation exists, if any, between positive attitudes and higher test scores.

Short-term results, however, are not enough. Just as a customer may report being very satisfied with a new washing machine a year after it was purchased, that same customer may be very unhappy with the purchase two years later if the appliance required extensive repairs and the service was poor. Students are often unaware of how much their education helped or hindered them until long after they've graduated, and teachers and principals have no way of knowing how what they do will affect a student in the future. Sometimes something good happens even when they think they have failed.

As a high school assistant principal in charge of discipline, for example, I had several confrontations with a student named

Mary Ann. She was often late to school and skipped classes occasionally, but I remember her best because I caught her smoking marijuana in the girls' bathroom twice. Each time she proclaimed her innocence despite the evidence to the contrary, and she was bitter and resentful about my suspending her from school. We never had one positive exchange during the years she was in high school. If someone had asked me how I had helped Mary Ann when she graduated, I would have said I didn't help her at all. My role as a disciplinarian had just increased her hostility to adults in general. Two years after Mary Ann graduated and I had left that school to be a principal in another town, I received a letter from her. She told me she was a college sophomore majoring in biology, wanted to thank me for all I had done for her, and said that she wished I were still at the high school so I could help her younger sister. I was very surprised and, of course, very pleased, although I had no idea exactly how I had helped her.

We need to collect data on student perceptions over time. The results of student satisfaction, both in the long term and in the short term, should be considered along with test scores in evaluating how well schools or school districts are doing. Teachers often say that they can't overcome the effects of students' personal or family problems outside of school, and they're right. But finding out how former students are doing, and what effect school may have had on their lives after they left, could help us better handle more immediate situations.

Many teachers are beginning to think of themselves as researchers. They want to know *how* students learn, so they can change their teaching methods to help students learn better. A math teacher, for example, may not correct students when they come up with the wrong answers but instead ask them to explain how they got them. By understanding their misunderstandings or idiosyncratic ways of approaching the problems, he can prevent students from using inappropriate strategies.

In order to find out more about how children learn to use language, both oral and written, many teachers of preschool and primary students collect a wide variety of data on individual students: notes on conversations with them, information from parents, examples of their writing, records of their classroom behavior and interaction with other students—in short, all the material one would collect for a case study. Of course, they can't do extensive case studies on every student, but as they focus on one or two students, they also gather some information on all of them. The more they learn about the process of learning, the better able they are to create a classroom environment and activities that promote rather than hinder learning.

This kind of information, much more useful to teachers than test scores, is also more meaningful to parents. Teachers no longer have to give parents impersonal checklists when they report student progress. Instead they can write profiles of students, which not only let parents know specifically what their children can do, but also how they go about doing it. Parents in turn can support classroom learning by giving children more opportunities to develop language skills at home. Such personal profiles of children collected as they progress through school become biographies of their school experiences, and reflect a broad range of information about the skills and weaknesses of individual students. Future teachers can build on students' past experiences, because their records reveal a depth and quantity of information that cannot be found in numbers. Unlike the random collection of anecdotal information that teachers sometimes included in students' records in the past, these profiles offer a continuous view of students' development over time.

Standardized test scores are not sufficient to evaluate school quality, any more than letter grades or test scores are enough to evaluate individual student achievement. We need to expand our views of how to assess education in general and students in particular. Human minds and personalities are too complex to be reduced to numbers and symbols. While we will probably always want to have some quantitative data to compare schools and students in general terms, we shouldn't limit our assessment to that kind of data, or use it as the basis for making all of our educational decisions. Much more research and development are needed for us to improve the whole process of assessment. And we must be willing to spend money to do it. Otherwise we will continue to waste our resources on reforms that will not produce the results we want.

Many critics of public education point to lower test scores and grade inflation as evidence that standards have eroded. They want schools to toughen requirements and raise students' test scores. Often they oppose innovative approaches because they fear we'll create schools where teachers and students will have a good time but won't be teaching and learning much. But more personalized learning and teaching will not lead to chaos and mediocrity.

SAT scores may not even be necessary to maintain high admission standards at colleges and universities. A study conducted at Bates College, a highly selective liberal arts college that no longer requires students to submit any test scores, found that those who didn't submit SAT scores performed as well as those who did. Moreover, applications have increased overall while applications from minority students have doubled since Bates dropped the SAT requirement.

Most standardized tests are norm-referenced, which means that half of all students who take them will be rated below average. How can we expect the less able students (or the school districts with large percentages of disadvantaged students) to stay motivated if they come out "below average" no matter how hard they try? Greater use of criterion-referenced tests would help. On a criterion-referenced test, an individual student is ranked against a pre-set standard, not others who have taken the test. (The driver's license exam is a good example of a criterion-referenced test. Consider how few teenagers fail to pass this exam.) Thus, it's theoretically possible for everyone who takes the test to earn top scores. And we shouldn't forget that test scores affect students' self-esteem; as Maslow points out, people cannot work to achieve if their esteem needs are not met. Therefore, we must be careful as we measure student achievement that the process itself doesn't *prevent* the achievement we are trying to measure.

Greater emphasis on test scores has forced teachers to teach to the tests. They limit classroom assignments to drill and memorization, because many of our present tests focus on recall of information and the ability to use rather simple skills. Students don't see meaning and purpose in work like this, so they do less and learn less. It's ironic that in our attempts to improve education, we've actually made the situation worse.

Good education lies not so much in placing more restrictions on teachers and students—mandated curricula, more required courses, more time in school, and more tests—as it does in reducing (*not* eliminating) the obstacles that stand in the way of teachers creating classroom environments where quality can flourish. We must value meaning more highly than measurement, and look for ways to make measurement more meaningful. And we must be willing to spend the extra money necessary to develop and administer better tests.

If we really want students to achieve in school, it's time to practice what we so often preach: those who fail to learn from history are condemned to repeat the mistakes of the past. Because we have focused too much on measurement rather than meaning, generations of students have had mediocre educations. Society has suffered from our misguided efforts. If we want students who view themselves as capable and worthwhile people; who know how to read, write, think, and solve problems; and who love and value learning, then we must expand the ways we assess and evaluate what they learn in school. The old ways clearly haven't been good enough. If the high standards we set and the means we use to determine how well they are being met cause students and schools to get discouraged and give up, then we might be better off not setting standards in the first place.

We must rethink our standards and design better ways of finding out how well they are being met. And in the process of doing this, we shouldn't forget that one of the school's most important roles is helping students set their own high standards, and assume the responsibility for achieving them.

Suggestions for Parents

Find out what kinds of tests are being given in your children's schools *and* how the results are being used. In the lower grades students may be assigned to reading or math groups for the entire year on the basis of one test score. There are many reasons why a child may do poorly on a test, only one of which is a lack of ability.

Let the school know in writing that you do not want your child placed in any group or class on the basis of a test score without your prior knowledge and permission. Schools are required to obtain your permission for special education placement, but some schools routinely give screening tests at the beginning of the year to determine placement for reading or math groups without telling parents. You may be unaware that your children are in lower (or higher) groups than they were the previous year.

Ask teachers or guidance counselors to explain tests and test scores to you, and do some reading on your own. The National Center for Fair and Open Testing (342 Broadway, Cambridge, MA 02139) provides publications that will help any parent become test-smart. One booklet, *Standardized Tests and Our Children: A Guide to Testing Reform,* should be required reading for every parent. It explains in understandable language what scores on standardized tests mean, how tests are used and misused, and why reform is needed. There's much that parents often misunderstand. A grade equivalent score, for example, does not mean that children who score high can do the work at a higher grade level. The grade equivalent is merely another way to report the score. If the test is given in the fifth month of the fifth grade, 5.5 is the average score for students in the fifth grade who take the test. A score of 7.5, then, doesn't mean a child is doing seventh-grade work, but only that the child has done very well on this test as compared to other fifth graders who have taken the test. As with any norm-referenced test, half the students who take it will earn scores higher than 5.5; half will earn scores lower than 5.5.

Work with other parents to lobby for changes in evaluation and assessment that will benefit students—portfolios, hands-on tasks—and to reduce or eliminate standardized test scores as a major factor in determining placement. Consider also the benefits of replacing ability grouping with more flexible classroom structures and teaching methods that accommodate children with developmental differences.

Chapter Ten

Helping Your Children Succeed

IT'S FASHIONABLE THESE DAYS for people to hold up Japanese schools as a model for us to emulate. There are many reasons why comparisons between American and Japanese education are not valid, but one important difference lies not in the schools but in our different cultures. Japanese people—as well as other Asians who have emigrated to the United States in recent years—provide a great deal more support for their children's education than does the typical American family.

The fact that fewer Japanese women have jobs outside the home, and that single-parent households (increasingly more common in the U.S.) are almost unknown in Japan means that Japanese mothers have more time to devote to their children's education. Support and encouragement for children in school is more important in Japan than it is here, because Japanese children are tracked for future careers very early, depending on how well they do in school. In the U.S., students who do poorly in school can still attend a community college, whereas Japanese students who do not perform well are diverted to vocational or other training. College is not a choice for everyone as it is here. In fact, in order to increase their children's chances of passing the exams that lead to college, Japanese parents also make school an extracurricular activity for their children. Many students attend special classes in private schools after their regular school day has ended.

University of Michigan psychologist Harold W. Stevenson, who compared more than 7,000 American students in kindergarten, first grade, third grade, and fifth grade with their counterparts in China, Japan, and Taiwan, found that Americans did the worst at all grade levels on a battery of math tests. Since he found no differences in IQ, and the performance differences are showing up even in kindergarten, something must be happening in the family even before children get to school.

These studies and others have led Sanford M. Dornbusch of Stanford University to conclude that Asian parents are able to instill more motivation in their children. His own study of high school students in the San Francisco area show that Asian-Americans spend more time on homework, cut fewer classes, and pay more attention to the teacher than other students.

Despite the differences in our cultures and educational systems, we can learn an important lesson from the Japanese: parental support can affect children's school success. Children who do well in school most often have parents who value education, who hold high expectations for their children, who get involved with their children's education, who provide opportunities for children to learn outside of school, and who are good role models for children. There's much you can do to help your children succeed in school.

Early Learning

Most of school learning depends upon children's ability to use spoken and written language. You can do a great deal to stimulate both your children's language development as well as their love of language, even before they are old enough for school. Some people even believe that reading aloud while children are still in the womb will have positive effects. Even if you are a bit skeptical about that possibility, you no doubt accept the idea that reading aloud to children and making objects, pictures, and books available for them, even when they're very young, makes sense. Perhaps even more important to their language development is the opportunity to hear and use language in a variety of situations. Many of the suggestions listed below apply not only to toddlers and preschoolers but also to children who are in school.

Provide a stimulating environment. Children need color, variety, and challenge—lots of things to explore and experiment with. There's no need to buy out the local toy store, though, since children may be better off playing with objects that require them to use their creativity. Blocks of wood or pots and pans may hold no fascination for us, but they are new and different to children. Young children can learn a great deal from fooling around with simple toys rather than fancy ones. Toys such as Legos, which allow them to be creative, will increase their ability to figure things out on their own and nurture their curiosity. Even if the toys themselves aren't creative, children can be encouraged to use them in creative ways. Ask children to make up their own stories about the Ninja Turtles or Barbie and Ken. Let them hear a variety of music as background for their play rather than just the sound emanating from the TV set.

Talk to your children. Don't use baby talk when you engage children in conversation. Begin talking to them early. They learn from hearing you speak even before they are able to speak themselves. As children get older, try to remember to listen more than you lecture.

Think aloud as you go about your daily chores. Children can pick up a great deal of language and information if you talk aloud to yourself as you work. "I'm taking this hamburger out of the freezer now so it will defrost for dinner." "I'm putting your jacket on because it's cold outside today." Of course, very young children won't understand what you're saying, but if you get in the habit of explaining what you are doing and why, they'll learn from you as they develop language skills. When you're out and about with your child, point out signs and words and read them aloud.

Discuss problems with your children. If children are afraid of the dark, don't automatically leave the light on. Talk to them about their feelings and ask them what they think might help. It's never too early for children to begin thinking about creative ways to solve problems. If children come up with an idea, they'll be more likely to use it than one you suggest.

Don't discourage questions. Children can easily drive you crazy by peppering you with one question after another. They learn by asking such questions, so don't try to squelch them. Instead, ask them what they think the answer might be, and later try to fill in with information you have that they don't. Even unanswerable questions are worth asking. That's the stuff of which philosophy and literature are often made. We want children to become lifelong learners, and question-asking is essential for that. When older children ask questions you can't answer, make finding the answers a joint activity.

Read aloud to your children and discuss what you read. Before children begin to talk, you can read to them, point out the pictures, and explain what's been read. When your children can respond, ask them questions about the text and the pictures. One study has shown that children learn language faster when they are active participants rather than passive listeners. Grover Whitehurst and researchers at the State University of New York at Stony Brook found that children actively involved at story time showed an eight-and-a-half-month advantage in verbal expression and a six-month advantage in vocabulary over children who were simply read to. The parents in the study were trained to ask open-ended questions on the child's answers and provide praise when reading to their two- or three-year-olds. Children who participate actively in this way are gaining experience for school, because teachers expect students to respond to reading in a similar way.

Don't stop reading aloud to children, even when they learn to read on their own. Let them read to you. Consider making family read-aloud time a regular event. The proliferation of books on tape shows that adults can benefit from and enjoy being read to. Get books with accompanying tapes or records for younger children.

Encourage your children to think aloud. If children talk as they play and explain what they are doing, they are actually developing metacognitive skills that later on will help them figure out how to approach school tasks more effectively. They are also developing more language fluency.

Ask open-ended questions. Questions like "Did you have a good time?" or "Is that a fort you're building?" require only a one-word answer. Even adult conversations are fostered by open-ended questions that encourage talk. You can learn a great deal by encouraging children to talk more. Instead of a question that can be answered with one word, try "Tell me about the party," or "Tell me what you've built there." As children talk, you'll pick up information that will help you understand them better and allow you to extend the conversation.

Encourage children to play with language. As soon as children can appreciate and understand them, make riddles, jokes, rhymes, and songs a part of the daily routine. Share them from other sources, make them up, and encourage children to create their own.

Tell stories to each other. Tell children stories about their family history and your own years growing up. Suggest that they ask older relatives to share their personal stories. Family stories can be a wonderful way to learn history from a primary source. Make up stories that include them as characters and encourage them to invent their own. When they're young, they can share them aloud. As they get older, they can also write them down. Older sisters and brothers will benefit from entertaining siblings with stories they create.

Reading

Provide a rich literary environment. Make books, magazines, and newspapers an important part of your home. If there's a variety of literary material around for children to explore and they see you using it, they'll make reading a part of their own lives almost naturally.

Encourage your children to read widely and regularly. Perhaps the best way to foster regular reading is to ask your children to tell you about the books they read.

Introduce children to the library. Take young children to library story hours and let them check books out. Encourage older children to use the library on a regular basis.

Give children their own books and magazine subscriptions. Help children build their own personal libraries by giving them books on birthdays and special occasions. Unlike toys and other items that break or go out of style, books can be treasured forever. Classics can be passed down from one generation to the next. Teach children to love books and to treat them with respect. Everyone enjoys getting mail, and magazine subscriptions are gifts that keep on giving. There are many religious and general interest magazines for young people of various ages and interests. Choose the ones that fit your children best. (See the list of children's magazines in the appendix.)

Let children see you read. What you do speaks more loudly than what you say. Let your kids see you read regularly—newspapers, magazines, and books. Children naturally want to imitate adults and older children. Give them worthwhile activities to copy. If you're more inclined to turn the TV on than pick up a book, they'll have difficulty believing you when you tell them that reading's important.

Share what you read with your children. Let children see how valuable reading can be by talking with them about what you read. Read children's books yourself and suggest to your children that they read the books you think they'll enjoy.

Writing

Specific suggestions for helping children develop as writers appear at the end of Chapter Five, but parents should keep these three general guidelines in mind.

Encourage children to read widely. The best writers are the most avid readers. Reading is also the most effective way for children to learn new words.

Let children see you write. Whether it be notes, letters, journal entries, or reports for work, if your children see you writing, they'll be more comfortable writing themselves.

Make writing activities part of your family life. Use notes to praise and communicate. Surprise children by putting a note in with their lunches. Keep a family journal. Write letters to friends, relatives, and perhaps the editor of the local paper. Ask children to share what they write with the rest of the family.

Television

Television isn't all bad. Children can learn a great deal from watching TV programs, but you may need to help them distinguish what is beneficial from what isn't. TV commercials, for example, are teaching even very young children to be voracious consumers. Explain the strategies companies use in commercials to sell their products.

TV should not be used as a babysitter. Like actively participating in story reading, children benefit from actively engaging in TV viewing.

Monitor the programs your children watch. Review the TV scheduling guides and select good programs for your children to watch. "Reading Rainbow" has value, as do other educational children's shows and a number of specials. If you aren't sure about a particular show and your children beg to watch it, view it with them and talk about it afterwards. Any TV program can be an occasion for learning – even if all that children learn is what not to do.

Combine TV viewing with reading. Many special programs are based on books (or – a more recent development – books have been written from the TV productions). Either before or after viewing one of these programs, have children read the book and then talk with you about the differences they noticed between the printed version of the story and the television production.

Limit the amount of time your children watch TV. Don't let your children become couch potatoes. Make sure they also spend time reading and playing. Consider setting limits, or get your children to agree to spend an hour reading in exchange for an hour watching TV or playing a video game. Let children select a certain number of programs to watch each day. Making good choices is an important aspect of learning.

Watch programs as a family. Choose some regular programs to watch as a family. Make them a special time for the family to get together and then talk about the programs afterward. Get children into the habit of evaluating and thinking about the TV programs they watch.

Make your children active viewers. Ask your children to tell you about the programs they watch. Ask questions. Get them actively involved with the stories and information they get from TV. Use the same techniques for TV viewing that you do when talking with them about books and stories.

Math

Help children see math used in the real world. Point out the occasions when math skills are necessary in cooking, shopping, and other activities.

Give children the opportunity to learn to handle money. Allowances, savings accounts, and payment for extra jobs around the house are all good ways to teach children the value of money and financial planning. One young girl wrote a letter to the Portland (Maine) *Evening Express* to share what she thought was an excellent way to learn about money. Rather than give her an allowance, her parents pay her for each chore she does so she can earn as little or as much as she wants each week–good training for a future job. She pointed out that she didn't get paid for feeding her cat or cleaning its litter box because that's a responsibility that goes with having a pet.

Play math games. On car trips and other times when the family must entertain itself, make multiplication tables and other math problems a way of passing the time.

Use shopping as an opportunity to learn. Children can learn more about math and become better consumers if you involve them in shopping. Teach them about pricing, comparison shopping, and reading product information, much of which includes math in some form.

Share some details of the family budget with older children. When teens want something the family budget can't afford, don't just say no. Show them electric, phone, heating, and other bills. Let them understand that running the home and family budget is a complex enterprise. They'll be less likely to feel resentful when they can't buy a new stereo or the latest-style jeans, and they'll have a more realistic idea of the cost of living.

General Knowledge

Discuss current events with your children. Follow up on TV and print news stories by looking up background information in reference books. Intelligent dinner table conversation supports children's immediate learning and builds good intellectual habits.

Visit museums and art shows. Many people travel to Europe and other far-flung locations to visit museums and historical sites, but have never visited such places in their own immediate area. Consider making a family day trip a once-a-month occasion for visiting interesting and important places close to home. Write entries about these outings in the family journal.

Take children to plays, concerts, and other cultural events. Except perhaps in very remote communities, cultural opportunities are available everywhere in the U.S. Take advantage of the events scheduled in your area. If live events are rarely scheduled where you live, pretend you're actually attending a concert or play by watching televised performances as a family.

Make family vacations educational as well as fun. Even if your major goal on your vacation is relaxation at the beach or in the mountains, take some time to visit historic sites or museums everywhere you go. If you can afford to do so, travel as a family overseas and in other parts of the U.S. What children study in school will be more meaningful if they have actually been to the city or country they are learning about.

Get books and pamphlets for children to read about the places you'll visit before you leave on a family trip. Teach them how to read maps and schedules. Let them help plan the itinerary for the trip as well as possible routes (if you're going by car). Have them keep a journal while you're traveling and make scrapbooks of the trip when you return home. They can collect items for the scrapbook as they travel.

Encourage children to get involved in sports and youth organizations. Go for quality rather than quantity. Some children rush around from one activity to another so fast that they don't have the time or energy to get deeply involved in anything. Children, like adults, also need unscheduled time. If they express interest in taking dance or music lessons, try to find a way to make it possible. If you can't afford private lessons, sometimes they're available free or at low cost through the school or some other organization. Encourage children to investigate their areas of interest—a foreign country or special topic, such as stars, rocks, or insects.

Invest in computer and video games that teach as well as entertain. There are so many products on the market that children should be able to find games they not only enjoy but can also learn from while they're having fun. Explore what's available and help children select games that do more than develop their manual dexterity.

Support for School

Several of the suggestions in this section appeared in earlier chapters. Consider the list below as a general review and an elaboration on some of the points raised earlier.

Provide a place and time for doing homework. Set aside a place and regular hours for your children to do homework. If possible, they should have their own desks and space to store the supplies they'll need. If they must use the kitchen table, get a crate or box for storing their materials that they can bring out when they sit down to work.

Make resources and supplies available. Paper, pens and pencils, rulers, scissors, paste, and other items should be readily available so that children don't have to waste time looking for them or have an excuse not to complete a task. Reference books—dictionary, thesaurus, encyclopedia, almanac, and English handbook—should be on hand. Maps and globes are also very helpful, and the whole family will have occasion to use them.

Teach children to use a personal computer. Word-processing programs make writing easier, and there are many wonderful tutorial programs available on a wide variety of topics. High school students, for example, may wish to prepare for the SAT by using programs developed especially for that purpose. Check with the school for recommendations of educational software that would help your children.

Ask children to show you the assignments they're working on. Children don't need to have parents correct their work so much as they need them to show an interest in what they do. Instead of checking on their homework like a jail guard, ask them to tell you what they've done and what they learned from it. As they explain an assignment to you, they are clarifying it for themselves.

Ask children to tell you what they learned. Talking about new information is an excellent way to reinforce the learning of it. You can help your children become more aware of what they're learning if you ask them every day, "Tell me about what you learned in school today."

Don't do children's homework for them. If children get stuck on an assignment, talk with them. Help them figure out strategies they can try to solve the problem. But remember that the assignment is theirs to do. You can help them best by encouraging them and helping them find ways to complete their work, but you shouldn't do their work for them.

Help children develop good habits for managing their time. Help your children plan their time and keep track of what they need to do by making sure they have a system for writing down assignments and plotting long-range projects on a desk calendar. If they work on long-term projects (such as research papers) over time instead of at the last minute, they'll do a better job. They'll also develop organizing skills that will benefit them later on in life.

A desk calendar is also the place to list other activities and time commitments. The way to stay ahead is to plan ahead. If they want to take a night off to do something special, ask them to use their calendars to show you when they'll get their work done. Consider telling them that their work must be done first if they want to take time off, although they may not be able to do this if their teachers give assignments day-by-day.

Do what you can to help your children become more organized in general. Books and homework papers won't be forgotten at home or at school if you help your children develop a system for carrying things back and forth. They should have a backpack or tote bag in which to carry everything. When they finish studying at night, they should put all their books and papers in the bag so it's ready to go in the morning. Even if they wake up late, they're already set to leave for school. The reverse is true when they leave school in the afternoon. Put the bag in an easy-to-spot location, right beside the door, for example, so it can't be missed in the morning rush.

Keep in touch with your children's teachers. Meet and maintain regular contact with your children's teachers. Make adjustments in the home schedule as needed when there's a problem. It's important to remember that children will be most successful when the home and school work together.

Show your children that adults learn, too. Take courses for personal enrichment or job advancement. Most community adult education programs offer a wide variety of courses. You're likely to find classes available in auto repair, carpentry, foreign languages, creative writing, word processing, income tax preparation, or flower arranging. Consider beginning a college program for an undergraduate or graduate degree. Join a Great Books discussion group. Children will learn to value what their parents value, and no child could do better than seeing parents as lifelong learners.

Teenagers

The teen years are almost as difficult for parents as they are for children. Just at the time when parents are perhaps most interested in having children do well in school, because college is just around the corner, children are less inclined to want to talk about school and the problems they're dealing with there. To maintain a friendly relationship with teens, parents must find that elusive balance between freedom and control. It's not easy.

Learn the meanings of slang words, but don't try to use them yourself. Teenagers sometimes sound as if they are speaking a foreign language. You'll sound silly if you try to speak the same way, but you'll have a better idea of what's going on in their lives if you can interpret what they say. Asking teens to explain the meanings of unfamiliar slang expressions shows them that you're interested in them. Even though teenagers don't always show it, they need to know they are loved and cared for, perhaps even more than when they were younger.

Listen. Let teens do most of the talking. It's too easy for parents to end up lecturing, even when they don't intend to. Children don't want to hear how tough things were when you grew up—they often won't believe you anyway. They want to know that you understand how tough things are for them. Listening is one way you can let them know that you understand and care for them. If you can remember some of the pain of your own teenage years, you really will be sympathetic to their concerns and feelings. Being a teen wasn't easy for me or anyone else I know.

Avoid criticism. No one is touchier than a teenager. Teens take remarks that weren't even meant to be critical as criticism. Instead of telling teens what they should do, engage them in a problem-solving conversation. Tell them how you view the situation, but first ask them how they see things. Help them come up with their own suggestions for resolving the immediate problem. If consequences for poor judgment or inappropriate behavior seem warranted, let them suggest what they might be.

Avoid long-term penalties. If, for example, your teenager gets a bad report card, it's not a good plan to ground him or her until the next report card comes out. Such a punishment is likely only to make the child resentful and hostile–and those feelings are likely to lead to lower rather than higher grades. Adding an extra hour a day to scheduled homework time is a better idea, because it serves not only as a consequence but also as a possible solution to the problem.

Look beneath the surface of your teenager's words. Listen between the lines to try to figure out what your teen may be feeling but not saying. You may be able to deal effectively with a situation your children aren't yet able to discuss if you try to understand their unexpressed feelings.

Be honest. If you want children to be honest with you, you must be honest with them. You may find that children will respond positively, rather than copy what you did, if you share stories of some of the bad choices you made as a teenager. Your children know that because you are human, you have made mistakes. Pretending otherwise creates more problems than it solves.

Don't be afraid to admit error. Parents can't help but make mistakes on occasion. You don't have to be perfect or always right. When children see that you can admit being wrong, they will be more likely to tell you when they were wrong.

Don't argue. Whatever the situation, arguing will make matters worse. When tempers flare, don't attempt to have a rational conversation. It won't be possible. Wait until later to discuss the problem.

Don't despair. The teen years don't last forever. Most parents discover that their children are wonderful people again when they finally make it over the threshold of adulthood. Even very troubled teens usually turn out to be capable and caring adults if they had supportive parents in their early years. It's just a lot more difficult for some kids to grow up than others. If you never stop believing in and caring about your children, they'll know it even if they can't show it. In the end they'll be O.K.

Preliminary results from a study of over 7,000 students and 3,500 parents conducted by Sanford Dornbusch of Stanford University show a relationship between parents' actions and children's school performance. The link was consistent for people of all ethnic groups and income levels. "Low-key, positive reinforcement, like praise and encouragement, work better than material rewards or big, exaggerated or emotional responses," says Dornbusch. In fact, parents who get "visibly disturbed" by a child's poor report card make the situation worse. They upset the child, and that tends to result in lower grades over time. Dornbusch says that creating rewards and punishments doesn't work because children become more concerned with them than the schoolwork.

You should be careful not to be too critical or demanding, nor to lavish praise. Your interest and assistance when needed will show that you care that your children do well, and they will respond by doing the best they can. Your goal should be to make your children independent of you – they must eventually be able to solve their own problems if they are going to be successful in life. Remember that they learn from what they see you do. If you love learning and do the best you can on what you have to do, they will naturally be inclined to do the same. Making your home a place where both learning is valued and practiced is the best foundation for children's success in school and in later life.

Parents should never forget that not only are they their children's first teachers, they are also their most influential teachers. The adults your children will someday become depends more on what you do than on what their teachers do.

Chapter Eleven

Improving Local Schools

STUDENTS DO BETTER in school when their parents are involved. A two-year study conducted by Stanford University's Sanford Dornbusch found that parental participation in school functions, such as open house nights, has a "substantial and positive association with grades" even when parental education and other factors were taken into account. Dornbusch says, "It's not clear why this is so, although it may be this is just a good indicator of underlying values or that contact with teachers may affect curricular assignments."

This finding shouldn't surprise anyone. The more information parents have about what their children do in school, the more they are able to work with teachers to help children achieve school goals. The converse is also true: the more teachers know about individual students, the better they will be able to help them succeed. Contact between school and home is not only desirable but necessary.

Teachers may be the experts on teaching, but parents are the experts on their own children. And, as educator Gene Maeroff points out, "Families cannot count on the schools to look after the educational needs of every child. It is not that teachers and principals and school board members are uncaring; they usually do what they can to protect the interests of schoolchildren. But with 45 million students in school, there is just so much even the most responsive and humane system can do for each child." Maeroff says that parents can take nothing for granted about the future of their children–including the quality and outcome of their schooling.

Most schools are not set up to make parent-teacher contact easy. Teachers, especially at the elementary level, have little time away from students. They aren't easy to reach by phone, although you can leave a message for a teacher to return your call. Recent concern about our public schools has led to suggestions that we find ways for the school and home to work in partnership. Thanks to funding from the General Mills Foundation for a three-year pilot project to improve Minneapolis public schools, some elementary teachers now have telephones in their classrooms. Teachers now call their students' parents at least twice a week. But don't wait for your children's teachers to contact you–they probably don't have phones in their classrooms yet. Take the initiative yourself. Here are some ways you can help.

Be informed. You need to know as much about the school as you can. Read the newsletters, notices, and handbooks your children bring home. Attend open houses and parent meetings.

Ask questions. When you're confused about something you read or something your child tells you, ask about it. Don't be afraid to call or visit the school to get more information. Many problems are caused by misunderstanding and could be avoided if matters were clarified. Children, intentionally or unintentionally, may give you only part of the story. Before you take action, check with the teacher to make sure you have all the information you need.

Take advantage of school services. Find out what services are available in your children's school and use them. Guidance counselors, for example, can be a big help when it comes time for students to apply to college. They can refer you to other school and community resources, such as psychological counseling and tutoring services, when the need arises. Many elementary schools now have counselors. The school nurse can provide information about health services and problems. If you suspect your child's difficulty in school may be caused by a learning disability, you can request that he or she be tested by contacting the principal or special education director. Even if you don't want your child placed in a special education class, you'll get information from the tests that may help you work with the child's teacher to figure out other ways of meeting your child's special needs.

Meet the teachers. You'll be able to work more effectively with your children at home if you know a little about their teachers. If the school has an open house or "Back-to-School" night, you'll be able to meet the teachers briefly. If you want to talk with them at greater length or if the school doesn't have such an open house early in the year, make an appointment to confer privately with them. Just as children try to play off one parent against the other, they will sometimes try to play off the parent against the teacher. If you know what a given teacher's expectations are regarding homework, grading, and misbehavior, your child won't be able to fool you with an account that is less than completely accurate. But whenever you're in doubt about your child's version of something that occurred at school, check with the school to get all the facts before you do anything else.

Visit the school in session. Working parents may find it difficult to get to school while classes are in session, and many children—especially older ones—would prefer that their parents never appear at school. If you can arrange a visit, however, you'll have a better understanding of what your children do every day. You may be surprised to find that your child is much different from the way he or she is at home. Some children who are outgoing and active at home are shy in the classroom. If you notice a discrepancy between home and school behavior, you may uncover a problem that should be addressed.

Make teacher-parent conferences more productive. Before you meet with a teacher, make a list of things you want to cover. Don't assume that the teacher will bring up everything that's important. Listen to what the teacher has to say, but ask questions. Here are some topics to consider discussing in addition to how your child's doing:

- What you can do at home to help.
- What the teacher's expectations and policies are regarding homework (how often? how much? typical assignments?), grading, late work, absences, make-up work, and discipline.
- What children study—some general idea of the overall curriculum.
- The teacher's philosophy and teaching methods.
- What children should do if they need extra help.

Work with the teacher when there's a problem. When your child has a problem at school, get in touch with the teacher right away. Don't accept your child's version of the situation until you get the teacher's side of the story as well. The teacher may be in the wrong, but many children will color the facts so it looks like a situation is more the teacher's fault than their own. You'll have to listen to both before deciding, but assigning blame is counterproductive in any case. Your objective should be to work with the teacher to solve the immediate problem and prevent problems in the future.

Always go through the chain of command. Don't call the principal, for example, before you talk to the teacher. A good principal will turn you back to the teacher anyway, and an ineffective principal may make matters worse by trying to handle the problem without involving the teacher. If after meeting with the teacher you aren't satisfied with the outcome, let the teacher know you are taking the matter to the principal and then proceed to do so. Your next step would be to contact the superintendent, but few problems will go this far without resolution. Don't contact a school board member even if he or she is a personal friend. School board members are elected to set policy and monitor the overall operation of the school system, not handle individual problems between parents and teachers. Trying to resolve a problem by going outside the chain of command will only cause more problems for more people, and will do little to take care of the original difficulty.

Suggest strategies for monitoring your children's progress. No matter what level they teach, teachers have their hands full all day long. At the high school level, for example, teachers often have more than a hundred different students, and they won't find it easy to communicate individually with parents. However, if you're going to work with your child at home, you'll want to know whether your efforts are paying off. When you meet with the teacher, set up some kind of system so that you can keep track of how well the child is doing between the scheduled report cards. Here are some ways the teacher can help you stay informed:

• Send home copies of graded tests or other assignments for your signature.

• Write you a note if the child's homework is not done or classroom behavior is inappropriate. Since you may not be able to trust your child to bring the note home, give the teacher a supply of stamped, self-addressed envelopes or postcards. (If you make the job easy, the teacher will be more likely to get it done. Your thoughtfulness will be appreciated.)

• Send home weekly progress reports. In some schools you can arrange with the guidance counselor for these reports to be issued. The guidance secretary fills the form out and sees that it's circulated to all the teachers and then sent to you.

• Set up a date and time for a phone call or conference to assess the progress that's been made.

• Let you know if a referral for testing or special services might be of some help.

Schedule a conference with all of your child's teachers at once. If your child is having difficulty in school generally rather than in only one class, ask the guidance counselor (or principal if the school has no counselor) to set up a conference with all of your child's teachers. This is an especially good option for working parents, since the conference can probably be scheduled early in the morning. Teachers benefit from meeting as a group. They can find out how children are doing in other classes and coordinate efforts to help them.

Support the school in disciplinary matters. Just as two parents should work with rather than against each other, teachers and parents should work together. Even if you disagree with the way a teacher handles a particular matter, don't put your child in the middle by letting him or her disregard the teacher's directive. If, for example, you feel your child was unfairly given detention, don't tell him or her not to stay. Let the child serve the detention and talk to the teacher about the situation. All kinds of problems result when parents and teachers don't present a unified front. You won't know what's wrong until you discuss the matter directly with the teacher. Meanwhile your children need to realize that they have obligations to meet even when there's a disagreement.

You may want to include your child in the conference with the teacher. What he or she will learn is that people don't ignore problems. They must work together to solve them. As a first step in such a case, you may suggest that your child report for detention and also make an appointment to discuss the matter privately with the teacher at a later time. Whenever possible, older children should try to work out difficulties themselves, but they may need some suggestions from you about how to do that. You should get involved only if the child is unable to work things out with the teacher on his or her own. All children and adults at one time or another feel they are unfairly treated. Everyone is better off when action leads to compromise rather than conflict.

Getting Involved

Some parents only get involved with the school when their children have problems. They're missing a golden opportunity to participate in their children's education in a more rewarding way. By volunteering your time and talents, you'll learn more about the school, the teachers, and your children's friends at the same time you help the school do a better job.

Attend school activities. Extracurricular activities are learning opportunities, too, and your child will be more likely to participate if you show interest. Your children can develop special talents outside the classroom, and your presence when they display their artistic or athletic accomplishments helps build their self-esteem, sense of belonging, and motivation to continue. If both parents work during the day, evening and weekend events may be the only ones you can attend, so they become doubly important.

One middle school in Massachusetts used school dances as a way of promoting family togetherness by making them parent-student dances. Records from the Fifties and Sixties are played for the parents along with those from the Eighties and Nineties for the kids. Parents didn't have to worry about their children being out at night alone, because students can't be admitted to a dance unless they are accompanied by a parent or guardian. Even if your children's school holds dances only for kids, there's always a need for adult chaperons. Your help would be very welcome.

Volunteer. There are plenty of opportunities for parents to help out at school, though more perhaps in the elementary school than the high school. Consider giving a few hours now and then to serve as a room mother, field trip chaperon, spelling-bee judge, or fundraiser. If you can devote a couple of hours on a regular basis you might work as a classroom or library aide. In the middle school where I was principal, parents supervised students in the classroom while students read books of their choice so that teachers were free to hold team meetings. The team concept was new, and the school district couldn't have afforded to implement it without volunteer help. If you have no free time during the school day, ask what you might do to help in the evening, on weekends, or at home rather than at the school. Most schools will be delighted to find ways for you to assist.

Consider substitute teaching. Most principals are desperate for good substitute teachers. In most states substitutes don't need to be trained as teachers, or even have college degrees. My most reliable and effective day-to-day subs were parents. They knew the kids, so they had few discipline problems—a major problem for substitute teachers—and I was happy to have them there. But there was another benefit as well: they learned a great deal about the school's needs, and thus they got other parents to join them in helping to make changes. They went to the school board to support budget requests and undertook activities to raise funds for items that had been excluded from the budget. Two parents volunteered to be advisers so we could start a school newspaper.

Be active in the parent-teacher organization. If your school doesn't have one, get a few parents together and meet with the principal to start one. The group can serve to inform parents as well as bring them together with teachers. One parent group, for example, sponsored a science fair that teachers didn't have the time to put together themselves.

Join special-interest parent groups. Most schools also have parent groups for extracurricular activities and sports, such as Band Parents and Sports Boosters. Support the groups that represent the activities in which your children are involved.

Serve on school and district committees. There are many opportunities for parents to get involved on committees. Some examples:

• school advisory council—meets with principal to discuss and advise on a wide range of issues relating to the overall operation of the school. Not every school has one, but if yours doesn't, you might consider trying to get one started

• school building committee–oversees the construction of new buildings or additions to an existing school

• positive action committee–makes suggestions for helping schools better meet the needs of students who are likely to drop out or already have dropped out

• curriculum committee–works with teachers and others to make recommendations regarding curriculum changes

• textbook adoption committee–reviews textbooks and other materials and makes recommendations for district or school purchases

• vocational advisory committee–monitors and recommends changes for vocational programs of various types. The idea is to get input from people who already work in the field–plumbing or auto mechanics, for example–so that the school program adequately prepares students for jobs in that area

• hiring committee–reviews applications and interviews candidates for positions (usually administrative rather than teaching)

• accreditation committees–A variety of committees must be set up when a school goes through an accreditation process, and all include citizen participation

• other–districts and schools often establish ad hoc committees for a variety of purposes. Follow the activities of your local school board and volunteer for an assignment that interests you.

As school budgets are cut, parents and other community-minded citizens have formed groups to raise money to fund special programs. In one community a parent group raised money to pay a teacher whose program had been cut, so the program wouldn't be lost. In another, several individuals established an educational foundation and raised money to fund special activities the school district budget could no longer cover.

Schools have changed little in the last hundred years. Even with all the recent efforts to reform and restructure them, most schools operate as they always have. The reform movement has led to additional requirements–longer school days, more required courses, increased testing–but the school structure and overall curriculum in most schools have remained the same.

At a recent meeting sponsored by the Education Commission of the States, educators, business representatives, and state policymakers discussed the reasons more hasn't been done to restructure schools. John Dorman, a businessman and member of the Public School Forum of North Carolina, said, "Overcoming institutional inertia has been our biggest struggle. It was far more difficult to build support within the education community than with the general public." Paula Evans, a project director for the Coalition of Essential Schools at Brown University, added, "Many educators often point to regulations as the biggest barrier to change. But state regulations and mandates can be worked through. Habit remains the biggest obstacle."

In fact, many states have relaxed or waived state regulations for schools that want to try innovative approaches, but there have been few takers. Frank Newman, president of the Education Commission of the States, said, "We've found that it's one thing to open the cage door, but quite another to get the bird to fly out." Other obstacles to restructuring identified at the meeting include "administrators who are reluctant to change, parents whose children are doing well in the current system, and state lawmakers who are unwilling to give up their control of the schools."

Educators are no different from the rest of us. Change is scary, and we naturally try to avoid it even when we realize that what we're doing isn't working well. Psychologists have long known, for example, that children who grow up in dysfunctional families unconsciously re-create similar family situations as adults. There's a great deal of security in the familiar. But even as we try to keep things the same, the world changes. Our children will not be able to survive in the next century unless we change the way they are being educated today. Parents and citizens must work within the system as it is today to institute changes that will give our children a more secure future.

You can't do much alone, but you can join together with others to coax your local school to try new approaches that will work better than the methods they're using now. The first step for everyone is to acquire new knowledge. A major reason we continue to do things as we always have is that we know no other way. Teachers, principals, and parents must educate themselves. An active parent-teacher organization can accomplish a great deal.

Bring in outside speakers and guest lecturers. Nationally recognized educators and child development specialists can share what they know with a local community and thus help set the stage for school change. In one community I know of there are monthly forums on education. Sometimes the speakers are experts who provide information to parents; other times they might be local teachers explaining school programs.

Because teachers are also likely to attend such events, the parent-teacher organization can get them to consider new ideas they might not be exposed to otherwise. You can also work with other interested parents to track down teachers and principals from other schools who have instituted new methods you'd like to see tried in your own school. Having people like these come as guest speakers after an expert has spoken is a necessary follow-up. Experts can only make people aware of what can or should be done; other educators can show how these ideas can be implemented. An occasional lecture or workshop won't make much of a difference, but a carefully planned series of talks will get local parents and teachers thinking and talking about change.

Invite parents and teachers to regular discussion groups. Just as students need to process new information in order to make it part of their own knowledge base, so too do adults. The parent-teacher organization can get teachers and parents talking about school issues on an informal basis by holding regularly scheduled discussion groups. Keep the groups small, even if it means having several meetings concurrently. Serve refreshments. Use the meeting time to talk about the information presented by guest speakers and to share the concerns of both parents and teachers. Participants might also read educational articles and books and talk about them.

The informal setting, however, will do more than just provide people with new knowledge. It will allow parents and teachers to get to know each other as individuals in a way they don't through normal school contacts. If you as a parent can better understand teachers' points of view, you'll be better equipped to figure out ways to make positive change seem less threatening to them. Both groups will come to appreciate each other's roles and trust each other; neither can accomplish much separately, but together they can work toward common goals.

Such informal get-togethers, even if they don't result in change, can dramatically improve school-community relations. In an age when communities are faced with tax caps and budget cuts, parent-teacher discussion groups can be an antidote to conflict.

Establish a scholarship fund for teachers. In many communities, funds aren't available for teachers to attend conferences where they can learn new methods and stay up-to-date on recent research findings. The parent-teacher organization can help raise the funds needed for teachers to attend such conferences, or take special courses—on whole language, for example, or writing-to-learn techniques. Keep in mind that teachers can't change what they're doing if they don't know any other way to teach. You can make sure that they have an opportunity to get the knowledge and then work to help them use it to benefit your children.

Support teachers' professional organizations. Most people have heard of the AFT and NEA—teachers' unions—because they negotiate contracts for teachers and lobby on their behalf in state legislatures and in Congress. Most teachers belong to a union. But there are other professional organizations to which many fewer teachers belong that could have a greater positive impact on the classroom if more teachers were actively involved in them. Each subject area has a national organization as well as affiliates in individual states. These sponsor conferences and workshops, and publish journals and books. Their main concern is improving the teaching of the particular subject, not lobbying for higher salaries and benefits. Teachers who are active in the National Council of Teachers of English or the National Council for the Social Studies, for instance, have access to the latest research in their fields and also meet teachers from other schools who have found more effective ways to teach. By attending conferences and reading the journals published by these organizations, teachers continue to learn and be renewed. See the appendix for a list of these organizations. They even publish some materials of interest to parents.

Teachers can also learn from reading recent books and articles in their fields, but often the funds for professional library materials are the first to go when there's a budget cut. Unfortunately, principals don't always realize how much their schools will benefit from getting their teachers such books and having them involved in such professional activities. There usually aren't funds available to pay for memberships or conference attendance. You can do a great deal to improve your school by finding ways to get more of the teachers to join and participate in these professional organizations.

Support activities that will lead to classroom change. Either as an individual volunteer or as a member of the parent-teacher organization, you may be able to get teachers to implement classroom changes by getting the activities started yourself. Research has shown, for example, that students are motivated to improve their writing and correct errors in spelling and punctuation when they write for an audience other than the teacher-as-evaluator.

If the teachers in your children's school assign writing that will only be seen and graded by them, the parents' group can introduce the idea of publishing student work by sponsoring a student literary magazine, a writing contest, or a book-publishing session. In one school that had such a publishing program, the parents typed children's stories and bound them into handmade books that were added to the classroom library for other children to read. An even better approach might be to teach children how to make their own books. Older students can use computers with word-processing programs to do the typing themselves.

These activities might begin as parent-sponsored projects, but once teachers see for themselves the motivational benefits, they will begin to look for more ways for students to share their writing with others. Gradually they'll make other changes in their teaching. Publishing student writing may be the first step in getting elementary teachers to adopt a whole language approach in their classrooms.

Recognize the teachers whose methods you'd like others to adopt. The parent-teacher organization can sponsor awards—complete with plaques and celebratory luncheons—to support and encourage change. Teachers need recognition and appreciation, and often the innovative, involved teacher stands alone in a school where others continue teaching as they always have taught and the principal doesn't want anyone rocking the boat.

By calling attention to teachers' good work, you can make those teachers want to continue their efforts and at the same time send a subtle message to other teachers. Awards are one way for parents to show the kind of teaching they value.

Making Policy

Once you get involved in working for change informally as an individual or as a member of a parent-teacher organization, you may want to become part of the power structure that sets policy and makes decisions about schools.

Don't be afraid to run for election to the local school board; every board needs dedicated, knowledgeable people without axes to grind. As a school board member, you'll be able to work toward the hiring of the kinds of individuals you'd like to see teaching and administering your local schools. You'll be directly involved in determining how financial and human resources will be allocated in your school district. It's also possible to move from local involvement to a higher level. One woman I know who worked hard for several years on the school board of a small community was later appointed to the state board of education, eventually becoming its chair.

Even if you don't want to become part of the power structure, you can still influence elected and appointed officials. Attend and speak up at local school board meetings. Follow the activity during the state legislative sessions: know what bills affecting education have been proposed, and go to the hearings and let your views be known. Get to know your own legislators. Let them know what you think about bills currently under study, and suggest legislation you'd like to see enacted. You might be surprised how much effect you can have in the legislative process. Too often legislators hear only from the same lobbyists, whose positions they well know even before they begin to speak. If you attend a hearing as a parent and present your views clearly and articulately, they'll listen to you and likely remember what you say. Too many people complain about laws after they are passed; we need more citizens to get involved in the process of making them.

No matter what activity is undertaken, a handful of people always end up doing the lion's share of the work. The parent-teacher organization will never be able to get every parent or every teacher to come to a workshop or lecture. As you become more knowledgeable about the kinds of changes schools need to make, you need to spread information to as many other people as you can. Consider these means of getting the word out.

- Write letters to the editor of the local newspaper.
- Get the local newspaper to do feature stories on innovative teachers and classroom practices.
- Publicize events sponsored by the parent-teacher organization after they've occurred as well as before. If the event was a guest speaker, people who read a news story afterward will have a general idea of what was said even if they didn't attend.
- Submit articles to the school or school district newsletter, or work to start one if none exists. Also look for other publications to which articles can be submitted, such as service club newsletters.
- Find speakers to present programs for service clubs (Rotary, Kiwanis), church groups, and community organizations.

Even though some of the suggestions outlined in this chapter could be construed as a bit Machiavellian, in that parents work to create a context in which educators are almost forced to change, you should always try to work within the system. If you become too assertive and try to make things happen too fast, you run the risk of creating conflict. Then no one wins.

The key to lasting change is working slowly, steadily, and carefully in a variety of ways. Change takes time. People must first change their attitudes and beliefs before they will change their behavior. But everyone enjoys comfortable social interaction. Much of what you and other parents must do involves creating settings in which parents, teachers, and others can be introduced to new ideas, talk about them, and explore possibilities for local schools. As people who are not used to working together come to know and trust each other, they'll be more likely to accept new ways of looking at teaching and learning.

Cooperation and collaboration will work, but they take time. Be ever watchful in order to avoid confrontation or conflict, because they can destroy in minutes what it takes months to achieve.

Reform and restructuring efforts will come to naught unless we can change the way teachers teach and relate to students in individual classrooms. Certainly other reforms are needed. The present structure of our schools and their schedules, which were devised a hundred years ago to serve a more agrarian society, will not prepare today's children for tomorrow's world.

Teachers who learn to personalize their teaching will not only make learning more meaningful for students, but they also will understand why and how they need to be more involved in the decision-making process of the school. Teacher empowerment can't be forced on teachers; it must come from within them. Many teachers are not yet ready for such empowerment.

In a world where values and moral standards seem elusive or nonexistent, children still somehow must develop such qualities. "Character education" and "moral education" are trendy concepts today, but the people who advocate including them in the school curriculum often view ethical and moral standards as something teachers can directly confer on students simply by teaching about them. It's hard to imagine why anyone would think such an approach could succeed. Values and standards, like teacher empowerment, must develop from within. They can't be imposed on students by either teachers or parents. The best way children can internalize them is by living them, and interacting with adults—both parents and teachers—who exhibit them in action, not just state them in words. Models are powerful teachers. If children do not see adults who practice the values they preach, children will not practice them either.

Children who learn from teachers who don't view teaching as a simple matter of transmitting information, for example, will more naturally experience for themselves (and thus internalize) a common core of values, such as those endorsed by the governor of New Jersey and state education officials: civic responsibility, respect for the natural environment, respect for others, and respect for self. We don't need special programs to inculcate values and moral standards; they must be an integral part of all school life. Merely adding a unit or course to the curriculum isn't the answer.

Perhaps the suggestions I have outlined here seem like a simplistic solution to school improvement, but complex results can stem from simple beginnings. We have wasted too much time and money doing what clearly doesn't work—and we have condemned thousands of students to less than fulfilling educations as a result. Isn't it time we used our common sense to make the one change that can make a real difference? Of course, there are other important issues that must be resolved: no child should go to school hungry, and no matter where they live, all children deserve to be educated in safe, clean, comfortable classrooms supplied with up-to-date books and materials. But while we debate the issues of equalizing educational funding or restructuring schools, we can take that first step, make that first change, and work to improve what happens in the individual classroom. Every child should have teachers who are lifelong learners and who understand that teaching is a relationship. To help children learn, teachers must pay as much attention to their personal needs as they do to their academic achievement.

Technology will continue to alter the landscape of the future, and many human problems are likely to become even more complex as a result. We need to make sure we provide an educational environment that will enable today's students to figure out effective ways to deal with tomorrow's problems.We have a lot to do and a long way to go, but as the Chinese proverb reminds us: "A journey of a thousand miles begins with a single step."

Chapter Twelve

Lifelong Learning: A Portrait of Public Education in the Twenty-First Century

THIS LAST CHAPTER presents a narrative portrait of what education might look like in the twenty-first century, now less than ten years away. In the fictional community of New Portland, John Weston finds an educational system that has solved many of the problems we're grappling with today. There, people of all ages–grandparents, parents, and children–learn together. The ideas in this chapter are not science fiction. While no community has yet combined all of the ideas represented here and put them into practice, they can be seen to varying degrees in communities across the nation.

As he hurried up the walk, John Weston noted the sign outside the low-slung brick building: "Community Association for Recreation and Education Administrative Center" and underneath, the slogan, "CARE Cares about Learning." Inside he stopped at the information desk. "Good morning," he said to the receptionist. I have an eight o'clock appointment with the CARE chief executive officer, Ms. Helena Forbes."

"One moment please," the young woman replied as she turned to the computer and tapped some keys. "I'll see if she's available." John looked around at the comfortably furnished lounge area. There were paintings and drawings attractively displayed on the walls, and pieces of sculpture graced the floor, window sills, and bookshelves.

"Your lounge looks like an art gallery," John said to the receptionist after she told him how to find Ms. Forbes' office.

"Yes," she replied. "We want the children's work to be seen by the public. We change our display here every month, and we've also arranged to have student art and other school work displayed elsewhere in town—in banks, grocery stores, and in the big shopping mall. Sometimes people even buy a student painting or sculpture."

"Really? That seems like a terrific way to recognize young artists."

"It's great for the kids' self-esteem and motivates them to work even harder." The receptionist continued, "I dabbled in art when I was a kid, but I didn't work at it the way some of our kids do, so I never got very good. Might have made a difference, though, if I had thought of myself as a budding artist rather than just a kid doing watercolors to pass art class. Times certainly have changed—and for the better." The receptionist sighed. "Well, Mr. Weston, you better get down to Ms. Forbes' office. She's expecting you."

As John walked down the long hall toward the CEO's office, he noticed that student work was displayed on these walls, too. Although he was anxious to visit some classes, he realized that he needed to get a picture of the whole system first. Public education in New Portland was very different from that in his own country.

Helena Forbes welcomed him with a big smile. If he'd seen her at a shopping mall, John wouldn't have guessed this attractive woman, probably fortysomething, was in charge of a complex school system in a city of 60,000 people. "I'm very pleased that you want to do a story on learning in our community for what I understand is the most well-respected and widely read magazine in your country. We're very proud of what we've accomplished. I'm sure you realize, though, that what we're doing in education is not so different from other places in the U.S. After fumbling around with many ineffective reform and restructuring efforts in the 1980s and 1990s, we finally managed to redesign the system in a way that works well for everyone in the community, not just the students we used to serve back then."

"That's why I want to do this story. We're still trying those old approaches you gave up on. And the emphasis on standardized testing in our schools now seems to prevent kids from getting the kind of education they'll need to survive in the coming decades. I hope my story will get people to change their attitudes and beliefs about learning and teaching. I think teaching should be more than stuffing facts into kids' heads and testing them to see if it sticks. We also have a big problem with kids dropping out of school–they don't do well and they hate it. I guess that's not a problem here."

"You're right. We don't have to worry about dropouts any more. For one thing, we've worked to make school a place where kids feel good about themselves and believe they're capable of learning almost anything. But we stopped talking in terms of graduation rates, too, because we believe that learning should never stop. Our whole system is organized to encourage people to become lifelong learners. In fact, our CEC division–short for Community Education Courses–is the largest one in our system. We offer courses on nearly everything for nearly everyone. If enough people want a course, we'll find a way to offer it. We design special courses for businesses, for example. They pay us to teach their employees. And, of course, we provide all the necessary courses for students who want to enter college. We have everything from fun-type, hobby courses–like flower-arranging and making Christmas decorations–to the academic–calculus, physics, and advanced English. And it may surprise you to learn that you'll find both senior citizens and teenagers in classes of every kind."

"You mean senior citizens sometimes take physics and calculus? Don't they feel awkward going into a high school filled with teenagers?"

Helena smiled. "Well, we've actually abolished high school. We teach most of the same courses–in part, because our colleges have changed very little in the last quarter-century–but classes are scheduled much the way adult education and some alternative programs were set up back in the 1990s. Some meet during the day, some at night, and most meet for varying lengths of time. We don't have many courses that meet for forty or fifty minutes every day. The old Carnegie units kids used to earn for high school graduation are as extinct as dinosaurs. My son, for example, has French for an hour everyday, but his chem class only meets on Wednesday and Thursday. The class runs from ten to four with a short lunch break, so there's plenty of time for labs."

Helena reached for a tabloid-sized newspaper on the shelf behind her. "Here, take a look at this week's CARE newspaper. You'll find course descriptions and schedules for upcoming courses along with times, dates, and places of the lectures, concerts, recreation, and athletic activities sponsored by our RCA division."

John took the paper and thumbed through it, noting that the bylines for several stories indicated that the writers were students. "What's RCA?" he asked.

"RCA's an acronym for Recreational and Cultural Activities. When we abolished high schools, we gave the job of organizing athletic programs to RCA. We replaced the interscholastic athletic competitions of the twentieth century with a greater emphasis on intracommunity leagues—sort of like the old school intramurals. Our best young athletes are invited to join community teams that compete with teams in other communities. New Portland has two community teams in all the major sports. Smaller towns have only one, and in the big cities, several teams are usually established for neighborhood-community regions within the city. Competitive athletics are not too much different from the way they used to be when individual schools competed with each other, but now fans are loyal to the community rather than a school. The big difference is that with the intracommunity leagues every kid gets to play rather than just warm the bench."

Helena Forbes paused as John Weston scribbled a few more words in his notebook; the newspaper she'd given him rested on his lap. "Perhaps it would help me understand things better if you could briefly describe how the whole system is organized. I think I understand RCA—although I'm sure I'll have questions later—and the idea of the Community Education Courses is pretty clear. CEC offers all kinds of courses for all ages of people. But surely you haven't abolished elementary schools. What are they like?"

"I'm sorry. I'm so used to our educational system now, I forget that it's a lot to take in all at once. You didn't live through the changes as we made them the way folks did here. I'll back up. The whole system operates as the Community Association for Recreation and Education. I think most people believe education is more important than recreation, but organizers liked the idea of using the acronym 'CARE.' That's what everyone calls us. And we emphasized our educational role by adopting 'Community Commitment to Lifelong Learning' as a permanent goal, but we use the phrase, 'CARE cares about learning,' as our motto."

"I noticed that it was on your sign outside," John said.

"It's on everything–our letterhead, newspaper, and posters. The first board of directors insisted on that when we instituted the new system."

"Is the board of directors like a school board?"

"Yes," said Helena. "It functions the same way, but two positions are new. One must be filled by a teenaged student and the other by a senior citizen over sixty. The other members must be over fourteen years of age and are elected at-large."

"I guess you're making sure that everyone who uses the system except the youngest students will be represented," John commented.

"You'd be amazed how helpful it's been to have those voices heard, especially the students'. Kids have often come up with the best ideas–maybe because they're not so resistant to change as we older folks sometimes are."

"I know what you mean. I think that's why education in my country has gotten worse rather than better. We haven't changed. Instead we've done more of what we did before. Crazy, isn't it? At least the article I'm writing may get people to talk about change, and that's a good first step," John said.

"That's the *only* first step," Helena said. "People have to agree on what needs to be done. That means, as you said earlier, changing our attitudes about teaching and learning. We found that conversation builds community. There was a lot of debate and discussion here, but once people realized that real learning was personal and idiosyncratic and much more complex than we could measure by using only standardized tests with multiple-choice answers, they began to question traditional methods. Ulti-

Community Commitment to Lifelong Learning

COMMUNITY ASSOCIATION FOR RECREATION AND EDUCATION (CARE)

CARE cares about learning

Board of Directors
(elected; includes student and senior citizen reps)

appoints

Chief Executive Officer (CEO)

SUPPORT SERVICES	EDUCATIONAL DIVISIONS			
Administrative and Support Services	Early Exploration Programs	Fundamental Education (Fun Ed)	Community Education Courses (CEC)	Recreational and Cultural Activities (RCA)
Finance/Records Facilities, Resources, and Equipment Central Lib. Media Ctr. Bookstore Computing Services Maintenance Transportation Bldg. Scheduling/ Management Planning, Personnel, Research and Development Testing/Assessment Teacher Inservice/Research Special Services Educational Counseling Social/Psych. Services Health Special Needs Public Info/Publications	Child Care to age 3 Preschool ages 3 to 5 Primary ages 5 to 8 (ungraded)	Age 8 and up 4-level interdisciplinary program—basic knowledge and skills Art, music, PE classes taken in CEC Students join Learn/Share group	Variety of courses, including some coded for college or vocational school admission Flexibly scheduled Open to anyone (adults/children) Apprenticeships/Internships Learn/Share Groups	Athletics Cultural Programs Special Events Support for Community Groups and Projects

Compulsory Education • Primary program and satisfactory completion of Fundamental Education (4 levels) plus 2 years of course work in Community Education Courses, including an internship and ongoing participation in a Learn/Share Group mately those questions led to the rethinking of the whole school structure. Let me explain the basic organization of CARE."

Helena opened the file drawer in her desk and took out a chart, which she spread out on her desktop. "This chart shows the basic organization and all the support services for CARE. I'll have my secretary get you a copy to take with you–reduced to legal size so you can refer to it more easily." John shifted his chair slightly and leaned over the desk so he could see the chart.

Helena pointed to the chart and said, "These are the two divisions we already talked about–CEC and RCA. The counselor you're going to see next will tell you about the Learn/Share groups and the internships/apprenticeships you see here under Community Education Courses. The other two educational divisions serve children from birth through ages twelve to fourteen when CEC takes over."

Helena pointed to the block letters and chuckled. "Fun Ed–great name, don't you think? We do want kids–and teachers–to realize that learning and teaching are enjoyable, but the name is short for Fundamental Education. Some people say Fun Ed's responsibility is the 'Four Rs'–reading, 'riting, 'rithmetic, and rudiments, meaning rudiments of knowledge–because that's what Fundamental Education provides. Children ages eight on up complete a four-level interdisciplinary program, usually in about four years."

"So there are four grades in the Fun Ed program," John said, reiterating what Helena had said to make sure he understood.

"No, not four grades, four levels. All of our school programs are ungraded, because we think in terms of developmental and competency levels rather than ages or grades. Each level is based on successful completion of the previous level, but children move from one to the other at their own pace. You'll understand how we personalize learning for each child when you visit some classes. When students have completed the four levels, they can read, write, think, and compute at the minimum level we feel is necessary to survive in the world–as a citizen, parent, and worker. We don't teach separate subjects, but we incorporate all the basic academic subjects into a series of interdisciplinary units and projects. Students take courses in other subjects–art, music, physical education–in CEC rather than in Fun Ed."

"What about so-called 'cultural literacy'?" John asked. "We have strong advocates for a rigid core curriculum and increased testing to make sure our kids learn basic history and geography, and know all about the great books and writers and thinkers. They want to make sure kids get a thorough knowledge of our cultural heritage."

Helena laughed. "We had those people, too, but over time we were able to show them how we could incorporate that knowledge and information into our interdisciplinary curriculum, and how kids could demonstrate their learning in many ways, not just on standardized tests. It took some time, but they finally came around. Fun Ed also incorporates other things people felt kids needed to learn, such as substance abuse, sex education, and so forth."

"What about people who feel kids won't learn to read without the basal readers?" John asked. "Did you have to deal with them, too?"

"Of course," Helena replied. "Everyone who grew up in traditional schools wanted their children to be taught the same way they had been taught. Like the cultural literacy advocates, they changed their minds once they visited our schools. They saw how much their children were learning and how much they enjoyed reading real books of all kinds—stories, including classics, biographies, history, and other nonfiction books. We make sure our kids read plenty about other cultures, something many of the old textbooks didn't do adequately. None of the books in any of our schools looks anything like the thick, boring, and sometimes misleading textbooks schools depended on for so many years."

She continued, "Our 'textbooks' are the books you see in libraries and bookstores. The kinds of books people choose to read because they're interesting, informative, and well written. Once we put these books into the hands of kids, they couldn't put them down. The number of books most of our kids choose to read in a year is much, much greater than the number they read when teachers assigned them."

"That sounds wonderful," John replied. "As you were talking, I kept picturing the kids in our schools grudgingly hauling those overweight hardcover literature anthologies and history books home only because they've got homework to do if they expect to pass. Your approach makes so much sense."

"Let me explain the other division, Early Exploration, so you'll have the big picture before you visit classes today. As I said, Fun Ed includes children from age eight. Until then, they're in one of our Early Exploration programs: Child Care to age three, Preschool for children three to five, and Primary School for those five to eight. Both Preschool and Primary classes are ungraded and are set up very much like Montessori schools. You must have those in your country."

"Yes, my daughter attended a private Montessori school until she started first grade. I always wondered why the public schools didn't adopt more Montessori methods, in the early grades at least. You mentioned that Child Care is part of the system. Is that free to parents?"

"Free public education begins at age five for all children. The Child Care and Preschool programs are open to anyone in the community, but we charge fees on a sliding scale. So if parents can afford to pay the full cost, they do, but kids from poor families pay nothing. We feed them free, too. You'll probably be interested to know that since we redesigned the educational system, we have fewer families living on welfare. Of course, the demographics helped—a greater number of older Americans now require more services from a smaller number of people in the work force, so there are jobs for everyone. But we have almost no one here who can't hold a job. We've been able to reduce other social problems as well. Far fewer kids abuse drugs and alcohol or engage in other self-destructive behavior. That means there's more money for education, since we don't have to spend it on things like the prison and welfare systems that were so necessary when our educational system wasn't working as well. I don't want to suggest that education alone can cure all the ills of society, but the reforms we made certainly have contributed to the solution of some tough societal problems."

"Do you have any statistical data that supports what you're telling me? That could be an important selling point to include in my article."

"No problem. I'll have my secretary gather some research reports and make copies for you while you're meeting with Hector Garcia, one of our educational counselors. Is there anything else you'd like to ask me before I walk you down to Hector's office?" asked Helena.

"Not at the moment," John replied, "but could you set aside an hour or so for me tomorrow afternoon? I'm sure there will be a few things I'd like to check on with you."

"I'll have my secretary set up an appointment for you. Stop at her desk on your way out. She'll have a packet of materials all ready for you. She'll also be able to tell you when I can see you tomorrow." Helena got up from her desk and motioned for John to follow her to the door. "Now let me introduce you to Hector Garcia, one of our counselors."

Hector Garcia's office was much smaller than Helena's. He had pushed his desk into a corner to make room for three well-worn upholstered chairs and a small coffee table. Hector welcomed John Weston warmly with a firm handshake as Helena Forbes returned to her office.

"Your office set-up is very appropriate for someone who does counseling," John remarked.

Hector laughed. "Well, my job as an educational counselor is limited to helping my kids figure out what CEC courses they should take. Providing career and college counseling. Informing them of the resources available through CARE. I also make sure my teenagers get the best placement for their apprenticeships/internships and that all my kids are involved in active, supportive Learn/Share groups."

"Excuse me, but it would help if you slowed down just a bit," said John, writing quickly in his notebook. "I want to get this all down. Can you tell me more about the apprenticeships?"

"Sorry. Don't hesitate to interrupt me. Did Helena explain what constitutes compulsory education for our kids?"

John shook his head, so Hector continued, "I'm sure you realize that in the old days we used to keep kids in school until they graduated from high school or reached age seventeen, and we weren't very successful. There were lots of reasons why kids dropped out, but I always believed that low self-esteem and the feeling that school imprisoned them had something to do with it. There wasn't any way they could leave sooner, even if they learned the minimum we expected them to know. Others dropped out without even learning to read and write. Only a few ever went back to school later on. Many ended up in prison or on the streets, never able to hold a job."

"That's exactly the situation in my country now," said John.

"I think we've found the answer," Hector replied. "We let kids move through the four levels of Fundamental Education as quickly as they can. Then they take courses for two years in CEC and spend eight to ten weeks as an apprentice or intern in some business or community agency that interests them. That's all that's compulsory, so some kids actually complete their formal education as early as age fourteen. By that time, they have developed the basic skills necessary to survive in jobs that don't require advanced training. But there's a psychological strategy in this arrangement that many people didn't believe in at first."

"A psychological strategy?" John asked.

"Exactly. What teenage characteristic would you say is most frustrating to adults?"

John thought for a moment, then said, "Rebellion, I guess. My teenage daughter is basically a good kid, but she drives me crazy because she absolutely resists doing anything her mother or I suggests. And we have friends whose kids are much more rebellious than Kelley."

Hector replied, "Rebelling against authority is part of growing up, and when we had laws that forced kids to go to school, some kids used dropping out as a way of declaring their independence. The more we hassled them, the more they resisted. Now that we've made it possible for them to finish school early by working hard, most do."

Hector chuckled, then added, "Of course, it also helps that they can't get drivers' licenses until they finish Fun Ed and two years of CEC. But since our major educational goal is lifelong learning, and we teach kids in ways that make learning enjoyable and relevant, most kids keep on taking courses long after they satisfy the basic requirements. The secret to getting teens to do what you'd like is not to order them to follow your rules, but to create a situation where they have freedom to choose. Peer pressure helps. Most kids choose to do what they see everyone else doing—in this case, taking classes and continuing to learn. Works like a charm. You'll see that when you visit some classes."

"Maybe I can adapt your strategy for my daughter. Maybe we should have a course for parents called 'A Subversive Approach to Dealing with Teens.' "

"That's not a bad idea," said Hector with a grin. "I'll mention it to the CEC coordinator. But there are two more components that make our educational system work—the internships and the Learn/Share groups."

"I'll bet you're going to say that kids realize the importance of continuing their education once they get a chance to work in the real world as an intern," said John.

"That's certainly true. But also, some decide that the job they thought they wanted isn't for them. When that happens, we arrange for them to do additional internships to help them find out what else they'd like to pursue. Actually, the broader their experiences, the better off they'll be, because we know that very few people today remain in the same job throughout their work years. We have to make sure kids are flexible because they may end up changing jobs three or four times in their lifetimes. And with fast-paced technological developments, even the same job may require very different skills in the future."

"That's why I'm so concerned about education in my own country. Our schools are still preparing students for a world that exists only in history books. Then people wonder why businesses complain that our graduates can't cut it," said John.

"The internships helped us break down the barriers between business and education. Once we realized we shared the same goals for our kids, we began to work in partnership with them. There's a personal advantage to the internships, too," added Hector. "Kids, no matter what their family backgrounds, get a chance to interact with an adult who serves both as a model and a mentor. This is also the reason for our Learn/Share groups. Both the internships and the groups work because adults in the community have a commitment to sharing their time and expertise with kids. People are very generous about volunteering their time to sponsor youth groups, coach athletic teams, and participate in ongoing personal and educational discussions with kids.

"The average person in the 1990s, for example, didn't realize there was hard evidence to show that the disadvantaged kids who later became successful adults had one thing in common: an adult who mentored and supported them. We made sure we got the word out by sharing success stories from our own community."

"How did you do that?" asked John.

"Well, one way was what you're doing now—feature stories in magazines and newspapers. Educators used to spend too much time talking to each other instead of the general public. We changed all that. We got out of the schools and spoke to Rotary and Kiwanis clubs and other groups. We took young adults who'd done well to those meetings and let them tell their own stories. It wasn't long before people realized that raising funds for scholarships wasn't enough. They had to get personally involved with kids. That's how the idea of Learn/Share groups was born. Admittedly, some people were initially moved to get involved because they saw it as a way to reduce the crime rate, but they usually ended up really caring about what happened to the young people they got to know."

"Am I hearing echoes of a Big Brother/Big Sister program here?" asked John.

"I guess you could say that the Learn/Share groups are a combination of Big Brother/Big Sister programs and the teacher/adviser programs that some schools, especially middle schools, had back in the 1990s. We realized that some kids came from disadvantaged homes and dysfunctional families and that adult mentoring was critical if these kids were going to make it. We knew we had to find a way to address that need, as well as figure out some way to guide kids through the loosely organized CEC. Every kid is assigned to an educational counselor to help them select courses, of course, but we counselors have a fairly large student load and can't give enough attention to every individual. The Learn/Share group picks up where we leave off. Did Helena tell you that kids get introduced to CEC as soon as they begin Fun Ed at age eight, because that's where they get art, music, and phys ed?"

"Yes, she did. That sounds like a good idea, letting them try out CEC with just a few courses while they're still in Fun Ed. Did you plan it that way?"

"Yes. The kids would be overwhelmed with choosing everything all at once if we didn't introduce them to the concept gradually. Their Fun Ed teachers and educational counselors are there to help, and that's when they also join a Learn/Share group. Each group is made up of about ten members–two or three adults, whose ages can range from early twenties to eighty–and children from eight to eighteen. You should meet Samuel Gordonson. He's eighty-eight and has been in the same Learn/Share group since we founded them. An amazing guy! The kids love him, and he loves them. We try to balance the ages of the kids in a particular group so there are always one or two who are just beginning Fun Ed, some who are at the third and fourth levels, and some who are completely involved in CEC and doing internships and apprenticeships. When one of the older kids joins the work force or goes on to college or vocational school, the vacant slot is filled by a younger student just beginning Fun Ed."

"The older kids, in sharing their past experiences, can advise the youngsters the way big brothers or sisters would," John said.

"That's right," Hector said. "And the adults function as parents–or grandparents, as the case may be. Kids stay in these groups for ten years, so they form really close relationships with the adults. And because people now view education as a community affair to which they must contribute, very few adults ever stop participating in a Learn/Share group. I guess everyone wants to feel useful and needed. The adults get pretty attached to the kids in their groups. When we do make changes–because someone moves out of the community or can't continue because of illness or death–we add a new person to an existing group. We try never to add more than one new adult to a group at a time. Of course, we've also formed new groups as the population grew."

"Are parents in groups with their own children?" asked John.

"No, never. We feel that every kid will benefit from getting to know adults other than their parents. If kids have family difficulties, we want them to be able to discuss their problems with trusted adults and others who are not involved. Siblings are not placed in the same groups either."

"It sounds like these groups might get involved in therapy," said John.

"Well, that's not their purpose, but it does happen–to a very limited degree. We make sure the adults in the group are aware of all the community resources for solving personal and family problems because we don't want people trying to handle situations for which they have no training. The group might discuss minor problems with kids, but if the adults see that a situation is serious, they talk to the kid's educational counselor or try to put the family in touch with Special Services. That division includes trained social workers who deal with families, and counselors to work with kids who have psychological or emotional problems."

"How often do these Learn/Share groups meet?" asked John.

"Usually twice a month for an hour or two–in someone's home or in one of our community rooms," Hector answered. "Our school buildings are open and in use from early morning until late at night year-round, so there's no problem finding a convenient meeting place. All it takes is a call to the scheduling office in the Facilities, Resources, and Equipment Division. A computer keeps track of what rooms are being used, when, and for what."

"Sounds like a more cost-effective system than we have. We spend a lot of money on buildings that sit empty much of the time. That may be another selling point. I'm not the only one in my country who's complaining about high taxes and wasteful expenditures of public funds. Getting more out of our expensive school buildings makes sense," said John. "Could you arrange for me to visit a meeting of a Learn/Share group? I'd like to get a firsthand look."

"I participate in one myself, but I also occasionally visit the meetings of groups my counselees are in. I'm going to one at five o'clock today. Can you join me? This group meets after dinner in the cafeteria at one of our schools."

John checked his schedule for the day. "Five o'clock would be fine. Dinner in the school cafeteria? How is that possible? I've heard of school breakfasts and lunches, but school dinners?"

Hector smiled. "We contract with a private company to provide food service for all of our schools, and since we have many classes scheduled in the evening, people asked why we couldn't provide an evening meal right on site. That way if people have a late afternoon class and another at six or so, they can stay right there. When we get to the cafeteria, you'll see that learning in this community is a family affair. Kids and their parents sometimes take courses together. You'll often see them having dinner together in the school cafeteria." Hector noticed the incredulous look on John's face. "I can understand your surprise. If someone back in 1992 had told me that families learning together and eating dinner in a school cafeteria would be a common occurrence, I never would have believed it."

"Families learning together . . . " John paused to look out the window. "Spending time with each other, sharing experiences . . . Have you noticed any improvement in parent-child relationships?"

"Oh, absolutely. Parents and kids have learned how to talk with each other, because they're sharing experiences where the parent doesn't have to behave in an authoritarian manner. The parent now isn't necessarily the expert. Today's world is so complex. Information continues to increase so rapidly that when parents and children take courses together, the parents are also learning something new. Because parents are more experienced learners, they can help their children with the process. The parent then is both a learner and a teacher. Do you see what I mean?" Hector asked.

"Yes," John replied. "Learning together must also help kids develop values, too. By spending more time—quality time—together, parents must be able to teach their children things some of our children never learn because their parents are too busy to spend time with them. Even in my own family most of our conversations—sometimes they're more like arguments—are about homework and chores, spending money, curfews, things like that. I'm sure families here have those discussions, too, but taking a course together must encourage conversations about more important matters—growing up, dealing with problems, the purpose of life."

"That's true. You'll see that we've tried to make our schools more personal as well. We keep the size of the classes small, hire the best teachers for our youngest students, and create a classroom climate that encourages personal development as well as the acquisition of knowledge and skills."

Hector's phone buzzed, and he picked it up. "Yes, we're all set. Send her down." He turned back to John. "We can talk more later. Your guide will be here shortly. She's an energetic sixteen-year-old who's currently doing an internship with CARE. One of her responsibilities is public relations – meaning she escorts visiting dignitaries around."

John laughed. "Well, I certainly don't consider myself a 'visiting dignitary,' but I like the idea of having someone to show me around!"

"Good morning," said a cheerful voice from the door.

"Hi," said Hector. "Come on in. John, meet one of our talented interns, Sara Roscow. She'll take you to visit some classes. I'll see you back here about four-thirty."

Sara directed John as he drove to one of the Fun Ed schools. Hector was right: Sara was energetic. The pert, dark-haired young woman radiated enthusiasm as she spoke about CARE, but she had a different view of her own first years in school.

"I started school in a backward community that still had the old-style schools and moved here when I was eight. What a difference! In my old school the first-grade teacher gave us nothing but Dick and Jane stories to read – and reams of worksheets. I can remember sitting at my desk circling words and filling in blanks and wondering if that's what school would be like for the next however-many years. We couldn't talk in class. If anyone did, our teacher would write our name on the board. For a second offense she would add a check, and then we had to stay in for recess. That happened to me once, and it was humiliating."

"I can see why you would have felt that way," John said sympathetically.

"I hated the teacher and told my mom that I wouldn't go back. The next day I tried to fake a stomach ache, but Mom made me go to school anyway. I was so glad that we moved here at the end of second grade. I didn't feel I learned very much in first or second grade. It was like being in jail. I couldn't figure out what we kids had done that so was bad we had to be punished. Learning here is fun. CARE really does care about learning! I had to take some tests when I first came. Then they put me in Fun Ed Level One. And I'll never forget the first day I walked into the class. It looked like the kids were having recess in the room. I mean they were all *over* the place. Some kids were working at computers. Two or three kids in one corner were working on a project of some kind. Another group was sitting together on the floor talking. They all had books open, but I could see that they were reading different ones. Library books—not Dick and Jane reading books. Some kids were sitting by themselves reading or writing. There were several tables of various sizes in the room, but not one desk except for the teacher's. It was way back in the corner. The teacher, who was talking to one little boy back there, didn't seem at all bothered by the noise. I quickly realized that all of the kids were working. This wasn't recess. And though they were talking and laughing, they weren't misbehaving. They looked like they were having fun. You'll see for yourself what I mean," Sara said. "That's the school up ahead on the right."

John parked the car and followed Sara into the building and down a long hall. "This is my old classroom, and my teacher, Ms. Harris, is still here," Sara announced as she opened the door. The classroom matched Sara's description of her first day there. Because the children, who all looked to be around eight or nine, were scattered everywhere, John had trouble counting them.

"Hi, Ms. Harris. I've brought another visitor. Mr. Weston is planning to write an article on our schools for a magazine."

"Come right in," Jena Harris said with a wide smile.

"I count twelve children here," John said. "Is that right?"

"That's how many are here today. Fourteen students are in the class, but two are out sick," Jena said. "Please make yourself at home and feel free to talk with the children. I'm just about to meet with a group of students who are revising stories they've written so our parent volunteer can type them up. Sara knows what we're doing here almost as well as I do, but if you have questions, I can answer them in a few minutes. If you'll excuse me . . . "

"She always leaves me to do the explaining," Sara said proudly, as Jena Harris gathered up four students from various places around the room and led them to a corner, where several comfortable chairs formed a conversation area. "After the kids get their revisions done and their typed copies back, they do their illustrations. Then a teen intern or parent volunteer helps them bind the pages together in a book. Their books are added to the classroom library for other kids to read."

"What a wonderful idea! I don't think anyone except the teacher ever read anything I wrote until I got out of school and became a writer," said John.

"I thought those kids' books were the greatest thing when I came here. In fact, Ms. Harris gave me one of them to read the first day. Jeremy Stevens' book—I'll never forget the story he wrote about his dog dying. It was so sad. But the story ended when he got a new puppy. He said something like you can't replace the dog you lost, but you have the memory to keep, and the new puppy is like making a new friend. His drawings weren't that great, but the story meant a lot to me because I had to leave my dog behind when we moved. I still missed her and didn't want to get a new pet. Jeremy's story changed my mind. I remember telling him how his story helped me. He ended up being a good friend—still is today."

John jotted down some notes. "That will make a nice anecdote for my article. Do you mind if I use it?"

"Not at all," replied Sara. "Reading Jeremy's book also made me anxious to learn more about writing so I could do a book of my own. I was asked to donate some of my later books to the school, but I kept the very first one I wrote. It was a story about the ants who invaded the kitchen of our new house. Publishing what you write starts early here. The older kids often do community research—history, current issues, and so forth—as well as creative writing. And when their work is outstanding or provides new information, it's either bound into a book and added to the CLMC collection or included in the data bank so everyone has access to it."

"CLMC? What's that?" John asked.

"Whoops. Sorry. I'm not supposed to mention things without explaining them, but sometimes I slip. CLMC is the Central Library Media Center. It maintains the electronic data bank and houses all the books, videotapes, and magazines for the whole system. We don't have individual libraries in any of our school buildings now. At first the change was made to save money and avoid duplication of efforts, but now we realize that services have been greatly improved as a result."

"So teachers have to take kids to the Central Library if they want them to get books? Or do they expect them to go by themselves?" asked John.

"I guess that's right if teachers want students to browse among the actual books, but everything that's available is accessible on the computer. Students can access the data bank from one of many terminals all over the community. The computer also tells them whether a particular book, videotape, or videodisc is out. The electronic system saves a lot of time and hassle. Kids request books by computer, and CLMC will deliver them right to the classrooms. Teachers can use the same process to set up classroom libraries. All the Fun Ed teachers do. See? Ms. Harris has a little library over there."

John looked where Sara pointed and saw that one area of the room contained bookcases used as room dividers to create a mini-library. A chubby, curly-haired girl was carefully inspecting the books on a lower shelf, one by one. "The centralized system does seem very workable and efficient. I've often thought how silly it is that our high school libraries, which presumably have the material students need for the courses they're taking, are closed at night and on weekends when students are most apt to be working on a term paper," said John.

"CLMC runs a bookstore, too, because many students, usually teens and adults, want to own the books they read for courses. But the CLMC bookstore only sells books that are used as texts. They don't want to compete with private business. Do you want to talk to some of the kids? Jason, the boy with blond hair over there by the window, is my neighbor. He's pretty neat."

"Sure. I'd like to know what he's working on." John and Sara walked across the room and sat down at the round table where Jason sat by himself, papers and books spread out around him.

"Mind if we interrupt you, Jason? Mr. Weston's writing an article on our schools. I thought you might be able to help him out," said Sara.

"No problem. I need a break," Jason replied.

"What are you working on?" asked John.

"I'm doing research on Puerto Rico. I have to miss school for two weeks next month to go with my parents. Ms. Harris said I could count the trip as school if I found out all about it first and then wrote a journal while I was there. I get to fill in the Puerto Rico page in my social studies learning book when I finish."

Before John could ask, Sara said, "Every student has what's called a learning book for every subject. It lists all the topics and concepts kids have to learn before they complete Fun Ed and go into CEC full-time. Since teachers teach interdisciplinary units and let kids do special projects all the time, the learning books are a way of keeping track of the curriculum each child has covered. When kids get to the fourth level of Fun Ed, the teacher has to make sure they study all the topics they haven't done yet. Most of the learning books are sort of like checklists, but the social studies one has maps, too. Kids fill in the maps as they study each country."

Jason pulled out a paperback booklet from the stack in front of him and opened it to the first double-page, which contained a blank map of the world. Only a few countries were labeled, but Jason proudly pointed out that he had neatly labeled the island of Puerto Rico on the map. He flipped to the Puerto Rico page, where he'd written nothing. "I can't fill anything in here until I discuss what I've learned with the teacher."

John patted Jason on the shoulder and asked Sara, "What happens if these books get lost?"

"They don't take the learning books home. The teacher keeps them and sends them on to the teacher in the next level. There's also a computer record of everything kids study in Fun Ed. The computer is even more necessary for CEC. There the courses can be quite different, so our CEC transcripts show every activity and course we've taken, along with the number of hours we spent on each. Some of the courses are also coded to show that they meet college or vocational school admission standards," Sara explained.

Turning back to look at Jason, John asked, "Tell me what you're doing to learn about Puerto Rico."

"Well, I've read a lot of books and looked at some travel magazines. Mom got me some brochures from the travel agency, too. The most fun thing, though, is talking to Carlos in San Juan."

"Carlos? On the phone?"

"Carlos is my kid-net pal. He's nine, too. We use the computer to send messages back and forth about our families, school, stuff like that. We can have kid-net pals anywhere in the world, but usually we don't get to meet them. Sometimes we write letters and trade pictures. This time I get to meet Carlos. I can hardly wait! He invited me to spend a day at his school when we go to Puerto Rico." Then Jason added in a discouraged voice, "I wish I were there today."

"What's the matter, Jason?" asked Sara. "You're usually so cheerful."

"Mrs. Montalvo didn't come in today. She's sick. She was supposed to help me with stuff about Puerto Rico I can't find in the books."

"Who's Mrs. Montalvo?" asked John.

"She's from Puerto Rico and is just learning to speak English. That's why she's in Fun Ed. Ms. Harris said it would help both of us if we worked together on my project."

"Mrs. Montalvo must be a Fun Ed student," Sara told John. "Adults often come back to school here, and they don't feel funny about enrolling in Fun Ed. They have separate classes, too, but they seem to learn even more when they work with the kids. Ms. Harris is especially good at working with adults. She makes them feel like her assistants at the same time she helps them with their basic skills. The kids benefit, too, as you can see with Jason."

"Amazing," said John, writing in his notebook. "It seems that the whole CARE system is based on the idea that everybody can learn and help others learn while they're doing it."

Sara nodded. "Well, we'd better let you get back to work, Jason. Hope Mrs. Montalvo's here to help you tomorrow."

"Thanks for talking with me, Jason. Have fun in Puerto Rico," said John.

Sara and John spent another hour talking to kids and looking at their work, then thanked Ms. Harris and left. In the car, John asked Sara to tell him how student learning was evaluated.

"We have many different ways. Teachers write profiles of the kids. In addition to the computerized records that show what kids have studied – the teacher's signature indicates that the student demonstrated understanding and knowledge of a specific topic or concept – kids take a basic skills exam in Level Four. Kids also select items for their individual portfolios each year—their learning books, sample papers, journal or learning log entries, projects, and other things that demonstrate what they have learned. Part of the portfolio is a videotape that contains an interview with the teacher at the beginning of the year, in which kids say what they want to do, what their goals are for the year. Then they make another at the end in which they say what they accomplished. There are also clips of projects, group presentations, and anything else the student wants to have taped."

"The videotapes sound wonderful, but they must make a great deal of extra work for the teacher," said John.

"No, not at all," said Sara. "The older kids do internships with the video department of CLMC. Kids can sign up to have any activity taped. The interns also teach kids how to use the equipment themselves. After Level Two most kids do their own videotaping and editing. They can always call on an intern if they need help."

"How does this system affect college admission?" asked John.

"Except for the way classes are scheduled, it's pretty much as I understand it was in the old days. Surprisingly, colleges haven't changed much—except for a few innovative schools. Most require basic courses, which CEC offers. Then kids take the SAT and achievement tests. The internships and the RCA activities give everyone a chance to show as much 'extracurricular' activity as they want on their college applications. The school I want to go to next year favors well-rounded students. Some CEC courses don't have grades, but all the college prep courses do."

By the time John and Sara arrived back at the CARE administrative center, they had visited a Child Care Center and a Preschool class. They'd stayed quite a while in a Primary class, because John was interested in comparing it to the Montessori school his daughter had attended. He found few differences. One group of kids was so involved in constructing an elaborate block city that they wouldn't stop even to chat with them. Sara, though, happily answered his many questions. She was so articulate and well-informed that he almost forgot she was no older than his own teenage daughter. He realized that much of the difference between Sara and Kelley was due to the differences in the educational systems. The system in his country forced students to be dependent and often turned them off to learning, while the approach here encouraged kids to become more responsible for themselves and enthusiastic about education.

As they parked the car, Sara looked at her watch and said, "I have to hurry. I'm almost late for my TV course. We don't have enough students to offer a course in Japanese so I'm taking it on the interactive TV network. The teacher's in New York, but there are hook-ups all over the country. We fax our assignments to the instructor and he corrects them and gets them back to us the same way."

"We've just begun to explore the possibilities of interactive TV," said John. "I can see the advantages, especially for people in remote, rural areas. Anyone anywhere could study any subject through interactive TV, couldn't they?"

"They sure could," said Sara, waving as she walked away from John's car. "Bye."

John headed in the other direction, back toward the building to meet Hector Garcia.

Inside the school cafeteria where John and Hector were to meet with the Learn/Share group, Hector said, "We're early, and I have an emergency of sorts to take care of, but I've arranged for you to talk with Suzan Robinson while I'm gone. She used to teach Fun Ed, but now she works in Research and Development and sometimes teaches CEC courses. I'll get back to you in time for the L/S group meeting." Hector introduced John to Suzan and then hurried off, leaving them to talk over coffee.

"Since you used to teach in Fun Ed, maybe you can clarify something for me," said John. "My guide today explained that students took a basic skills exam and developed a portfolio for Fun Ed, but she didn't say anything about how kids were evaluated. I mean, who decides whether they've learned enough to graduate? And what happens if they don't?"

"Good question, although the term we use is 'satisfy'—as in 'satisfied Fun Ed' rather than 'graduate.' A panel made up of educators and citizens reviews students' test results and portfolios, as well as teachers' profiles, before they schedule interviews with the students. If students have made it all the way through Level

Four, they're pretty much set on the basics, but everyone has different strengths and weaknesses. The panel decides whether to issue a certificate of satisfaction with either no conditions or else with recommendations for further study in specific CEC courses. Because of the way we define compulsory education, all students have to spend two years in CEC anyway, but the kids who need to fill in some gaps have required courses to take, while others are free to choose all of theirs."

"But what about the kids who are really slow and can't learn? Surely you must have students like that."

"Not very many," said Suzan. "Except for the mentally retarded, who have special programs that include participation in some CEC courses so they aren't isolated completely, all of our kids learn because we personalize the curriculum and teaching methods for each student. Of course, it takes some kids longer than others to get through Fun Ed, but it makes a big difference when teachers really believe that every kid is able to learn. Special Services provides tutors if they're needed in special cases. ESL kids, for example, always have tutors until they learn enough English to get along by themselves. But I think the biggest reason why our program works for everyone is that we assign only the best teachers to Fun Ed. College students may do their student teaching in Fun Ed, but they begin their actual teaching in CEC. Then, the best ones get 'promoted' to teaching Fun Ed. And they're chosen not just because they're knowledgeable, but also because they care about kids and know how to encourage and bring out the best in each one. Plus we have a wonderful in-service program based on the idea that good teachers never stop learning about teaching."

"Tell me more about the in-service programs. In my country they use what I call the inoculation approach,' a series of one-day workshops on a variety of topics – substance abuse, AIDS education, or classroom management. They haven't been very effective. I did a story on a three-hour presentation in one school district on using writing as a tool for learning. The consultant was good, but I realized that there was no way three hours of listening to someone talk would really help teachers learn to use the new methods in their classrooms."

Suzan laughed. "That's just the way in-service used to be

here. Now we combine our in-service efforts with teacher research. We expect teachers to do classroom research on whatever aspect of teaching and learning interests them. They keep journals, collect data, and experiment all the time. Each teacher belongs to a teaching-learning group consisting of about four or five other teachers. They meet regularly to share information, discuss articles and books they've read, and support each other. Every year they're required to submit an informal report on their research. That's probably the most important part of the in-service, but we also sponsor programs on topics teachers request. We sometimes bring in outside consultants or arrange for presentations on the interactive television network. We pay teachers' expenses to attend conferences and encourage them to visit classes in other communities. Sometimes those visits lead to teacher exchanges—teachers are often given visiting status in another district just as college professors have done for years. We've found that the best way to spread new ideas is through informal contacts, word-of-mouth."

"Being able to teach somewhere else must help avoid teacher burnout, too," John commented.

"Our teachers have so many different opportunities to learn that few of them ever burn out. But we're also quite generous about granting sabbaticals and leaves-of-absence. You're right—being able to recharge the batteries by doing something different for a while is all most people need to return to their jobs renewed and refreshed."

"What else does Research and Development do?"

"We provide mentors for beginning teachers and maintain an extensive professional library, which includes some of the results of the research our teachers do. But we're also responsible for monitoring student achievement and progress in the whole system. That means collecting and analyzing the data from the standardized tests we give. It was test results that first gave us the idea to study the classrooms of our most successful teachers to find out what works for them and why, so that we could help other teachers improve. That's another option teachers have. They can take leaves from classroom teaching to serve as research assistants for a year at a time. We discovered that our best teachers were the most enthusiastic learners, so we encourage all teachers—along with everyone else in the community—to keep learning in a variety of ways. Adult learners—whether teachers or parents—are good models for our students."

"People say that children learn more from what they see than what we say. I've seen the truth of that with my own children," said John.

"That was the biggest obstacle we faced when we tried to get teachers to go beyond simply lecturing and testing. They needed to experience these new methods for themselves before they felt comfortable trying them out with students. But we should have expected that—their only models for teaching were teachers who lectured and tested. I first worked in R and D while I was still a Fun Ed teacher, because there were so few teachers who understood the new methods well enough to help others learn them. At first I worked with teachers in intensive summer workshops, but with so many teachers wanting help, they assigned me and several others to R and D full-time. Now teachers take mini-sabbaticals for a month or two to participate in our workshops. Most of them are CEC teachers who want Fun Ed jobs because there's more continuity working with the same kids for a whole year."

"I'd like to take you home with me to work with the teachers in my community! Does the system allow international exchanges?" asked John.

"Yes, but—" Hector Garcia's return interrupted Suzan's reply.

"Has Suzan been helpful?" Hector asked.

"She certainly has. I asked her to come back with me," John said with a smile.

"Sorry," Suzan laughed. "Now if you'll excuse me, I have to get going. My husband's meeting me. Tonight's our Great Books discussion group. It's been a pleasure meeting you, John. Good luck."

As Suzan walked quickly toward the cafeteria exit, Hector pointed out the table at the other end of the large room where the Learn/Share group was gathered.

Hector introduced John to the L/S group members, explaining that he was gathering information for a magazine story and just wanted to observe. After shaking hands with everyone, John took a seat beside Hector at the far end of the long table where he could see everyone and opened his notebook. They had already finished eating and cleared the table.

Mark Johnson, a sixteen-year-old whose passion for repairing cars was evident from his grease-stained hands, led the meeting. Hector had explained that only the youngest students were excused from taking a turn as discussion leader. In fact, leading the discussion in the L/S group for the first time at age eleven or twelve had become something of a rite of passage. The group included six other students: Cori and Casey, both eight and in Level One of Fun Ed; Marcus, eleven, in Level Three; Eric, twelve, whose Fun Ed satisfaction interview was scheduled next month; Kristen, fourteen, now in her second year of CEC; and Chris, fifteen, who was taking mostly college-coded CEC courses. John noted that the three adults–Vickie, a young mother in her thirties; Ken, a middle-aged insurance executive; and Philip, a retired postal worker–were careful not to dominate the discussion. Vickie made a special effort to draw Cori and Casey into the conversation.

Mark began the meeting by asking if anyone had a special situation they wished to discuss.

Chris said, "I have a problem I'd like some help with, but let's do the reports first and let me be last. I'll bring it up then."

"Okay, we'll begin with reports. Who wants to go first? Casey, why don't you tell us what you've learned and how things have been going since the last meeting?"

Casey smiled shyly. "My teacher's letting us do frogs. I named mine Joe. And I write in my journal every day. We wrote poems about the frogs and saw a video. Joe's not a frog yet, but he will be. Right now he's just a polliwog."

Casey answered several questions from the group about the frog unit she was doing in Fun Ed. Then Cori talked about the story she was writing that would be published in a book when she finished. Vickie again helped to make the group's newest members feel welcome by describing a new children's book she had just read to her own children. Marcus talked about the CEC course on whales he was taking with his father. He was excited because the whole family was going to join him and his father on the class whale watch on Saturday. Eric said he was worried about his upcoming interview with the Fun Ed Satisfaction Panel. After Mark and Kristen described their experiences with the panel and convinced him he had nothing to worry about, he felt better.

Everyone laughed when Ken described how things were going in the cooking class his wife insisted he take. "Some people complain that they can't understand the jargon in their insurance policies. Well, I'm having trouble with the cookbook. The teacher says there's a difference between 'saute' and 'fry,' but they seem the same to me. It's a good thing I'm not getting a grade!"

"I wish I'd taken that course," Philip said. "Since my wife hasn't been able to get around, I've taken over in the kitchen. I'm getting sick of soup and take-out. My wife spoiled me by making everything from scratch. I was used to eating well. You might not think this cafeteria food is anything to write home about, but it's a darn sight better than what I've been eating lately. I'm happy to be here for more reasons than one!"

"What above microwave meals?" asked Vickie. "Some of them are really good." When Philip admitted he'd never eaten one, Vickie explained how easy they were to prepare and where Philip could find them in the grocery store. When Cori mentioned that she often fixed her own microwave dinners, Philip said, "You convinced me, Cori. I'll try one."

Kristen and Mark both talked about their internships. Mark proudly announced that the owner of the auto repair shop was so pleased with his work that he offered him a permanent job there when he finished his internship next month. "You know, I have you guys to thank for this. Tom, the social worker you got to help my family out when my father overdosed on drugs a few years back, kept me off the streets by getting me interested in fixing cars. Since we didn't have a car, I might never have fooled around with them otherwise. Who would have guessed that's something I'd be really good at? My father's doing good now, too. He just started a new job."

Kristen was not as enthusiastic about her placement, however. "I thought I would go to college and then to law school, but I've changed my mind. My ideas about what lawyers did came from TV shows and they weren't very realistic. I thought you got to take exciting cases to court, but now I know that much of the time you're reading, writing, and researching. Court is only a small part of the job. And most of the cases are pretty routine." Ken suggested that Kristen investigate some other career options and consider doing another internship before she went to college.

"O.K., Chris, you're on," Mark said. "Everyone else has had their say. What can we help you with?"

"It's this college-coded course I'm taking on World War II. We have to do a hypermedia project on some aspect of the war."

"Hypermedia," said Kristen, "that's fun. An electronic research paper is better than a written one because you can put in pictures, music, and everything."

"I know," said Chris. "I did one last year in another course and it was good enough to be accepted for use in Fun Ed classes. I designed it to be interactive so kids could learn from it. But I did that one all by myself. This time Mr. Baker's making us do these in groups. And he said everyone had to help – one or two people couldn't do all the work. We're being graded on the process as well as the final project. I'm worried because this course is graded and counts for college. There's one person in the group who won't do anything. We've been covering for her because she's had a problem at home. We thought we'd help her out at first, then she'd pitch in and do her share. But it hasn't worked out that way. The problem's taken care of, so now she's just taking advantage of us."

Mark said, "That happened to me in a Fun Ed class once. We finally had to go to the teacher. She helped us work things out eventually, but I learned a valuable lesson. You should never cover for anyone because then they don't have to be responsible for themselves. Some people naturally look for the easy way out – I do it myself sometimes. But you can't make it easy for them to do that."

"I agree," Kristen said. "Why don't you go and talk to the teacher? I'm sure he'll be able to help."

"I don't want to be a rat fink," said Chris.

"Some things never change," said Philip. "When I was a kid, we had the same worries. But, take it from me, kids worry too much about what their friends will think instead of doing what's right or sensible. Just tell Mr. Baker you'd like to talk to him in confidence. He may be able to suggest something you can do without that girl or anyone else even knowing you talked to him."

"I second that idea," Mark said. "Me, too," echoed Kristen and Marcus. Even Cori said, "I think Mr. Philip's right, Chris."

"O.K., I'll try," replied Chris. "But I'll blame you if the other kids find out and get mad at me for ratting."

"Chris," said Ken with a smile, "what happened to the idea of people assuming responsibility for their own actions? Shouldn't that include you?"

Chris laughed. "You're right. It's your suggestion but my decision. I'll talk to Mr. Baker and let you know what happens next meeting."

"Anything else we need to discuss tonight?" Mark asked. When no one said anything, he continued, "Ken wants us to read a story and discuss it next time. I have copies for everyone. Cori and Casey, if you need help reading it, let one of us know. It's not too hard, though. Ken said it's about making a tough decision, so maybe you'll want to read it before you see Mr. Baker, Chris. Before we sign off for the night, I guess I should ask Mr. Weston if he wants to ask us anything."

"No questions," said John, "but thank you for letting me sit in. It was interesting and I learned a lot. Is it all right if I include what you've said in my article?"

Everyone nodded affirmatively, so Mark said, "Guess that's it. Two weeks from tonight. Same time. Same station. Ken's the discussion leader. See you then. Have a good one!"

After a quick dinner in the cafeteria, Hector walked John to his car. "So what do you think of what you've seen here?"

"Impressive. You've found ways to bring people together by defining education much more broadly than we do. The public education system here has really changed the culture. I want people in my country to know what can be done. It's really amazing that it all seems to be based on very simple premises. Everybody counts, everybody cares, and everybody learns," said John.

Hector said, "So simple that we had trouble getting people to realize how much we could accomplish in building a system based on such simple beliefs. Everyone here is a teacher and a learner. You're right about the most important element. The system works because its main purpose is making sure that people–adults and kids–really believe that they count and others care. The result, as you can see, is a community committed to lifelong learning."

Notes on Sources

Chapter One

The National Commission on Excellence in Education, *A Nation at Risk*. Washington, DC: U.S. Department of Education, 1983.

Robert Rothman, "Judging Schools: The Focus Shifts to Results," *Teacher Magazine*, January 1990.

Jonathan Kozol. *Savage Inequalities*. New York: Crown, 1991.

Karlene K. Hale, "Maine man is finalist for National Teacher of the Year," Portland (ME) *Press Herald*, January 10, 1990.

Chapter Three

Robert Hilliard quoted in *Engfo: A Resource for Teaching and Learning*, Vol. V, No. 1, Fall 1989. Colorado Dept. of Education.

See John I. Goodlad, *A Place Called School*. New York: McGraw-Hill, 1984.

For more detailed information, see Rita Dunn, Jeffrey Beaudry, and Angela Klavas, "Survey of Research on Learning Styles," *Educational Leadership*, March 1989.

Bernice McCarthy. *The 4MAT System: Teaching to Learning Styles with Right/Left Mode Techniques*. Barrington, IL: Excel, 1987.

Myra Sadker and David Sadker, "Sexism in the Classroom: From Grade School to Graduate School," *Phi Delta Kappan*, March 1986, and (with Sharon Steindam) "Gender Equity and Educational Reform," *Educational Leadership*, March 1989.

See Linda Kreger Silverman, "What Happens to the Gifted Girl?" in *Critical Issues in Gifted Education*, ed. C. June Maker. Rockville, MD: Aspen, 1986.

See Carol Gilligan, *In a Different Voice*. Cambridge, MA: Harvard University Press, 1982, and Carol Gilligan, Nona P. Lyons, and Trudy S. Hamner, *Making Connections*. Harvard University Press, 1990.

Robert J. Sternberg, "Three Heads Are Better Than One," *Psychology*

Today, August 1986. See also Sternberg, *The Triarchic Mind: A New Theory of Human Intelligence*, New York: Viking, 1988.

Robert J. Sternberg, "Thinking Styles: Keys to Understanding Student Performance, *Phi Delta Kappan*, January 1990.

"Seven Ways of Knowing, Not One," *Education Week*, January 27, 1988. See also Howard Gardner. *Frames of Mind*, New York: Basic Books, 1983.

See Anne Wescott Dodd, "The Big Mac Approach to Teaching Grammar," *Connecticut English Journal*, Spring 1985.

Richard P. Feynman. *Surely You're Joking, Mr. Feynman*, New York: Norton, 1985, and *What Do You Care What Other People Think?*, New York: Norton, 1988.

Chapter Four

Geoff Davidian, "The making of a killer," *Maine Sunday Telegram*, January 21, 1990.

Abraham Maslow. *Toward A Psychology of Being*, New York: Van Nostrand, 1962.

Cameron Seymour, "School dropouts: Administrators seek answers to the problem, Brunswick (ME) *Times Record*, November 14, 1989.

Ellen Mahoney Sawyer, "School dropouts younger," Brunswick (ME) *Times Record*, May 4, 1989.

Letters to the editor, Brunswick (ME) *Times Record*, November 22, 1989.

"Iowa Poll Spurs Guide To Pare Dropout Rate, *Education Week*, November 8, 1989.

Joseph F. Gastright, "Don't Base Your Dropout Program on Somebody Else's Problem," *Research Bulletin*, Phi Delta Kappa, April 1989.

"Thinking about Grades" in "Kidding Around," Brunswick (ME) *Times Record*, March 27, 1989.

June Cox, Neil Daniel, and Bruce O. Boston. *Educating the Able Learner: Programs and Promising Practices*. Austin, Texas: University of Texas Press, 1985.

"Trooper knows anguish of youth suicide," Portland (ME) *Evening Express*, October 18, 1989.

Amy Stuart Wells, "Plan speeds pace of remedial study," Augusta (ME) *Kennebec Journal*, June 5, 1989.

Stanley Pogrow, "Challenging At-Risk Students: Findings from the HOTS Program," *Phi Delta Kappan*, January 1990.

Debra Viadero, "Foreign Language Instruction Resurfacing in Elementary Schools," *Education Week*, November 6, 1991.

Linda McNeil. *Contradictions of Control*. New York: Routledge & Kegan Paul, 1986.

Linda T. Sanford and Mary Ellen Donovan. *Women and Self-Esteem*. New York: Penguin, 1984.

Chapter Five

Part of this chapter is adapted from Anne Wescott Dodd, *A Handbook for Substitute Teachers*, Chapter Six, Springfield, IL: Charles C. Thomas, 1989. The publisher has granted permission to reprint.

Chapter Six

Shirley Brice Heath in an address. Maine Council for English Language Arts Spring Conference, Portland, ME, March 17, 1989.

Anne Ruggles Gere. *Writing Groups: History, Theory, and Implications*. Carbondale, IL: Illinois University Press, 1987.

Deborah Burnett Strother, "Cooperative Learning: Fad or Foundation for Learning?" *Phi Delta Kappan*, October, 1990.

Gene Stanford and Barbara Dodds Stanford. *Learning Discussion Skills Through Games*. New York: Citation Press, 1969.

Alfie Kohn, "It's Hard To Get Left Out of a Pair," *Psychology Today*, October 1987. For a full discussion of the negative effects of competition, see Alfie Kohn's book, *No Contest: The Case Against Competition*. Boston: Houghton Mifflin, 1986.

Dewey J. Carducci and Judith B. Carducci. *The Caring Classroom*. Palo Alto, CA: Bull, 1984.

William Glasser. *Control Theory in the Classroom*. New York: Harper and Row, 1986.

Pauline B. Gough, "The Key to Improving Schools: An Interview with William Glasser," *Phi Delta Kappan*, May 1987.

For more information on the jigsaw method, see Elliot Aronson et al. *The Jigsaw Classroom*. Beverly Hills, CA: Sage, 1978.

Yael Sharan and Shlomo Sharan, "Group Investigation Expands Cooperative Learning," *Educational Leadership*, December 1989/January 1990.

Yael Sharan and Shlomo Sharan, "How Effective Is Group Investigation?", *Educational Leadership*, December 1989/January 1990.

"Special Education," *Education Week*, November 8, 1989.

Deborah Burnett Strother, "Mediation, Conflict Resolution, and Cooperative Learning," *Phi Delta Kappan*, October 1990.

Anne Ratzki and Angela Fisher, "Life in a Restructured School," *Educational Leadership*, December 1989/January 1990.

Chapter Seven

"New Ideas about Learning," *USA Today*, November 7, 1989.

Bill Stonebarger, *Hawkhill Science Newsletter*, Winter 1990.

Harriet Tyson and Arthur Woodward, "Why Students Aren't Learning Very Much from Textbooks," *Educational Leadership*, November 1989.

"Smarting from Critics, Textbooks Bounce Back," *ASCD Update*, May 1989.

Robert Rothman, "McGraw-Hill Technique Will Allow Schools To 'Customize' Textbooks," *Education Week*, November 1, 1989.

"English Associations Call for Major Changes To Improve Student Learning," *Council-Grams*, Volume LI, No. 5, May 1989.

Robert Rothman, "Sciences Group Unveils Plan To Revise Curricula," *Education Week*, March 1, 1989.

James A. Minstrell, "Teaching Science for Understanding," in *Toward the Thinking Curriculum*, edited by Lauren B. Resnick and Leopold E. Klopfer. Alexandria, VA: ASCD, 1989.

Robert Rothman, "Academy Urges Nation To 'Wake Up' and Revamp Mathematics Education," *Education Week*, February 1, 1989.

John A. Dossey, "Transforming Mathematics Education," *Educational Leadership*, November 1989.

"Math gets boost," Portland (ME) *Evening Express*, October 16, 1989.

Charlotte Crabtree, "Improving History in the Schools," *Educational Leadership*, November 1989.

Peter Schmidt, "European Upheaval Sparks Curriculum Debate," *Education Week*, January 10, 1990.

Gilbert M. Grosvenor, "The Case for Geography Education," *Educational Leadership*, November 1989.

Bob Forkey, "Industrial arts to get retooling," Portland (ME) *Evening Express*, February 22, 1989.

John O'Neil, "Foreign Languages," *ASCD Curriculum Update*, January 1990.

"The Need for 'Informational Literacy,' " *Council-Grams*, Volume LI, No. 5, May 1989.

Peter West, "Some Are Seeing Computer 'Magic' in a New, But Costly Software Tool," *Education Week*, March 29, 1989.

Chapter Eight

Elizabeth Schulz, " 'The Dog Ate It': Study details homework hassles," *Teacher Magazine*, January 1990.

What Works: Research about Teaching and Learning. U.S. Department of Education, 1986.

William Snider, "NAEP Finds Basic Skills Up, Higher-order Skills Lacking," *Education Week*, February 22, 1989.

Sylvia Fraser. *My Father's House*. New York: Ticknor and Fields, 1982.

Powell, Arthur G., Eleanor Farrar, and David K. Cohen. *The Shopping Mall High School*, Boston: Houghton Mifflin, 1985.

Vita Wallace, Letter to the Editor, Portland (ME) *Press Herald*, January 30, 1990.

James Alvino, "12 Learning-to-Learn Skills," *Learning 90*, February 1990.

Robert J. Sternberg and Marie Martin, "When Teaching Thinking Does Not Work, What Goes Wrong?", *Teachers College Record*, Vol. 89, No. 4, Summer 1988.

Marvin J. Cetron. *Schools of the Future*. New York: McGraw-Hill, 1985.

Chapter Nine

Scott Willis, "Transforming the Test," *ASCD Update*, September 1990.

Robert Rothman, "NAEP Will Make Its Most Extensive Use of Performance Items," *Education Week*, January 24, 1990.

John O'Neil, "New Exam System Debated," *ASCD Update*, November 1991.

Tina Blythe and Howard Gardner, "A School for All Intelligences," *Educational Leadership*, April 1990.

Chester E. Finn, Jr., "The Need for Better Data on Education," *Education Week*, February 7, 1990.

Mark Pitsch, "Study Affirms Bates College Officials' Hunch in Dropping Requirements for Admissions Tests, *Education Week*, November 27, 1991.

Chapter Ten

Fox Butterfield, "Why They Excel," *Parade*, January 21, 1990.

"Grades, parent actions linked," Portland (ME) *Evening Express,* February 12, 1986.

"Story Hour Power," *Learning 90,* February 1990.

Chapter Eleven

"Grades, parent actions linked," Portland (ME) *Evening Express,* February 12, 1986.

Gene I. Maeroff, " 'School Smart' Parents Strengthen Education," *Education Week,* October 25, 1989.

David Hill, "Making Schools Their Business," *Teacher Magazine,* January 1990.

"School Dances: A Different Approach," *The Maine Principal,* January 1990.

If you decide to try substitute teaching, see Anne Wescott Dodd, *A Handbook for Substitute Teachers.* Springfield, IL: Charles C. Thomas, 1989.

Reagan Walker, "Single Definition of 'Restructuring' Remains Elusive," *Education Week,* February 21, 1990.

Peter Schmidt, "Despite Controversy, Consensus Grows on the Need To Teach Values in the Schools," *Education Week,* February 7, 1990.

Chapter Twelve

This chapter is based on Anne Wescott Dodd, "A New Design for Public Education," *Phi Delta Kappan,* June 1984.

Organizations and Resources for Parents

Active Parenting Publications
810 Franklin Center, Suite B
Marietta, GA 30067

Books and videos on parent education

Alliance for Parental Involvement in Education
P.O. Box 59
East Chatham, NY 10260-0059

Newsletter, publications, and resources about education options and parent and student rights

ASPIRA Association, Inc.
1112 16th Street NW, Suite 340
Washington, DC 20036

Administers a national parent-involvement demonstration project in Hispanic communities in nine cities, and produces booklets to help Hispanic parents with their children's education.

American Association of Parents and Children
560 Herndon Parkway, Suite 110
Herndon, VA 22070

Making the Grade: How Parents Can Help Their Kids Do Better in School This Year ($1.50) and *Tuition Software Guide* (planning for college expenses, $3.00)

Barbara Bush Foundation for Family Literacy
1002 Wisconsin Avenue NW
Washington, DC 20007

First Teacher: A Family Literacy Handbook for Parents, Policymakers, and Literacy Providers ($4.00)

Educational Resources Information Center (ERIC)

A nationwide information service designed to make educational literature readily accessible. For more information about the various centers and services or a free subscription to *The ERIC Review*, call ACCESS ERIC toll free at 1-800-USE-ERIC.

ERIC/RCS
Indiana Research Center, Suite 150
2805 East 10th Street
Bloomington, IN 47408-2698

You Can Help Your Young Child with Writing (Baghban, $1.75)
Beginning Literacy and Your Child (Silvern and Silvern, $1.75)
Helping Your Child Become a Reader (Roser, $1.75)
101 Ideas To Help Your Child Learn To Read and Write (Behm and Behm, $4.00)

Heinemann/Boynton Cook Publishers
361 Hanover Street
Portsmouth, NH 03801-3959

Write for a catalog. Although books are addressed to teachers (literacy education and elementary teaching), some are excellent for parents.

Institute for Responsive Education
605 Commonwealth Avenue
Boston, MA 02215

National research and advocacy organization that studies schools and helps them become more responsive to citizen and parent involvement. Write for information about the journal *Equity and Choice* and reports.

International Reading Association
800 Barksdale Road
Newark, DE 19704-8139

Works with parents, educators, and researchers to improve reading instruction. Write for information about publications that help parents develop lifelong reading habits with their children. (Some titles listed under ERIC/RCS above are IRA publications and are also available from IRA.)

Mexican American Legal Defense and Educational Fund
634 South Spring Street, 11th floor
Los Angeles, CA 90014

A civil rights organization that conducts a Parent Leadership Program for promoting the participation of Latino parents at their children's schools.

National Association for the Education of Young Children
1834 Connecticut Avenue NW
Washington, DC 20009

Free catalog of resources on all aspects of child development and early childhood education.

National Black Child Development Institute
1463 Rhode Island Avenue NW
Washington, DC 20005

Provides direct services and conducts advocacy campaigns to improve the quality of life for black children and youth. Speakers and publications available.

National Center for Fair and Open Testing (FairTest)
342 Broadway
Cambridge, MA 02139

Standardized Tests and Our Children: A Guide To Testing Reform ($3.00) *FairTest Examiner*, published quarterly. Write for information on other publications available.

National Committee for Citizens in Education
10840 Little Patuxent Parkway, Suite 301
Columbia, MO 21044

A variety of books for parents and citizens, such as *Your School: How Well Is It Working?* ($5.50) and *The Middle School Years: A Parents' Handbook* ($9.95). A newsletter, *Network for Public Schools*, published six times a year, describes innovative programs and provides information and resources to parents and others concerned about schools.

National Coalition for Parent Involvement in Education
Box 39
1201 16th Street NW
Washington, DC 20036

Free brochure, "Developing Family/School Partnerships: Guidelines for Schools and School Districts" (Send business-sized SASE with 52 cents postage).

National Council for the Social Studies Publications
c/o Maxway Data Corporation
225 W. 34th Street
New York, NY 10001

Charting a Course: Social Studies for the 21st Century, a report by the Curriculum Task Force of the National Commission on Social Studies in the Schools ($7.00 plus 2.00 postage and handling).

National Council of Teachers of English
1111 Kenyon Road
Urbana, IL 61801

How To Help Your Child Become a Better Writer (single copy free) Other publications for English language arts teachers may also be of interest to parents. Write for catalog.

National Council of La Raza
810 First Street NE, Suite 300
Washington, DC 20002-4205

Research and advocacy organization that works on behalf of U.S. Hispanics and provides technical assistance to community-based organizations.

National Parents and Teachers Organization
700 N. Rush Street
Chicago, IL 66611

Looking In On Your School ($1.00) Request a list of other publications.

National School Boards Association
1680 Duke Street
Alexandria, VA 22314

National Urban League
500 East 62nd Street
New York, NY 10021

The Urban League National Education Initiative: What Students Need To Know ($10.00) Includes chapters on what parents and community members should know about academic competencies, career planning, and testing; planning and conducting parent/community workshops; and additional resources, such as information on homework and tests.

Parent Outreach Project
2805 E. 10th Street, Suite 150
Bloomington, IN 47408-2698

Parents and Children Together, a forty-eight-page monthly magazine with an accompanying audiocassette, includes information for parents and activities for children, read-along stories told by professional storytellers with prereading and prewriting activities and literature extensions. ($60.00/year)

The Parent Power Foundation
1010 W. Orange Grove Road
Tucson, AZ 85704

Offers workshops and keynote presentations for parents, schools, and PTA's as well as publications.

Phi Delta Kappa
Eighth and Union
P.O. Box 789
Bloomington, IN 47402

Phi Delta Kappan is perhaps the best journal covering educational issues and trends for a general audience. Write for subscription information.

Reading Is Fundamental
600 Maryland Avenue SW, Suite 500
Washington, DC 20024

Encouraging Young Writers
Developing a Family Library
Family Storytelling
Summertime Reading
(all guides 50 cents)

U.S. General Services Administration
Consumer Information Center
P.O. Box 100
Pueblo, CO 81002

Request the *Consumer Information Catalog*. Most publications cost 50 cents, but some are free. Titles include

Becoming a Nation of Readers
Books for Children #6 (recent titles preschool through junior high)
Developmental Speech and Language Disorders
Take Pride in America with Mark Trail (coloring book)
Summertime Favorites (reading list)
Timeless Classics (400 titles published before 1960 for children of all ages)
Choosing a School for Your Child
Help Your Child Become a Good Reader
Help Your Child Do Better in School
Help Your Child Improve in Test-Taking
Help Your Child Learn Math
Help Your Child Learn to Write Well
Helping Your Child Learn Geography
Helping Your Child Use the Library
Helping Your Child Learn Science
The Importance of Play
Learning While Growing
Matching Yourself with the World of Work (lists requirements for 200 jobs)

Professional Education Associations

These organizations, as well as some in the previous list, are professional groups for teachers, but most publish books and pamphlets of interest to parents. If you would like to know more about a particular subject area, contact the organization representing that discipline.

American Council on the Teaching of Foreign Languages
Six Executive Plaza
Yonkers, NY 10701

Association for Education Communications and Technology
1126 16th Street NW
Washington, DC 20036

American Educational Research Association
1230 17th Street NW
Washington, DC 20036

American Home Economics Association
1555 King Street
Alexandria, VA 22314

American Association of Physics Teachers
5112 Berwyn Road
College Park, MD 20740

Association for Supervision and Curriculum Development
1250 N. Pitt Street
Alexandria, VA 22314

Council for Exceptional Children (Special Education)
1920 Association Drive
Reston, VA 22091

International Technology Education Association
1914 Association Drive
Reston, VA 22091

Music Teachers National Association
617 Vine Street, Suite 1432
Cincinnati, OH 45202

National Art Education Association
1916 Association Drive
Reston, VA 22091

National Association for Sports and Physical Education
1900 Association Drive
Reston, VA 22091

National Business Education Association
1914 Association Drive
Reston, VA 22091

National Council for the Social Studies
3501 Newark Street NW
Washington, DC 20016

National Council of Teachers of Mathematics
1906 Association Drive
Reston, VA 22091

National Middle School Association
P.O. Box 14882
Columbus, OH 43214

National Science Teachers Association
1742 Connecticut Avenue NW
Washington, DC 20009

Magazines

For Parents

Horn Book (children's books and book publishing), 14 Beacon Street, Boston, MA 02108

Parenting Magazine, 501 Second St., #110, San Francisco, CA 94107

Parents Magazine, 685 Third Ave., New York, NY 10017

Sesame Street Parent's Guide Magazine, Children's Television Workshop, One Lincoln Plaza, New York, NY 10023

The Single Parent, Parents Without Partners, 8807 Colesville Road, Boston, MA 02108

For Children

Animal Tales, 6015 N. 35th Avenue, Phoenix, AZ 85017 (Stories about animals for people who love them)

Calliope: The World History Magazine for Young People, Cobblestone Publishing, 30 Grove St., Peterborough, NH 03458 (World history to 1800 for ages 9–15)

Careers, The Magazine for Young Achievers, E.M. Guild, Inc., 1001 Avenue of the Americas, New York, NY 10018 (The working world and careers for high school students)

Chickadee Magazine, The Young Naturalist Foundation, 56 The Esplanade, Suite 306, Toronto, Ontario M5E 1A7 Canada (World and environment for ages 4–9)

Cobblestone: The History Magazine for Young People, same as *Calliope* (American history for ages 8–14)

Cricket Magazine, Carus Publishing Co., 315 5th Street, P.O. Box 300, Peru, IL 61354 (Literary magazine for ages 6–12)

The Dolphin Log, The Cousteau Society, 8440 Santa Monica Blvd., Los Angeles, CA 90069 (ages 7–15)

Faces, The Magazine about People, Same as *Calliope* (World cultures, anthropology, folktales, and legends for ages 8–14)

Highlights for Children, 803 Church Street, Honesdale, PA 18431 (ages 2–12)

Hopskotch, The Magazine for Girls, Hopskotch, Inc. P.O. Box 1292, Saratoga Springs, NY 12866 (ages 6–12)

Humpty Dumpty, Children's Better Health Institute, 1100 Waterway Blvd., Box 567, Minneapolis, MN 46206 (ages 4–6)

Jack and Jill, same as *Humpty Dumpty* (ages 7–10)

Kid City, Children's Television Workshop, One Lincoln Plaza, New York, NY 10023 (ages 6–12)

Ladybug, same as for *Cricket* (ages 2–7)

Merlyn's Pen, The National Magazine of Student Writing, P.O. Box 1058, East Greenwich, RI 02818 (Publishes writing by students in grades 7–10)

National Geographic World, National Geographic Society, 17th and M Streets NW, Washington, DC 20036 (age 8 and up)

Odyssey, Kalmbach Publishing Co., 21027 Crossroads Circle, Waukesha, WI 53816 (astronomy and outer space for ages 8–12)

Owl, The Discovery Magazine for Children, same as *Chickadee* (Science and nature for age 8 and up)

Ranger Rick, National Wildlife Federation, 1400 16th Street NW, Washington, DC 20036 (ages 6–12)

Skipping Stones, 80574 Hazelton Road, Cottage Grove, OK 97424 (Multicultural children's quarterly for ages 7–13)

Spark!, The Magazine of Creative Fun for Kids, P.O. Box 5028, Harlan, IA 51593-2528 (Imaginative projects for ages 3–12)

Sports Illustrated for Kids, Time-Warner, Time and Life Bldg., New York, NY 10020 (age 8 and up)

Stone Soup, The Magazine by Children, Children's Art Foundation, P.O. Box 83, Santa Cruz, CA 95063 (Publishes writing and art by children through age 13)

3-2-1 Contact, same as *Kid City* (Science, computers, and scientists for ages 8–14)

The World of Business Kids, Business Kids/America's Future, Lemonade Kids, Inc. Suite 330, 301 Almeria Avenue, Coral Gables, FL 33134 (entrepreneurs and business for teens and preteens)

Your Big Back Yard, same as *Ranger Rick* (animals and nature for ages 3–5)

Ask at your local library for information about children's magazines affiliated with religious denominations or other organizations, such as Boy Scouts and Girl Scouts. Older children should be encouraged to read magazines published for adults, such as *National Geographic.*

Books for Parents

Bettelheim, Bruno and Karen Zelan. *On Learning To Read: The Child's Fascination with Meaning.* New York: Knopf, 1982.

Bergstrom, Joan M. *School's Out—Now What?: Creative Choices for Your Child.* Berkeley, CA: Ten Speed Press, 1984.

Bloom, Jill. *Help Me To Help My Child: A Sourcebook for Parents of Learning Disabled Children.* New York: Little Brown, 1990.

Brenner, Barbara. *The Preschool Handbook: Making the Most of Your Child's Education.* New York: Pantheon, 1990.

Calkins, Lucy M. *The Art of Teaching Writing.* Portsmouth, NH: Heinemann, 1985, and *Lessons from a Child,* 1983.

Cogen, Victor. *Boosting the Underachiever: How Busy Parents Can Unlock Their Child's Potential.* New York: Plenum, 1991.

Clay, Marie and Dorothy Butler. *Reading Begins at Home,* 2nd ed. Portsmouth, NY: 1987.

Clay, Marie. *What Did I Write?* Portsmouth, NH: Heinemann, 1975.

Cutright, Melitta J. *The National PTA Talks to Parents: How To Get the Best Education for Your Child.* New York: Doubleday, 1990.

Goodman, Kenneth. *What's Whole in Whole Language?* Portsmouth, NH: Heinemann, 1986.

Graves, Donald and Virginia Stuart. *Write from the Start: Tapping Your Child's Natural Writing Ability.* New York: New American Library, 1985.

Hearne, Betsy. *Choosing Books for Children.* New York: Delacorte, 1990.

Kimmel, Margaret Mary and Elizabeth Segel. *For Reading Out Loud!* New York: Delacorte, 1983.

Larrick, Nancy. *A Parent's Guide to Children's Reading,* 5th ed. New York: Bantam, 1982.

Lipson, Eden Ross. *The New York Times Parent's Guide to the Best Books for Children.* New York: Random House, 1991.

Maeroff, Gene. *The School-Smart Parent.* New York: Times Books, 1989.

Reaves, John and James B. Austin. *To Find Help for a Troubled Kid: A Parent's Guide to Programs and Services for Adolescents.* New York: Holt, 1990.

Rutherford, F. James and Andrew Ahlgren. *Science for All Americans.* New York: Oxford University Press, 1989.

Sanford, Linda T. and Mary Ellen Donovan. *Women and Self-Esteem: Understanding and Improving the Way We Think and Feel about Ourselves.* New York: Penguin, 1984.

Silverman, Arlene. *Growing Up Writing: Teaching Our Children To Write, Think and Learn.* New York: Times Books, 1989.

Stewart, Lynn and Toni Michael. *Parent's Guide to Educational Software.* San Diego: Computer Publishing Enterprise, 1990.

Stillman, Peter. *Families Writing.* Cincinnati: Writers Digest, 1989.

Tchudi, Stephen. *The Young Learner's Handbook.* New York: Charles Scribner, 1987, and *The Young Writer's Handbook,* 1984.

Temple, Charles et al. *The Beginnings of Writing.* Newton, MA: Allyn and Bacon, 1988.

Trelease, Jim. *The Read-Aloud Handbook.* New York: Penguin, 1985.

Whitin, David J. et al. *Living and Learning Mathematics: Stories and Strategies for Supporting Mathematical Literacy.* Portsmouth, NH: Heinemann, 1990.